# TOM JONES

## the life

Also by Sean Smith

*Kylie*
*Gary*
*Alesha*
*Tulisa*
*Kate*
*Robbie*
*Cheryl*
*Victoria*
*Justin: The Biography*
*Britney: The Biography*
*J. K. Rowling: A Biography*
*Jennifer: The Unauthorized Biography*
*Royal Racing*
*The Union Game*
*Sophie's Kiss* (with Garth Gibbs)
*Stone Me!* (with Dale Lawrence)

# TOM JONES
## the life
### BY SEAN SMITH

*'I wish I was immortal
so I could bloody sing for ever'*
Tom Jones, 2009

HARPER

## HARPER

An imprint of HarperCollins*Publishers*
1 London Bridge Street
London SE1 9GF

www.harpercollins.co.uk

First published by HarperCollins*Publishers* 2015

1 3 5 7 9 10 8 6 4 2

A catalogue record of this book is
available from the British Library

HB ISBN 978-0-00-810445-0
PB ISBN 978-0-00-810446-7
EB ISBN 978-0-00-810452-8

Printed and bound in Great Britain by
Clays Ltd, St Ives plc

MIX
Paper from
responsible sources
FSC⁻ C007454

FSC™ is a non-profit international organisation established to promote
the responsible management of the world's forests. Products carrying the
FSC label are independently certified to assure consumers that they come
from forests that are managed to meet the social, economic and
ecological needs of present and future generations,
and other controlled sources.

Find out more about HarperCollins and the environment at
**www.harpercollins.co.uk/green**

*To HB*

# CONTENTS

# PART ONE
# TOMMY WOODWARD

# 1

# THE SHOW-OFF

---

Even as a small boy, it was always about the voice. Tom calls it his 'God-given gift'. Freda Woodward believed her son was musical as a baby when she held him in her arms: 'As soon as music came on the radio, he would start to move like a jelly. And if you left him in his cot, he would make musical sounds at the top of his voice. I remember thinking, "What's eating this boy?"'

Tom's first memory of impressing his mother was when he was a blond, curly-haired five-year-old and she heard him singing the popular wartime novelty song 'Mairzy Doats'. She asked him to sing it again, and when he had finished, she told him, 'You've got a lovely voice.' That parental approval was all the encouragement Tom needed to believe that he would be a singer one day. 'I had this voice and the love of it. So any chance I could get, I wanted to get up and sing.'

Tommy Woodward liked an audience as a little lad. His first cousins, Jean and the twins Ada and Margaret, would come over to his parents' house on Laura Street for a concert. There would just be time to have a fight with Margaret, which Tommy usually started by trying to stick a spider down the back of her neck, before it was showtime. His doting mother Freda knew the

3

routine, because he used to pester her almost daily to announce him dramatically, in a proper show business fashion.

'I would be cleaning the lounge and there was a deep window-sill and Tom would get up there and pull the drapes over and he would say, "Mum, call me out now." And I would say, "Wait a minute now, because I'm busy." And he would say, "No, call me out now." So I would say, "Tommy Woodward, he will be out next" and he would jump out and start to sing. Well, I knew there was some talent there. He was never shy.'

Margaret remembers the concerts well. 'He would be up in auntie's window, pretending that he was on stage then. And we would all have to clap. He was always very talented, but none of us children were allowed to be shy.'

The Woodwards were originally from Cornwall, but moved to the small village of Treforest overlooking Pontypridd at the end of the nineteenth century, drawn by the prospect of finding work in the mines that were thriving at the time. Thousands of families poured in to transform the landscape of South Wales. Row upon row of small terraced houses were built for the 'immigrants' who created the mining communities for which the Valleys became famous. Tom's father, Thomas John Woodward senior, was the first of his family to be born in Wales.

It is a huge simplification to describe these areas as poor, deprived or underprivileged. Working down the mines was considered a good job and, more importantly, it provided a regular wage. Being a miner was exceptionally hard work, but Tom's dad was proud to follow in the footsteps of his father and two elder brothers. He earned his first wage at the age of fourteen, when he went down Cwm Colliery in Beddau, three miles across the mountain from Treforest.

For forty years, rain or shine, frost or snow, he would rise at 5.15 a.m., pull on his hobnail boots and go to work to shovel fourteen tons of coal. It was man's work – hard, physical and dangerous. A year after he began, the General Strike of 1926 saw proud mining families having to queue at soup kitchens because they had no money to put food on their tables. It was the worst of times.

Tom senior was a dapper man, polite and popular with the ladies. He met Freda Jones at a local dance in 1933, when she was eighteen and he was twenty-three. Theirs was a whirlwind courtship. She was much more sociable than her quieter suitor, but those who knew him well would often remark on his dry sense of humour. The vivacious and statuesque Freda was already pregnant when they married on 3 September of that year. Their first child, a daughter called Sheila, was born on 11 March 1934. She was a quiet child, taking after her father by being more of a listener than a talker.

A further six years had passed and the Second World War was raging before a much wished-for son was born on 7 June 1940. He was given the same name as his father, Thomas John Woodward. As many babies were then, Tommy was born at home, 57 Kingsland Terrace, Treforest. When Tom was one and a half, the family swapped houses with his father's widowed mother and moved into her larger house at 44 Laura Street.

Treforest was spared the worst of the German bombs, but the village didn't escape the warning sound of the sirens or the planes rumbling overhead. Mothers used to tell their children that it was thundering outside, before ushering them under the stairs or the kitchen table until the 'all clear' was sounded. If you looked out of the window, you could see the searchlights illuminating the night sky over Cardiff, twelve miles to the south.

The house in Laura Street had a cellar, so Tom's family would shelter under the steps leading down to the basement level. The village wasn't a specific target for the Luftwaffe, which was seeking to destroy the factories engaged in wartime production on the Treforest Trading Estate a few miles away. There was always the chance, however, that unused bombs would be jettisoned when the planes turned back for Germany, as the pilots needed to lighten their load so they would have enough fuel to make it home.

These were dangerous days. One older boy had his leg blown off by stepping on a mine that had ended up on the recreational area known as the White Tips, where schoolchildren played rugby and football. Nobody escaped the blackout, or the eerie sense created by the darkness when the street lamps went out at sunset.

Tom was too young to remember much of the rationing, the long shop queues or the nights lit only by the moon. The noise of it all stuck with him though: 'I can remember the searchlights and there were always guns going off. At the time I thought that's the way the world was.'

There were no supermarkets in the post-war days when rationing was still enforced. You could, however, get everything you needed for your family, without leaving Treforest, at the grocer's, Hale's the butcher's or Howells the baker's. All the housewives bought their groceries in a little shop and post office called Marney's in Wood Road.

Tom Marney, a bustling, popular figure, had run his store for as long as anyone could remember. The shop was a bit like the Valleys' equivalent of *Open All Hours*. It was the place to go to catch up with your neighbours, while the shopkeeper in his trusty brown overall leaned on the counter and amused everyone with the latest gossip. He'd heard Freda telling a friend what a talented singer her little boy was, so he wanted to hear for himself.

He persuaded Freda that she should let the lad give everyone a song the next time they went in. Sure enough, the waiting queue was transfixed as Tom clambered on to a crate and burst into his then high-pitched vocal. According to local legend, Mr Marney told the small crowd that had gathered to put their hands in their pockets and 'give the boy a few coppers'. Despite Freda's protests, Tom's hands were filled with pennies, much to his delight. It was his first paying gig.

Tom was always encouraged to sing by his extended family in and around Pontypridd. He was by no means the only good singer among the Woodward and Jones clans, but he was the only one taking an interest in the popular songs on the radio. Others, like his Uncle George and Uncle Edwin, his father's brothers, had magnificent voices, but stuck to the more traditional hymns and ballads.

Uncle George gave Tom an early piece of advice, which he always followed. One Saturday, when everyone had gone back to Laura Street for a last drink and a sing-song, he told young Tommy, half asleep and wanting his bed, that he should always sell a song to people's faces. Never stare at the floor or the ceiling or close your eyes, because then you are trapping the song and keeping it prisoner. 'Let people see what you are singing about,' said George.

Tom had an edge, even as a youngster in short trousers. He didn't just sing a song; he performed it with verve and passion. In 1946, when Tommy was six, the Oscar-winning film *The Jolson Story* was released. The biopic, starring Larry Parks, told the life of the star who, from humble origins, became the most famous entertainer in the world. Fortunately, it glossed over the singer's marital problems brought about by his inveterate womanising.

Tom was transfixed when he saw the film with his parents at the Cecil Cinema in Fothergill Street, Treforest. He recalled, 'I thought Al Jolson was great, because he was a great entertainer.' Back at the house in Laura Street, he would stand in front of a mirror and practise the famous Jolson gestures and hand movements, so he could impress his audience the next time he gave a performance in the lounge. He wanted to be like Jolson, because 'he's moving *and* singing.'

Performing in front of an audience for Tom was like swimming for other youngsters: after you have overcome an initial fear of the water, it becomes second nature. Tom wasn't overawed when Uncle Edwin stood him on a chair to sing to a crowded pub or when his mother showed him off at the weekly meetings of the Treforest Women's Guild, which met in a small hall at the top of Stow Hill, a short, lung-busting walk from home.

Little Tommy was, in fact, a big show-off. Looking back at his childhood self, Tom admitted, 'It was my strength. A lot of boys in school were great rugby players or football players. But I was lucky that I had this voice. It gave me confidence.' In that regard, Tom took after his vivacious mother. His cousin Margaret, who was very close to Tom growing up, used to tell him that he would always have another career if his voice ever gave out: 'He has my auntie's personality. She was a very natural woman and would be the life and soul of the party. Tom was the same. I told him he would make a marvellous stand-up comedian.'

The one member of clan Woodward who was a reluctant singer was his father. Tom recalled, 'My father was a shy man. But he could sing if he had had enough beer.' His mother had no such inhibitions, however, and would happily burst into song. Unfortunately, she couldn't match her husband as a singer, although her son says she could just about hold a tune.

Tom's universe was very small when he was growing up. He usually says he hails from Pontypridd, but he is a Treforest boy through and through. Until he left school, his entire life was acted out within a few hundred yards of his home, and even then his first job was only a five-minute stroll away. His mother's sister, Auntie Lena, lived with her husband, Albert Jones, in adjoining Tower Street, so his first cousins were so close you could almost hear the kettle going on. His best friends, Brian Blackler and Dai Perry, were within shouting distance and he never had more than a ten-minute walk to school.

The boy was called Tommy at home and among family to avoid confusion with his father, but his school friends always knew him as Tom, or sometimes Woodsie. The local children would never have dreamed of referring to Tom senior as anything other than Mr Woodward. Proper respect for your elders was very important in this small, insulated mining community. One story in particular illustrates this. When both her children were of school age, Freda took a job in a local factory to bring in some much needed extra cash. One day she and her husband were queuing for the cinema when a boy shouted out to them, 'Hello, Freda.' Tom senior was enraged by the impertinence and wanted to know who he was. Freda said he was just a young lad who worked at the factory. Her husband was incandescent. 'You're not going to the factory any more,' he insisted. 'If they can't call you Mrs Woodward, then you don't work there!'

Freda never took another full-time job, but she was the woman local families called on when someone died. She would be asked to lay out the body, which involved dressing the deceased so they looked their best for the funeral. It was a sign of the regard in which she was held that she was trusted with such a significant task.

Tom was decidedly spoiled and, perhaps because he was indulged, he was slightly on the chubby side. His sister was six years older, so he was very much the little one in the family. Coincidentally, his mother was the youngest sibling, eleven years younger than Lena, and the baby of her family too. The Woodwards were relatively better off than many in the area, because they were a household of only four. Both Tom's mother and father were one of six children, so there were lots of cousins living in Treforest. Lena and Albert alone had seven children.

As far as young Tom was concerned, it was entirely normal to grow up with such an extended family in close proximity. He loved it and has always stressed that family is of paramount importance to him. It would come as no surprise to those who knew him well that his immediate family would later live within five minutes of him in Los Angeles or that he made sure his cousins were always welcome there.

Tom enjoyed a traditional and idyllic childhood, despite the dismal landscape of an impoverished area. The house in Laura Street was an end of terrace and bigger than some of the others in the street. Freda liked the decoration to be bright and colourful – a cheerful place for her family. 'It was a beautiful home,' recalls Cousin Margaret. 'Auntie Freda was very house-proud but she would always give you a welcome.' Like so many housewives then, she would invariably have a pie or a tray of Welsh cakes baking in the oven of her kitchen on the lower ground floor and the smell would waft enticingly up the stairs.

A coal fire kept the house warm. Tom and the other boys in the neighbourhood used to enjoy helping when the coalman came round with a delivery. He would lift up a round, steel plate in the pavement and tip the coal in. The boys would then push the coal down the hole, so it would land in the room on the bottom floor known as the coal house.

Visitors always came to the back door, which was never locked. The house had no bathroom, but hanging on a hook outside was the small tin bath that Freda would fetch down every night and put in the scullery across the hall, ready to fill with hot water so her husband could scrub himself clean of the coal dust and grime every evening.

On Tom's birth certificate, his father listed his occupation not as miner but as Assistant Colliery Repairer (below ground). The work was just as dirty, dark and forbidding as digging the seam. It was also hugely important, because it involved repairing the wooden joists that kept the tunnels from collapsing, preventing calamitous results.

The daily rituals in the Woodward home never changed and the roles that his mother and father had within the household had a profound effect on young Tom's outlook on life and the development of a set of values that many would see as old fashioned. His father worked hard to provide for his family, and his wife was equally diligent in making sure his house was spotless, his children were clean and tidy and he was cared for from the moment she could hear the click of the garden gate announcing he was back. Tom observed, 'Most of my values have been formed from that working-class environment. They were good people.'

Freda was always up first to light the fire, make breakfast, lay out Tom senior's work clothes and prepare his packed lunch ready for his journey over the mountain to the colliery. He usually walked with Brian Blackler's father, Cliff, and the many other miners from Treforest. While he spent the day with a pickaxe in his hand, Freda would make sure the children were safely at school before beginning her daily tasks of shopping, baking and cleaning. She took particular care in polishing the horse brasses that were dotted about the best room and were her pride and joy.

At the end of a strenuous day, a miner needed his hot meal. Freda always had her husband's tea ready on the kitchen table for him to enjoy as soon as he had washed his hands. Tom and Sheila, hair brushed and tidy, were there to welcome their father home.

After he had eaten, he would take his bath. It was far too small for a grown man. Tom described his father's routine: 'He would have to kneel on the floor first of all and take his shirt off and wash his top half and when he had done that he would stand in the bath and wash his bottom half. And he would shout for my mother to come and scrub his back.' Freda would wash his back with a flannel, unless they'd had a tiff and she wasn't speaking to him, in which case she would send Tommy in to do it instead.

Sometimes Tom senior would pop out to the Wood Road Non-Political Club – known locally as 'the Wood Road' – for a beer with his friends, but on Saturdays he took Freda with him. It was a traditional working men's club that tended to be all male during the week and more family oriented at the weekend.

Mr and Mrs Woodward always made a handsome, smartly turned-out couple. Freda looked glamorous with her blonde hair styled immaculately, and favoured beads to accessorise her dress. Her husband would wear a three-piece suit with a brightly coloured shirt and tie and pristine suede shoes. His son always appreciated his sharp dress sense and sought to emulate him when he became older.

At the club, Freda and the other wives sat together and gossiped while the men drank their beer at the other end of the room. Only one topic of conversation was banned – politics. That was why it was called the Non-Political Club. Sometimes there was singing. Freda's tour de force was her version of the old favourite 'Silver Dollar', which she performed with great verve and humour. She relished the memorable first line 'A man without a woman is like a ship without a sail'. Afterwards, they would usually finish the evening off at Lena and Albert's, because Tom's aunt had a piano, which she would play, making a late sing-song even jollier.

The piano was in much demand at Christmas time. Tom would join the other young children at his aunt's at teatime for a lucky dip. Aunt Lena would buy a lot of little gifts and wrap them in preparation. The children would then draw numbers out of a hat to see which present they received – it was Santa's lucky dip. As Margaret explained, 'The money wasn't there to be extravagant, but we never realised this, because our home was so nice. All of us would be there with the piano going. Tom said to me once that we never realised we were poor, because we were all together and it was absolutely lovely.'

Everyone in the village was in the same situation. Nobody had a car, but everything was so near that they walked everywhere. The children could easily get to the Cecil Cinema for a matinée. They had to pay just once and could stay all day – they could watch the feature as many times as they liked. Of course, if it were something the girls found scary, then Tom would make it his mission in life to race around or jump out and frighten them as much as possible on the way home. He could be a rascal, but he was never rough, especially with his younger cousins. 'We were very close, I've got to be honest,' said Margaret.

Sometimes they played on the White Tips, or in summer walked to Ponty Baths, as it was called, and swam and splashed around in the enormous paddling pool that had been an attraction in Ynysangharad Park since the 1920s. Tom didn't spend all his time with the girls, however. Most afternoons, after tea, he joined his pals to muck about or kick a ball in the old quarry behind Stow Hill. These days, health and safety officers would have a fit at the sight of so many small boys in short trousers scaling the sides and scrambling around in the earth and stone.

Even better was when they were allowed, in the holidays, to go and play and camp on the Feathery, the spectacular mountain behind Treforest. In the late forties and early fifties, children had to find amusements that didn't revolve around television, computers and phones. Invariably, about ten of the younger boys from the Laura Street area would be together – all the usual suspects, including Tom, Brian, Dai and the Pitman brothers. The older boys would be on one side of the mountain, ignoring the youngsters. Brian recalls, 'It was good fun in those days … Great times! We never slept – never slept all night.'

# 2

# THE PRISONER
# OF LAURA STREET

Tom didn't enjoy going to school. He was a poor student and, like most of his pals, couldn't wait for the time to pass so he could leave and become a man. In later years, he was able to attribute his slow academic progress to dyslexia, but that diagnosis wasn't readily available in the 1940s, and Tom was perceived variously as being disinterested or not very bright. Even the basics of reading, writing and arithmetic failed to inspire him.

He began in the local infants school before moving on to Treforest Primary School in Wood Road and then to the Central Secondary Modern School at the top of Stow Hill. He wasn't much interested in playing football or rugby, like his friend Dai Perry, but he did enjoy watching boxing. He liked drawing, but his principal interest was singing. Surprisingly, he showed little desire to join a choir. He knew he was the best singer in the school, but he wasn't a team player and, from an early age, was very much a solo artist in the making.

That inclination extended to traditional carol singing at Christmas, when a group of his friends called for him at the house and asked if he would join them. He responded, 'No, I don't think I will tonight,' and let them carry on, before slipping out to sing by himself. 'If I was singing with four or five fellas, they drowned you out. They would always cock it up. You couldn't shine. And I made more money singing by myself.'

His family obviously knew about his talent as a singer, but his friends didn't realise he was gifted until they heard him sing at school one Friday afternoon. The teacher told the class to entertain themselves for a while during a free period. Tom started drumming his fingers hard upon the desk – he was beating out the sound of galloping horses. Then he began, 'An old cowpoke went riding out one dark and windy day.'

The melancholy song 'Riders in the Sky' had been written in 1948 by Stan Jones, a friend of the multi-Oscar-winning director John Ford, the master of the Western genre. Jones composed songs for some of the most famous Westerns of all time, including *The Searchers* and *Rio Grande*, both starring John Wayne. The hugely evocative 'Riders', one of his earliest compositions, became his most famous, mainly because it was covered by a string of singers that included Bing Crosby, Johnny Cash, Peggy Lee and Frankie Laine.

The lyrics are based on an old folk tale about a cowboy told to change his ways or end up damned and forever chasing a thundering herd of cattle across the endless skies. Tommy Woodward was less concerned about the moral of the story and more interested in the famous chorus of the song, which was tailor-made for a young boy with a big voice who loved Westerns: 'Yi-pi-yi-ay, Yi-pi-yi-oh, ghost riders in the sky'. It was his party piece and he never tired of singing it. Fortunately, his classmates didn't get bored of his rendition, which became a weekly favourite. For many, their abiding memory of school was of Tom Jones singing that song.

His preferred version of the classic was by bandleader Vaughn Monroe, whose rich, resonant baritone vocal suited the ethereal nature of the song. Tommy could only imitate it by cupping his hands together, covering his mouth and pretending he was in a cave. Monroe's recording was called 'Riders in the Sky (A Cowboy Legend)' and was the most successful of all, reaching number one in the *Billboard* charts in the US in 1949. If you listened to the radio, you couldn't fail to hear it. Later versions added the word 'Ghost' at the beginning of the title, but Tom always remained loyal to the original. He acknowledged the significance of the song when he recorded it as the rousing opening track of his 1967 album *Green, Green Grass of Home*.

'Riders in the Sky' was important to Tom not just because it was a song he performed so much as a child, but because it told a story. He observed, 'I love songs that paint a picture.' Many of Tom's best-loved songs, such as 'Delilah' and 'Green, Green Grass of Home', are hugely descriptive and evocative. He wasn't a fan of repetitive pop chants like 'She Loves You'.

One of Tom's favourite stories is about the time he sang the Lord's Prayer in class, performing it not as a solemn church song, but as a negro spiritual. His teacher was so amazed that he was asked to sing it again in front of the whole school. Schooldays weren't filled with too many highlights for Tommy Woodward, but that was one of them.

Tom had recently celebrated his twelfth birthday when he started complaining to his mother that he was feeling tired. The normally lively boy had no energy. It was difficult enough at the best of times to get him up for school, but Freda couldn't help noticing how listless her son had become. Sensibly, she decided that a trip to the doctor was called for. A precautionary X-ray revealed that Tom had a dark shadow on his lung: he had tuber-culosis. The only good thing about such upsetting news was that the condition had been diagnosed early.

TB, or 'The Black Spot' as they grimly called it in the mining communities of South Wales, was a killer. The disease, which usually affects the lungs, is caught through the air by coming into contact with an infected person coughing or sneezing bacteria near you. Wales had one of the highest rates for TB in Europe – hardly surprising in close-knit communities where nearly every miner coped with a cough all his life.

The Woodwards were touched by the disease, as so many families were. His father's side of the family experienced several instances of TB during Tom's lifetime. His cousin Marie died from the disease at the age of twenty-one. Her sister Valerie was also stricken, but survived after spending two years in Sully Hospital, near Penarth, which specialised in tuberculosis cases and where the fresh sea air helped young lungs to heal.

The first decision that had to be made was whether to send Tom away to rest and recuperate and break up the family or accept the difficult challenge of nursing him back to health at home. Even if victims of the wretched disease survived, they faced the prospect of being crippled for life.

Freda decided she wanted to nurse her boy back to health at home. His condition was extremely serious, but he wasn't a sickly child by nature and the disease had been identified at an early stage. As a result, the chances of him making a complete recovery were good. He was infectious for only a short time, while the treatments he received fought the bacteria. During that period, he needed to be kept isolated from his friends, so he wouldn't cough and spread the infection. There was no magic cure, however. He needed absolute rest and a long period of convalescence to rebuild his strength, which wasn't easy for an active boy.

His mother decided he should be moved down to the middle floor of the house, to a bigger room where the coal fireplace could keep him warm when the days became chilly. He needed to have the windows open at all times, lowered only slightly when a bitter wind whistled down Laura Street.

After the initial elation of not having to go to school, life became pretty boring. He explained, 'Bed was a novelty at first. I didn't have to go to school, which was great, since I wasn't a good student. But being forbidden to sing during the first year was a real drag!' In his boredom, he would drive his poor mother to distraction by frequently banging on the floor with a stick to attract her attention in the kitchen on the floor below. She would drop everything to rush and see what he needed.

Freda did her best to amuse her son. Sometimes she would sing and dance around the room to cheer him up. She urged him to draw with a set of Indian inks she bought for him. When he was allowed to have visitors, she encouraged friends and family to see him.

Cousin Margaret, who was ten at the time, recalls, 'We realised it was serious. We were up there visiting him most of the time. Auntie Freda would say, "Come up and keep him company." We would tell him about school and what we were doing. We were never bored with Tom.

'But we could never play cards. My mother wouldn't have us playing cards. Auntie Freda was the same. Cards were like the devil in the house. We were chapel – only a man could play cards, not a woman.' Tom, perhaps as a result of his mother's disapproval, has never had any inclination to play cards and has always shown a strong dislike of any form of gambling.

From his bed, Tom could look out of the window and see all the way down the valley. He recalled, 'As good as that view was, I'd grow restless. So my parents would routinely move the bed around the room to change the scenery for me.' Freda was forever cutting out pictures of cowboys from magazines and sticking them to the wall, so he would have something fresh to look at. Margaret observes, 'It was lovely, his bedroom.'

The lifesaver for Tom was when his parents rented a heavy, dark-brown radio for him. It was the sort of old-fashioned wireless you could imagine listening to when the declaration of war was announced. Tom loved it. His parents didn't mind if he listened to it late at night, when the BBC played American music into the small hours – time didn't matter when you were in bed for twenty-four hours a day. Pirate radio and Radio 1 had yet to change the musical taste of a nation. In 1952, 'Rock Around the Clock' was still two years away. Instead, Tom grew to love the records of Mahalia Jackson, the 'Queen of Gospel', an influence he carried with him throughout his career. He also discovered the music of Big Bill Broonzy, the acclaimed master of the Chicago blues, whom Eric Clapton once called his role model and both Keith Richards and Ronnie Wood of The Rolling Stones identify as a key figure in the development of their guitar-playing.

This was music to stir the imagination of a twelve-year-old boy in Treforest. These wonderful performers helped shape his destiny and Tom never forgot the effect they had on him. He included Mahalia's uplifting recording of the traditional American hymn 'The Old Rugged Cross' and Big Bill's protest song 'Black, Brown and White' among his Desert Island Discs in a programme broadcast shortly after his seventieth birthday in 2010. Tom had heard the song 'The Old Rugged Cross' many times, because it was a favourite of Welsh choirs and was often sung at funerals and formal occasions. Tom had never heard it sung like this, however, and he was keen to try out the style.

After a year confined to his room, Tom had shown enough improvement to be allowed to get up for two hours a day. He still couldn't go out, but was well enough to stand by the front door and wave to his friends as they walked up the hill to the quarry or the White Tips to play or gathered around the gas lamp-post as darkness fell to laugh and chat. Tom was frustrated and jealous. 'I promised myself that when I could walk to that lamp-post, I'd never complain about anything again.'

Once he was stronger, Tom was allowed to resume singing. When he turned thirteen, his parents rented a black-and-white TV set in time to enjoy the coronation of Queen Elizabeth II. Tom was able to watch the performances of popular artists of the fifties, like the snappily dressed Frankie Vaughan. Ever since he'd first seen Al Jolson on screen, Tom was a magpie when it came to imitating other entertainers. He would absorb a hand gesture or a facial expression and file it away to use himself.

His parents also bought him a guitar, on which he could strum a few basic chords as rudimentary backing. Freda never forgot his delight when he saw the parcel wrapped up at the bottom of his bed: 'There was happiness! To see Tom smile was all I wanted.' Through the open window of his second-floor bedroom, he would serenade the neighbourhood. It was like a scene from the period drama *Call the Midwife*, as the mums in the street would pause their chores to listen to young Tommy Woodward sing.

Just imagine if *The X Factor* had existed back then. Tom's would have been the ultimate sob story – young boy stricken with TB raises himself from his sickbed to 'nail' 'Riders in the Sky'. There wouldn't have been a dry eye on the judging panel.

Brian Blackler remembers visiting his friend, who was sitting up in bed singing 'Riders in the Sky' and other songs he had picked up from the radio, including 'That Old Black Magic'. Artists from Marilyn Monroe to Frank Sinatra had recorded the song, but the version that had caught Tom's ear was by Billy Daniels. Nobody sang the standard like the great black singer and Tom was struck by his unique phrasing. He decided he wanted to sing it that way too.

Eventually, after two long years, the fourteen-year-old Tom was considered well enough to venture into the outside world once more. Holidays during his childhood – as for most mining families – tended to consist of a day trip to Barry Island, but this time his parents thought he deserved a proper summer treat. Brian Blackler remembers the boys had borrowed bicycles and, as they were riding, Tom shouted over, 'I'm going now to Porthcawl for a week. Do you fancy coming down?' Brian, who was one of eight children and had never had a proper holiday either, jumped at the chance, and joined the Woodward family in a caravan by the seaside in the popular resort some thirty miles west of Cardiff. There wasn't much to do other than muck about on the dunes or 'freeze your balls off' in the water – it was always cold in Porthcawl. Tom found a place to sing though: the back of an old lorry by the beach, where he could entertain other holidaymakers.

The holiday was a positive outcome at the end of his two-year sentence in Laura Street. The resumption of school wasn't particularly welcome, however. A teacher had come in from time to time to help the patient with his lessons, but Tom's heart had never been in it. For his age, Tom was well behind and hadn't mastered the most basic elements of education. His handwriting and spelling were hopeless – not that he cared much. After all, he had met the girl who would be the love of his life.

# 3

# A TEENAGER IN LOVE

Being laid up in bed with tuberculosis isn't an ideal situation for a lad struggling through adolescence. Tommy could only gaze out of his 'prison' window in frustration and watch the local schoolgirls laughing and gossiping in the street below. One in particular grabbed his attention – Melinda Trenchard was the prettiest girl in the neighbourhood.

Linda was the daughter of Bill and Vi Trenchard, who lived in Cliff Terrace, just a few hundred yards away from Laura Street across Wood Road. Her parents ran the County Cinema, near the railway station in Pontypridd, and were well known in the area. Vi was friendly with Tom's mother, Freda, and, like her, was outgoing and popular.

As youngsters, Tom and Linda's paths seldom crossed. Boys and girls played separately, unless they went to the same school. Linda, who is six months younger than Tom, went to a Catholic primary school, so he was only vaguely aware of who she was at that age. He noticed that she wore little crucifix earrings, like many of the local Catholic girls, but that was about all.

Tom first became aware of Linda properly, before he was struck down with TB, when she was playing marbles in the street with some friends. He recalled light-heartedly, 'I must have been eleven. I walked down her street and she was bending down and playing marbles. I saw those great legs and all of a sudden I thought of her in a new light.'

He did pursue Linda, after a fashion, but it was more for a game of kiss chase than anything else. All the boys would chase the girls and if they were lucky enough to catch up with one, they had to give her a kiss. 'My first proper kiss was with Linda and it was her first kiss too. Afterwards I had to run my wrists under cold water. I was an early starter.' It was nothing more than a playground romance at this stage, although Tom has always been disarmingly frank and earthy about growing up: 'I can remember the first time I got to know myself better – I thought I had broken it!'

When he was confined to his room, Linda was the girl he would watch out for most. He would quietly seethe when he saw her talking to the other boys, but he could do nothing about it. She never came to visit him, because, in those prim and proper days, girls who weren't family didn't visit boys in their homes. Linda, as Tom could see from his window, was maturing into a lovely teenager. Her old school friend Vimy Pitman observes, 'She was very, very attractive. She was everybody's cup of tea. She had a lovely figure and was the sweetest girl. She would never say anything nasty about anybody or get involved in arguments or anything. She really was a nice girl.'

When Tom emerged from Laura Street, he had changed. He was taller and broader and his hair had turned the colour of coal. Linda hadn't seen him for two years. She recalled, 'When we met up after he went back to school, I didn't recognise him at first, but I was immediately attracted to him again.'

Tom was equally smitten. 'I don't know what the feeling was. All I knew was I had a feeling for this girl. She looked fantastic.'

It was a classic case of opposites attracting – good girl in the A stream meets a boy who couldn't care less and was languishing in the Ds. Tom's lack of interest in all things academic had become even more pronounced. He had fallen so far behind during his two years away from school that he saw little point in trying to catch up. Linda, on the other hand, was particularly accomplished at drawing and illustrating – an interest she might have had in common with Tom if he had stuck with it. Perhaps art was too closely associated with the boredom of TB, because music took over as soon as he was allowed to sing again.

The girls at school weren't too bothered about Tom's classroom credentials. Vimy acknowledges, 'Lots of the girls, well, most of the girls, I suppose, found him very attractive. He seemed a bit rough to me, but he definitely had the charisma. He had a way with him – a swagger.'

Linda had no idea at first that he was a gifted singer. She hadn't been present at any family sing-songs, nor had she heard him entertain classmates. Instead, she had to wait until his sister Sheila's engagement party to hear him. She described it in a rare interview in the 1960s: 'Tom's mother and mine knew each other well, so it was quite natural that when his sister got engaged he should invite me to the party. It was there I first really heard him sing. He sang "Ghost Riders in the Sky" and accompanied himself by tapping his fingers on the table. I wish it had been recorded.'

The opportunities for teenage courtship in Treforest were few. Linda and Tom got together first of all at the local youth club. She recalled, 'We were too young to say we were going together, but we always seemed to end up with each other.' They would synchronise running errands for their mothers, just so they could walk to the local shops hand in hand.

Tom and Linda became an item almost without anybody noticing. It wasn't a case of them going into class one day and announcing that they were going out. His cousin Margaret can't remember a time when they weren't together: 'I used to think they were like Darby and Joan – like an old pair of slippers. They were always together, with their arms around each other. They were very loving.'

Many of her contemporaries have likened Linda to Doris Day, the epitome of movie-star niceness. Tom, on the other hand, had a touch of Marlon Brando about him, being more brooding than clean cut. But something clicked between them. Looking back on those days in 2006, Tom said, 'Teenage love is great. It never really happens like that again. We were so wrapped up with one another then and we've never really lost that. We like one another's company. We are friends, we laugh and we are natural with one another. That's something you can't learn. It's either there or it's not.'

Things soon became more serious. If it was dry, they would walk for hours in the hills above the village. If it was raining – and it rained a lot in the Valleys – they would shelter in the old red phone box at the end of Laura Street. Fortunately, it was a fine day when they decided to make love for the first time. Tom was fifteen and Linda was fourteen when they found a secluded spot in a field overlooking the village. Tom said simply, 'It was very special.'

Tom's devotion to his girlfriend was clear from his reluctance to brag about her to his mates. He didn't provide them with a blow-by-blow account, and flatly denied they had done the deed. It was all right to indulge in some swaggering talk with the lads about sex, but he wouldn't talk about his sweetheart. As Vimy Pitman perceptively observes, 'Linda was sacred.'

Tom had only a year of school left after recovering from TB. As well as Linda and singing, his other interest when he resumed his education was smoking Woodbines. He would join the boys and pop into the shop opposite the school gates, where they would buy one fag for a penny. Brian Blackler recalls, 'Then we would go up the White Tips and smoke it and die on the way home. You think you are big when you have a fag in your mouth when you are a young kid.'

Tom left school at fifteen, as did practically everyone in Treforest. You had to be at the grammar school in Pontypridd to stay on and take A levels. Tom had no qualifications, but one thing had already been established: he wouldn't follow his father down the mines. Even before his brush with TB had ruled it out, his parents wanted a different life for their son. Margaret observed, 'He was brought up that he wasn't going down the mines. Uncle Tom would never have agreed to that.'

In any case, Tom belonged to the first generation of Welsh sons who weren't expected to follow in their fathers' dusty footsteps. Instead, he found his first job as an apprentice glove cutter at the Polyglove factory in the Broadway, the main road between Treforest and Pontypridd.

His friend Brian joined him there when he, too, left school. Brian recalled, 'We just used to shift some gloves. That was about it and a machine would do the rest.' It was hot, dull and repetitive, and all for thirty-eight shillings a week in old money. Tom admitted that he hated it – not least because the cutting room was men only. The female staff were in another part of the factory, dealing with sales, packaging and retail.

At least he was earning just enough money to indulge his interest in records, clothes and beer. Far more important than work was the emergence of rock 'n' roll, with the release of the film *Blackboard Jungle* and the impact of the theme tune 'Rock Around the Clock' by Bill Haley and His Comets. The song, with its hugely catchy, danceable melody, played over both the opening and closing credits. The film transformed a minor hit into a sensation. 'Rock Around the Clock' was everywhere.

The song was released at the start of 1955 and made some waves in the UK before the movie came out in March. It re-entered the charts in November 1955 and marched all the way up to number one. Bill Haley was no Elvis though. He was already thirty, on the chubby side and just as likely to be performing an old country and western song as anything cutting edge. His music was much more influential than the man himself.

Tom first heard the song blaring from the radio that was constantly playing at the factory to keep the workforce entertained as they faced the daily grind: 'All of a sudden this "Rock Around the Clock" came on and I thought, "This is jumping out of the radio".' His workmates were less impressed and failed to understand what he found so exciting about it. An exasperated Tom told them to 'just bloody listen to it'.

At least Tom's enthusiasm for the new music gave him a head start when it came to the two Christmas parties he attended during his time at the factory. All the staff had the opportunity to mix together, but the men tended to stand around drinking, while the girls wanted to dance. Tom had a big advantage, 'I was the only one who could jive. I was like a kid in a candy store.'

Tom's ability on the dance floor had been finely tuned by Linda when they went out dancing on the weekend. She had left school a few months after her boyfriend, and she found a job in

Pontypridd, working as an assistant in a draper's shop, where one of her tasks was looking after the window display.

By this time, Tom had embraced the new Teddy boy culture that was sweeping the country and Linda was happy to wear the uniform of the girlfriend. Becoming a Teddy boy was part of growing up for many young men who left school at fifteen and wanted to announce to the world that they had arrived. This was nothing like the gang culture of today, although it helped if you could handle yourself in a fight.

Teddy boys weren't a natural product of rock 'n' roll. The famous attire had been around for several years, ever since fashion leaders in Savile Row, London, had tried to reintroduce the Edwardian style to affluent upper- and middle-class young men after the end of the Second World War.

Gradually the uniform filtered down to working-class youths. They were known as working-class Edwardians until the *Daily Express* printed a story in September 1953 with a headline shortening Edwardian to Teddy and the term 'Teddy boy' passed into mainstream usage. The fashion lost its appeal to the middle classes when that happened, so the famous suits could be picked up for bargain prices on second-hand market stalls.

Tom was a Treforest Ted. He wore all the gear: gaudy waistcoats, cowboy hats, bootlace ties, black suede crepe-soled shoes, known as brothel creepers, and, his pride and joy, a sky-blue suit, consisting of a long jacket with a velvet collar and narrow trousers. Local journalist Colin Macfarlane memorably described Tom in the 1950s: 'He could be seen walking along the streets with his Teddy boy coat and trousers that were reckoned to be as narrow as the thinnest drainpipe in the village.'

Tom always fancied himself in his Teddy boy finery. The proprietor of Linda's drapery shop wasn't so impressed when this dandified vision came to call during working hours. Tom may have thought he was the height of fashion but, to others, Teddy boy was synonymous with young hooligan. Linda had to make sure he stayed out of sight at the back of the shop during working hours.

Linda, who was always smartly turned out, had a figure that looked good in anything, especially the pencil skirts that were fashionable in the mid-fifties. She also had a DA haircut, which was a polite shortening of the coarser 'Duck's Arse', so called because it resembled the rear end of a duck. In the US, where it originated, the style was known as a 'Duck's Tail' or a 'Tony Curtis', after the heart-throb actor who popularised it. The cut was short at the back and long and curled over in a quiff at the front. The general idea was to pile as much of your hair onto the top of your head as you could, using slabs of hair gel to hold it in place. Tom had one as well, lovingly teased and shaped by Linda.

The young women were more impressed with his efforts than the men. One of the lads recalls Tom's image: 'He looked like a dipstick. Always did when he was younger – a greasy-haired gypsy.'

Brian Blackler, whose Teddy-boy suit was silver, remembers: 'We would go down to Cardiff and see the boys down there with their hair like Tony Curtis and we would come home and copy them. We all looked the same then.'

After the working week was over, Saturday was dance night. The Teds would meet up in a pub for a few bevvies to start off the evening. Tom and Dai, who was a year younger but didn't look it because of his size, would generally be served, because they seemed older than they were. The girls, meanwhile, would usually congregate at someone's house before making their way to that night's chosen venue. 'We girls never touched alcohol,' confirms Vimy. They would make do with crisps and lemonade and wait for the boys to arrive. The Ranch in Pontypridd, St Luke's Church in Porth and the Catholic hall on the Broadway were popular for a night of jiving – at least until 10.30, when they had to play the national anthem and finish for the night.

Boys and girls would put on their best clothes on a Sunday afternoon and meet up in the centre of Ponty for what was known locally as the Monkey Parade – a weekly ritual in which the young men were like peacocks trying to attract the best-looking female. They would pair off for an innocent stroll through town. If Tom were delayed for any reason on the Saturday or Sunday, none of the local lads would chat up Linda, because she was strictly off-limits. She was Tommy's girl.

# 4

# THE MAKING OF A MAN

Another rainy day in the autumn of 1956 changed Tom's life for ever. As usual, he and Linda were sheltering in the phone box at the end of Laura Street, when she plucked up the courage to give him some news. Tearfully, she told him they were expecting a baby in the spring. Tom was now sixteen and she was fifteen.

They hadn't bothered with contraception. There was no family-planning clinic in Treforest in those days. Tom admitted that he didn't care about precautions, because he knew 'I loved this girl'. He hadn't given it a second thought until it was too late. He described his shock, 'I thought, "Oh my God, what is my mother going to say. Or my father, what is he going to say!" The initial thing was "I am in hot water."'

Despite his youthful swagger, Tom was still living at home and young enough for his mum to give him a clip round the ear and tell him to get his hair cut, which she frequently did when she noticed it was longer than Linda's. He had huge respect for his parents and didn't want to disappoint them.

Tom was right to be nervous. He later confided in bass guitarist Vernon Hopkins that his father was very angry at the news that he was going to be a grandfather. He thrust a wad of notes into his son's hand and told him to head off to Cardiff and join 'the bloody merchant navy'. When everyone had calmed down, Freda and Tom senior called a family conference to decide what should be done.

The meeting to decide the teenagers' future was held in the best room at Laura Street, which was usually reserved for special occasions. While, strictly speaking, this was a very special occasion, it wasn't a celebration. Linda walked round with her parents, Bill and Vi, then settled in a corner of the room with Tom, as the two families tried to agree a plan of action.

One option was ruled out right away. The Trenchards were a good Catholic family, so there was no question of an abortion, which, in any case, was still illegal in 1956. One solution, followed by many families, was for Linda to go away and 'visit relatives' for the later stages of her confinement, give birth and have the baby adopted. She could then return to Treforest refreshed and rested after a lovely 'holiday' and none of the neighbourhood gossips would be any the wiser.

A third possibility was that Linda could leave Treforest for a while, give birth and then hand the baby over to her aunt, who had no children, which would at least have kept the child within the family. None of these possibilities seemed ideal and the adults continued to try to reach an agreement. The whole time, Linda and Tom sat together, holding hands and whispering affectionately to one another.

Eventually, Freda noticed them. Tom recalled the moment, 'My mother, God bless her, said, "Look at them. We're trying to decide what's going to happen and they're oblivious to what's going on. How can we get in the way of that?"'

Thomas senior asked his son what *he* wanted to do. Tom replied without hesitation: 'I said, "I want to get married to

Linda and she wants to get married to me." My father just looked at me, it all went dead quiet for a moment, and then he said, "Go ahead." I always loved him for it.'

It wasn't quite as simple as that, though. Linda was not yet sixteen and was therefore too young to be married legally. They would have to wait until after her next birthday, on 14 January, and by that time there would be no hiding her condition. There was the wider family to convince that this was the right course of action as well. At least Tom's mother and father weren't hypocrites about their son's situation: they, too, had married after Freda became pregnant – and that was in the 1930s. Tom's cousin Margaret remembers her Auntie Freda telling her that Tom wanted to get married: 'He wasn't forced at all. Some parents might have done that, but he wanted to.'

Linda's friends weren't judgemental. While there was some inevitable gossip behind closed doors, Vimy Pitman recalls, 'Everybody felt immensely sorry for her, because she was such a nice person. Nobody put her down. I didn't know of any other pregnancy when we were that young. It was all so shocking. She was far too nice to say anything nasty about. You wouldn't say, "Oh look, what has she been up to, then?"'

Any childhood dreams Linda may have had of a romantic wedding were put firmly behind her when, eight months pregnant, she and Tom made their way to the Pontypridd Register Office in Courthouse Street on 2 March 1957. At that time, it was still important to be married before giving birth, however late in the day.

Register offices haven't changed much. It was an impersonal affair, with the cheery registrar, the master of ceremonies, seated behind a plain wooden table, while immediate family sat in rows on the facing chairs. Tom's sister Sheila was there with her new husband, Ken Davies, who was one of the two main witnesses on the marriage certificate. Tom's grandmother Ada, Aunt Lena and Uncle Albert, parents of the twins, were there and, of course, so were his parents, watching their teenage son grow up before their eyes. Linda's parents were joined by some of her close relatives, including her aunt, Josie Powell, who was also a witness. Nobody realised then that Linda's father, Bill, a quiet man like Tom senior, had only a short time left. He was battling tuberculosis – a grim reminder of how close to death Tom had come.

The ceremony was mercifully brief and the family retired to the Wood Road for a celebratory drink on the way home. It was very low key, but there were more pressing matters for the newlyweds to consider – where they were going to live and how they would provide for their child.

The living arrangements were easily sorted. Tom just packed his clothes and sauntered round to Linda's, where the now Mr and Mrs Woodward were given the basement area of 3 Cliff Terrace as their first marital home. Linda's parents and her younger sister Roslyn were on the floor above. Their living quarters were below the level of the street, so there wasn't much natural light, but Linda set about making the place presentable. It was very basic, however, with no fridge, Hoover or phone. The old stove she had to cook on was something from the 1940s. Visitors would bang on the grill with a boot to attract their attention, although that was liable to set the dogs barking up and down the road.

Tom had taken on some extra shifts at the Polyglove factory to try to build up a nest egg to get them started as man and wife, but it soon became clear that he would have to look for something better paid. He started work as a general labourer at the

British Coated Board and Paper Mills on the Treforest Industrial Estate.

Tom was just leaving on his bike to cycle to work for a night shift, when the ambulance drew up to take Linda to the maternity hospital in Cardiff. 'I couldn't even take a shift off when my wife went into hospital.' Even if he hadn't been working, this was the 1950s and long before prospective fathers were expected to hold their partner's hand while she gave birth.

On his return from the mill the following morning, Tom dumped his bike on the pavement and excitedly rushed into the all-too-familiar phone box to ring the hospital. It was 11 April 1957 and Tommy Woodward, aged sixteen, was informed he was now the father of a baby boy.

Tom dashed to the hospital in Glossop Terrace. He can chuckle now about what he must have looked like. He told the 1991 TV documentary *The Voice Made Flesh*, 'I walked to the hospital with a shopping bag, which I wouldn't have been seen dead with the week before. I had this bloody Teddy suit on with a shopping bag. And I walked into the hospital and I saw Linda and my son and I came out of there and I thought, "Who can touch me now!"'

He took the bus home, but decided to stop along the way at one of his favourite dance halls to toast the birth. 'I went into the toilet and one kid said, "Oh, we heard that you had to marry Linda Trenchard." And I grabbed him by the throat and lifted him up, you know, on the wall and then people pulled me off. I was so "lifted" by the fact that I had a wife and little boy. It made me feel much stronger than I was a week before. It made me a man.'

* * *

Despite that feeling of masculine bravado, Tom's situation was far from promising. He was a teenage father of one with no prospects. To a certain extent, Tom's life was following the norm for this part of South Wales: boys would leave school at fifteen, go down the mines or find a factory job and then look to marry and settle down. Circumstance may have dictated that Tom started a year or two earlier than most, but the majority of his school friends were married, with young families, while they were still teenagers.

Family life for Tom began with some grim news. Linda's father had to go into hospital as his tuberculosis worsened. Bill Trenchard died from TB just six weeks after the birth of his grandson, Mark. He was forty-two. Linda tried to rally round her mother and younger sister, but she had to care for her baby. Tom did his best to be supportive and, for a short time at least, was very attentive to his young family. He went everywhere they went. Brian Blackler recalls that the first time he saw Mark Woodward was when Tom was walking on the Feathery with his little boy perched on his shoulders. He was clearly a proud new dad.

Tom's routine began to follow a pattern remarkably similar to that of his father. During the week he worked hard, and on Friday nights enjoyed a beer with his mates at the Commercial Inn in Treforest or the White Hart pub in the area between the village and Pontypridd known as The Tumble.

Brian also left the glove factory and started work at a local pit, the Maritime Colliery in Maesycoed, on the outskirts of Pontypridd, so Tom inevitably saw less of him as time passed. Tom still enjoyed the company of his old friends, but his best mate as the years went by remained Dai Perry. In Dai's own words, they were like brothers, and they forged a lifelong bond, supping pints together and getting into scraps. It was a time when Tom's nose was reshaped many times. He later complained to the renowned journalist Donald Zec, 'I hate my horrible nose – it's been worked over, bent sideways and patched up more than any other part of me. And always hit by a head – we liked to keep our hands nice and smooth like.' His crooked teeth weren't much better.

Generally speaking, Tom and Dai didn't go looking for trouble. It had a habit of finding them, however, usually when one beer too many had been downed. On one memorable occasion, Tom was head-butted so hard, he ended up flying through the plate-glass door of a fish and chip shop.

The fight had been brewing for several days, after a row and a frank exchange of insults outside an Indian restaurant had resulted in Tom punching a man he described as a hooligan. The word went out in the days that followed that the man's friends were looking for Tom to even the score. Dai warned him to be careful, but Tom was sure he could handle any trouble. He told Dai overconfidently, 'He's got no chance.'

Sure enough, the man – and his father – caught up with Tom as he ate some chips in the doorway of a Ponty takeaway. Tom has never been slow to tell the story of his comeuppance: 'I told him, "Why don't you run along?" Dai whispered to me, "Keep an eye on him," but I didn't care. I said, "Where do you want to go?" and while I was talking, he suddenly let me have it and I smashed right through the door into the fish and chip shop.'

He was still scrambling to his feet, ready to continue the fight, when the police arrived and moved everybody on. Tom, fuelled by the beer, followed the pair up to the Graig, where they lived, and jumped on them without even bothering to take his overcoat off. It was a big mistake, because there were two of them.

That became three when the man's mother charged out of their house, and four when his brother arrived as well. As Tom put it succinctly, 'They beat the shit out of me.' He still has the scar where one of them bit him on the finger.

Dai Perry looked on while his friend took a beating. Although he could have sorted things out for Tom, he did nothing because of an unwritten code of conduct: you couldn't fight a woman or a much older man, especially if he was someone's father. It was a question of respect, and Tom never held it against him.

On the streets of Pontypridd, the Teddy boy rules did not, for the most part, include the use of knives. Drugs weren't a feature of the lifestyle either, and Tom never saw the point of narcotics. Instead, it was a macho culture of beer, Woodbines and the occasional brawl. Brian Blackler is adamant that Tom didn't deserve his reputation as a ruffian: 'He could look after himself, Tom, but he wasn't a fighter. I think most of the boys were like that in them days. We wouldn't get bullied, would we? I never liked a bully and I wouldn't get bullied and Tom was the same.'

Despite not looking for trouble, there were many nights when Tom greeted his wife with a black eye or a fat lip after a night out. There must have been a lot of bullies in Pontypridd then. An evening rarely ended without some sort of punch-up between those Teds who were looking for trouble. If you went out to a dance hall in town, you needed eyes in the back of your head to keep watch for any menacing Ted sneaking up on you from behind. The British Legion in Rhydyfelin was so notoriously rough that it became widely known as the 'Bucket of Blood'.

The history of that era reveals that there were some massive fights between rival gangs of Teds. But Keith Davies, who later played guitar alongside Tom, observes: 'Sometimes I think the whole Ted thing is overcooked. It was just a way of life for every-one. Everybody was a Teddy boy. I wouldn't say Tom was a tough Ted. He was aggressive on stage though.'

Tom, meanwhile, was promoted at work to a job as a machin-ist. As a result, he was earning more money, but alternate weeks he had to work a night shift from 6 a.m. to 6 p.m. Even that small advancement was threatened by an overzealous trade unionist, who complained that he was too young to receive a man's wage. Tom had to hold his tongue – and his fists – when some of the other staff tried to sabotage his machine so he would be out of favour with management. He began to hate his job.

Letting off steam with his mates was poor compensation for his general unhappiness at the way things had turned out for him. He was linked to some petty crime in the area, which gave Freda some sleepless nights, worried that the next knock on the door might be someone ready to arrest Tom. Mostly, though, it involved sneaking into the cinema without paying or nicking the occasional 45 from the record store.

He laughed the troubles off: 'When the officials came to see my mother with the brasses nicely polished in the front room and a picture of granddad with his medals on, they went away saying, "No ruffian could live here!"'

Perhaps most alarmingly, he temporarily lost his appetite for singing, weighed down by his responsibilities. Linda, whose contribution to Tom's career should never be underestimated, had to prod and cajole him into singing again, starting off while shaving in the mirror before work. She was delighted when he came home one afternoon in early 1957 with a new single in his hand.

Tom had been walking through the centre of Pontypridd, when he heard 'Whole Lotta Shakin' Going On' by Jerry Lee

Lewis for the first time. It was blasting out from the speakers at Freddie Feys' record shop. He was immediately stopped in his tracks: 'Good God. To me that was it! I loved that record and it was a white man singing boogie-woogie that he had heard black men play.'

Tom would never forget the effect Jerry Lee's music had on him. He admired Elvis and would spend afternoons listening to Brian's elder brother John's collection of The King's records. But he loved the man from Louisiana, who was known as 'The Killer'. Tom liked his aggression and the way Lewis would chew his audience up and spit them out. He was a white man who sounded like he was black, and that was the effect Tom had always wanted.

At least money wasn't as tight and he could buy a new Hawk guitar. He was earning £18 a week and they weren't paying any rent. Until now, Tom had sung at school and family get-togethers. It was time for him to start singing in public.

Urged on by Linda, he approached his uncle, Albert Jones, to ask if he could perform at the Wood Road. 'Could you put us on, Uncle Albert – you know, do a gig down there?'

Albert, who was quite a stern chap, replied, 'It will never go down well here – rock 'n' roll.'

Tom persevered, however, and eventually he had a lucky break, when an act they had booked failed to show one Sunday evening. Tom stepped up and sang three numbers, including the classic Elvis hit 'Blue Suede Shoes' and 'Sixteen Tons', a number one for Tennessee Ernie Ford in 1956. The reaction was much more favourable than Albert had expected, so Tom came back after an interval and sang three more. Afterwards, the club's entertainment secretary, Charlie Ashman, was so pleased, he put his hand in the till and handed Tom a £1 note. In those days of pre-decimal money, he could buy thirty pints in the club for a quid. The only problem was that everyone knew how old he was and he could never get served there.

Tom was encouraged to think he could sing for money, or at least beer money, in the pubs and clubs around Treforest and Pontypridd. His mates supported him, especially when he started singing at one of their favourite pubs, the Wheatsheaf, at the bottom of Rickards Street. They would have a few beers in the downstairs bar before adjourning to the room upstairs, where Tom would belt out his mix of Jerry Lee Lewis, Elvis and Ray Charles numbers, accompanying himself as best as he could on his guitar.

The audience loved him at the Wheatsheaf, but it was practically his local and didn't really count. The landlady, Joan Lister, recalled that the audience wouldn't get up for a pint when Tom was on, which may or may not be true. He needed more than that generous appreciation, however, and for a while joined a local beat group called the De Avalons. He was the drummer, not the singer, but soon tired of that arrangement, much preferring to be the centre of attention.

He joined a concert party called The Misfits. These variety ensembles, which often included a comedian and a group, were very popular. They were like a mini evening of *Britain's Got Talent*. Tom liked the set-up, because the money was good – anything from £2 to £5 for a night's work – and he found he could earn almost as much at a weekend as the rest of the week in the paper factory. Tom was one of three acts, which included a singer who specialised in Frankie Laine numbers.

Linda had no objection when Tom decided to quit his job at the paper factory and sign on the dole. Tom was reassured by a workmate, who told him, 'If you fail, you can always return. It doesn't take a genius to work in a paper mill.' He needed to be free from shift work so he could accept evening bookings. From time to time, he would take a job selling vacuum cleaners or working on a building site, carting bricks, but his heart wasn't in it and these jobs rarely lasted more than a few weeks. His only ticket out of the Valleys was with 'singer' stamped on his passport, so he was much happier concentrating on that ambition than grafting for a few pounds a week. The reality was that he had started to drift.

The most significant member of a Tommy Woodward audience during this time was a young guitarist from Rhydyfelin called Vernon Hopkins. He had heard about a rough and ready lad with a big voice doing his time on the pub and club circuit around Pontypridd, so he turned up at the Wheatsheaf one night to watch Tom perform. Vernon was unimpressed with his act, but admired his voice.

'His voice was great, but he would just stand there and sing. He wouldn't even introduce a song. It was like he didn't want to be there at all, but he had to do it, because he wanted the money. It wasn't a good picture. He looked intimidating.'

# 5

# THE GIRL WITH
# THE RED DRESS ON

Not everyone found Tom scary. One of his long-standing drink-ing pals, Alan Barratt, wasn't overawed, even though he was the smaller man. According to local legend, he once gave Tom a fearful pasting in an argument over a girl. Tom literally had to drag himself home on his hands and knees. The pair remained good friends and Tom was later rumoured to have helped Alan buy the newsagent's in Church Village, where he settled, just a few miles from Pontypridd.

They were together one evening eating a takeaway outside a curry house, when Tom met a curvaceous fifteen-year-old called Gill Beazer. When he came across a girl he liked, Tommy Woodward was no longer one of the lads. He acted in a completely different manner. He had been impressed when, as a boy, he walked with his father around the terraced streets where they lived. The local housewives would come to the front door just to smile and say to his dad, 'Good morning, Thomas.' The friendly greetings brightened his day. He learned from his father and the other men in his family that women were to be treated with respect, consideration and as equals. He didn't swear or act the macho man in front of them, and it made no difference how pretty they were.

Gill was most definitely attractive, though. The tabloid papers of today would describe her as a stunner. Tommy's relationship with the shy teenager was a million miles away from his later image as Tom Jones, sex-obsessed superstar.

In the early summer of 1960, the curry house had just opened in Central Square, Trallwn, on the other side of Pontypridd. It was a general store as well, and Gill was browsing there when Tom, then aged twenty, showed up with Alan Barratt. They were there for two reasons: Tom loved curry and, to this day, lamb curry remains a favourite dish; he also liked a pint. He and Alan would pop into the Llanover Arms on the corner or the Central Hotel across the square. The hotel had a music room, where Tom would appear occasionally, so he knew it well.

Gill lived with her nan, Ruth, around the corner at the top of East Street, third house down on the right. Her mother left when she was a baby, and her father, a carpenter called Elias Beazer, made a new life in Rhydyfelin, where he remarried and had a large family. Gill still saw her dad, but was brought up by her grandmother.

In the evenings, Gill, who was a bit of a loner and had few friends of her own age, would often take a stroll around the square to soak up the atmosphere and have a passing conversation or two. It was a much more innocent time, when people looked out for one another. Gill was well known in the neighbourhood and would pop in and out of the shops – a cobbler's and a hairdresser, a sweet shop, a greengrocer and the Co-op at the end. 'I just used to like to go out of my door, onto the square and talk to whoever was around.' There never seemed to be any girls her age, so she usually ended up talking to the boys, who would be chatting and trying to look cool on their motorbikes.

She began joining other underage girls to sneak into pubs where they could get served, providing they stayed at the back, away from the men-only bars. Perhaps because of that and her large bust, the boys would talk about her and she developed a bad reputation that was entirely unjustified.

She knew nothing about Tom when they met. Treforest seemed a world away from Trallwn. She didn't know he was a local singer and she had no idea he was married with a young son – information that he certainly didn't volunteer. It would be a common theme, where Tom was concerned, that women he became involved with didn't know his marital status. Gill told him she had just left school and was working as a shop assistant in the Star Supply Stores in Pontypridd, waiting for a better job to come up in the Aero Zip factory on the industrial estate.

One thing struck Gill at that first encounter: Alan, who was a couple of years older than Tom, was much more handsome than his friend. Gill observes, 'Alan was a very good-looking guy. He had black curly hair and was smartly turned out. He was looked-after smart, if you know what I mean. He was slighter than Tom, although Tom was slight, mind. Tom wasn't particularly hand-some, because he had this long jawline.'

Alan may have been better looking, but it was Tom who had the charm. He had a bent, lopsided nose, crooked teeth and an elongated jaw, but he was easy to talk to. 'He just had this lovely personality as far as I was concerned,' recalls Gill, who readily agreed to meet up a day or two later by the railings on The Parade, the street below the curry house.

'He told me when he wanted to meet me there, but he didn't come. I just hung about for an hour and eventually he turned up. No matter when he made arrangements with me, it would be an hour or two later that he would turn up.' Gill didn't realise that he had responsibilities elsewhere.

Nothing happened between them on The Parade other than a walk and a chat. They just seemed to like each other's company. It was very relaxed and Tom suggested that she might like to hear him sing at a gig or perhaps take in a dance one evening soon; he would call her to let her know when.

The next time she saw him, he was walking underneath the bridge by the railway station in Pontypridd, looking unrecognisable in a double-breasted navy blue pinstriped suit. Gill assumed he had paid a trip to the magistrates' court nearby: 'He might have been a naughty boy, but he was very smartly dressed.' She didn't quiz him about it. It wasn't her business and she wasn't a pushy sort of girl anyway. She admits, 'I never had any confidence in myself.'

Tom's luck with the law had, in fact, run out when, desperately short of cash, he had broken into the old tobacconist's shop in Treforest with a pal. They were hardly criminal masterminds. The stupid petty crime was unearthed when, by all accounts, they tried to sell their haul down the Wood Road. The police, hearing the rumours of some dodgy cigarettes for sale, put two and two together and found the goods hidden in Tom's mother's house.

Even the dole office knew of his misdeed, noting in its records: 'Applicant is on bail pending being heard for a charge of breaking and entering at the next quarter session.' Tom has not denied this transgression and later admitted he had once been placed on probation.

Tom started calling Gill to suggest when they might meet up. Neither of them had a phone. Tom would step out to his red phone box and she would be in hers outside the Central Hotel, just across from the top of East Street. Tom would dial the number – 2026 – and wait for someone to answer the ringing phone. It didn't matter who it was, he would simply ask the person to pop over the road and tell Gill that he wanted to speak to her. She would dash for the phone, pleased to hear from him.

Gill had the same routine if she was staying the night at a friend's house. She would simply ring the phone box and ask whoever answered to go and tell her nan what she was doing, please, so she wouldn't worry. She never knew the number of Tom's phone box, presumably because he didn't want to run the risk of his wife answering. Gill recalls, 'I would have to wait for him to do things and I suppose I was patient enough to wait without even thinking about it.'

She loved it when they went jiving at Judges in Porth or the Bucket of Blood in Rhydyfelin: 'I was a good jiver and so was he.' But, in the main, she would just be his girl when he went to a gig. Often she had no idea where they were, although Franchies in Taff Street was one she enjoyed. Neither of them had any money – Gill used to make a lot of her clothes – so it would be a trip on the bus to the gig, where she and sometimes other friends would cheer him on. Tom would usually be paid a couple of pounds and perhaps some beer. Afterwards, there was no hanging around. He needed to get home to his family, so they would catch the bus back to Pontypridd, get off in Merthyr Road and he would set off for Treforest, while she walked back to East Street. She recalls, 'He would do the gig and then he would be gone. We never had any money. We never had anything at all.'

Looking back with the privilege of hindsight, Gill believes Tom wanted company: 'He needed someone when he went to these gigs – he needed someone in the audience there for him, someone whom he could focus on or relate to. He didn't want to go on his own.' He was clearly fond of her, however.

On one evening she was due to accompany him to a gig in Caerphilly, eight miles away. Tom suggested she get the bus, which left from the Broadway, with him and his friend Gwyn Griffiths. The bus ran only once an hour, so Tom had to catch it or he would be late. Gill and Gwyn, whom she already knew, caught the bus as arranged, but, typically, there was no sign of Tom. As they travelled down the Broadway, they saw Tom running along, clutching his guitar and trying to catch them up. He banged on the side to attract the driver's attention and Gill started shouting to him to stop the bus as well. Thankfully, he stopped and let Tom on board.

She had dolled herself up for the occasion, wearing her long brown hair up and putting on a red dress that an aunt had brought over from Jamaica as a present. Gill will never forget that gig, because after his usual smattering of Jerry Lee Lewis and Elvis, Tom turned towards her, midway through his next song, focused his gaze directly on her and sang, 'See the girl with the red dress on …' It was his power-packed version of 'What'd I Say', the song that took the legendary Ray Charles into the mainstream in 1959. Jerry Lee had made a rock 'n' roll recording of the track at the famous Sun Studio in 1960. 'I was elated,' says Gill. 'He was singing to me.' It was lovely for Gill, but it also revealed that Tom hadn't forgotten the advice of his Uncle George and was selling the song to his audience. It was a technique he continued to employ as a Las Vegas headliner.

Gill thought there was more to the relationship than there was. Perhaps she was naive, but she acknowledges simply: 'Yes, I thought he was my boyfriend.' That changed when she saw him in Pontypridd with a young blond boy who was clearly his son and turned out to be Mark. 'I didn't have bad feelings towards him about it. I'm a "what will be, will be" sort of person. I think that a little bit of something is better than nothing. That's the only way to explain why I went on seeing him.'

Gill admits that she and Tom enjoyed plenty of 'kisses and cuddles', but she denies there was anything more. If they weren't going to a gig or jiving, then they would simply stay and chat on a street corner or go for a walk in Trallwn or the nearby village of Ynysybwl. She strongly believes that the image of Tom as a rough and ready macho man is completely wrong. She explains: 'I think people got the wrong impression of him. He wasn't at all as he was portrayed. I never found him to be a forceful person. He never expected anything from me and he told me that, and it was very important to me. He said to me that whatever I wanted physically would be OK. He was never, ever nasty with me and treated me as an equal. He was a gentle person.'

Everyone assumed that Gill was sleeping with Tom, because for nearly two years they were often seen together. They never went all the way, however. Eventually Gill found a proper boyfriend, whom she would marry. She still saw Tom occasionally. He would pop in to find out how she was doing and make sure she was all right. They lost touch when Tom's career began to move forward, although Alan Barratt would call round to catch up from time to time. When Gill had a son, Alan brought her a card from Tom on the boy's first birthday that contained two crisp pound notes. By strange coincidence, in later life, she became the best friend of Marion Crewe, who was Dai Perry's sister and was close to Tom, whom she adored. Gill remained on the fringes of Tom's world and would say hello on the sad days he came home for funerals.

Gill paints a contrasting picture of the young Tom Jones from those who have portrayed him as some sort of yob. The most likely explanation is that there were two sides to Tom, fashioned from his upbringing in this quiet part of South Wales. He would act the big man over a pint or two with his mates, swear like a navvy and was quite prepared to nut someone if they were threatening him. Facially, he looked much tougher than he actually was. He wasn't a huge man by any means, being slim and fit and about 5ft 10in tall. But his badly misshapen nose and teeth meant he could look menacing without even trying. He liked dressing as a Teddy boy because he thought he looked 'slick', as he put it.

The reality, at least as far as women were concerned, was entirely different. 'I think he was quite shy underneath,' says Gill. Her view of Tom is one endorsed by Linda: 'He is the most mild-mannered man you could wish to meet – and so patient with everyone. He is kind and gentle.'

The real man doesn't sound like a love-them-and-leave-them stud. Inevitably, he changed when he became a superstar and had to live up to his image as a sex god. Women were willing and readily available to him then, but at this stage of his life that happened only occasionally. Looking back on her own experience with the man who would become Tom Jones, Gill reveals the moral dilemma of Tommy Woodward: how to reconcile becoming involved with other women while being happily married. She observes, 'He loved his wife dearly.'

# 6

# SENATOR TOM

Vernon Hopkins hadn't forgotten about Tommy Woodward; he just didn't need him. He had seen Tom once or twice around the Pontypridd pubs, apparently flogging a dead horse, still in Teddy boy gear, the Hawk guitar around his neck, banging out the same Frankie Laine, Jerry Lee Lewis and Ray Charles numbers. Tom didn't seem to be getting anywhere. Although he always believed it was his destiny to be a singer, he was stuck in a rut.

Vernon, a young man filled with energy and a passion for music, changed that for him. He had a steady job as an apprentice compositor with the *Pontypridd Observer*, while playing with his group, The Senators, who were gradually building a local following. They had even appeared on television.

The band had started out as a three piece – just Vernon and two Rhydyfelin teenagers, Keith Davies and Jeff Maher, who lived next door to one another. By coincidence, the trio had their first gig at the Wood Road in Treforest. Keith, who was a devoted fan of The Shadows, played their famous hit 'Apache' and other Hank Marvin classics, but it was clear they needed a singer if they were going to progress.

One of the club members told them his son could sing and would come on stage with them. Keith already knew Tommy Pitman from Rhydyfelin, but didn't know he could sing. The Senators were happy to give him a try the next time they played at the club. It went well. Tommy jumped up, sang 'Blue Suede Shoes', 'Jailhouse Rock' and some other Elvis songs, with a dash of Buddy Holly for variety.

Tommy had recently been demobbed after finishing his national service with the RAF in Cyprus. While there, he had joined a group that wanted an Elvis-style singer. They performed regularly on the island, on television as well as in live shows, so he was an accomplished performer by the time he sang at the Wood Road.

Everything seemed set fair for the group. They added a drummer, Brian Price, and decided to call themselves The Senators after the model of Vernon's Höfner guitar. They soon became much in demand, with some regular gigs, including the YMCA near the Old Bridge in Taff Street, Pontypridd, on Friday nights. They were also booked to appear on a new pop show called *Discs A GoGo*. This was hosted by the former Radio Luxembourg DJ Kent Walton, who would become much more famous as the commentator on professional wrestling every week on ITV's *World of Sport*. They had to audition at the studios in Pontcanna, Cardiff. Tommy sang a Cliff Richard song – only to learn that for the show, a Christmas special, the producers wanted the band to perform 'Jingle Bells'. 'Well, that's me out for a start,' said Tommy. 'I'm not going to sing "Jingle Bells". I'm a rock 'n' roll singer.' So the rest of The Senators went ahead without him and performed it as an instrumental.

The Senators were going places. The one problem for the band that Vernon couldn't have foreseen was that Tommy Pitman was losing his enthusiasm. He was older than the others and didn't relish playing for what was, in effect, a teenage jive club. He recalls, 'I wasn't mad on singing, to be honest. I got a bit fed up with the YMCA on Friday nights. There were no drinks or anything like that – just dancing. I used to go down with my mates and have a couple of beers in a nearby pub and then we'd start playing a few cards until I'd go, "I'm not going up to the Y tonight."' Friday night, he decided, was drinks night with the boys.

The rest of the band coped the first time, but something had to be done when it happened again. They laboured through the first set, but Keith Davies observed, 'I can only play "Apache" so many times.'

Vernon said, 'I know a fella who goes round the clubs. He's called Tommy Woodward and he'll probably be in the White Hart.' So he set off down the High Street to try to find their substitute.

Sure enough, Tom was with his friends, propping up the bar, when Vernon dashed in. He said Pitman hadn't turned up and asked if Tom would like to earn a few bob by singing the second set. Vernon remembers Tom giving a little cough into his hand. He has the same mannerism today; it's a sign that he's nervous about something. He downed the rest of his pint, 'OK, Vern, I'll do it for a couple of quid.'

Just when Vernon thought it was all settled, Tom remembered that the YMCA was a booze-free zone. He stopped in his tracks: 'I'm out for a good drink, Vern. Out with the boys, like.' Vernon, thinking quickly, said he would buy a crate of beers and smuggle them in just for Tom. That sealed the deal.

They ran back to the Y as fast as they could go without exhausting Tom, who wouldn't be able to sing if he was gasping for breath. It's not easy to get up and start singing with a band you've never really met before, let alone rehearsed with. The Senators had also just gone through some changes: Jeff and Colin had left to start their own group and had been replaced by rhythm guitarist Mike Roberts, who was in television, and Alva Turner on drums.

The legend of that first gig has it that Tom bounced on stage and was off. That's not strictly true, because he was fretting about not knowing what the first number was going to be. 'Christ,' he said to Vernon, 'we've never even practised together.'

The familiar swagger was back, however, when he walked on and turned to Keith, who had no idea who he was, and said confidently, 'Do you know "Great Balls of Fire" in C?'

'No,' came the reply, 'but you sing it and we'll play it.'

With a voice so strong it made the walls tremble, Tom burst into 'You shake my nerves and you rattle my brain …'

The rather square and sober 200-strong audience had never seen anything like the menacing figure now before them. He looked as if he would jump off the stage and nut you if you didn't applaud in the right place. They were too shocked to clap after the first number. Tom marched off to take a lusty swig of light ale from behind a curtain, before continuing in the same vein, standing defiantly in centre stage, legs braced as if he were pulling a cart. Gradually, however, freed from the restrictions of playing his guitar, he began to move about and engage with the audience, who responded by starting to dance. Tom found his rhythm, and Vernon recalls, 'He was like a man possessed.' He was helped in that regard by polishing off four light ales while he performed.

Tommy Pitman was a good singer, particularly effective with ballads, but Vernon realised that night that the other Tommy,

Tom Woodward, was the future for the band. Keith Davies agreed, 'He had a much stronger voice than Tommy Pitman. He was just more aggressive all over. They were just two different types of singer.' Tom wasn't concerned about that – he just wanted to grab his couple of pounds and make it back to the White Hart before they called last orders.

Tom went round to Vernon's house a few days later for a run-through and sang an old-fashioned Edwardian ballad called 'Thora' in his best gospel style. 'I'm not having no bugger in this band who sings hymns,' said young Keith, who would ultimately be persuaded by the obvious quality of Tom's voice.

Tom began rehearsing regularly with the band on a Wednesday at Vernon's house in Glyndwr Avenue, Rhydyfelin. Five young men were crammed into the front room, with amplifiers on every chair, and a piano and drum kit wedged in as well. Vernon recalls fondly, 'You wouldn't believe the size of it. We rehearsed many of the numbers that he later made famous in that room.'

Five became six the day that Tommy Pitman came down to find out if he was still in the band. Vernon was nervous about so many blokes in a confined space, worried that the two Tommys would come to blows as they competed to be The Senators' vocalist. He even persuaded his sisters to lay on tea and sandwiches in an attempt to keep everything civilised. In the end, the two Toms behaved impeccably.

Vernon knew he wanted to keep his new singer, but they put it to the vote. Keith supported Vernon's view that Tom Woodward should stay. Tommy Pitman pointed out that he owned part of the equipment. The next suggestion was that they should have two vocalists. Tom wasn't having that and told them, 'It's either me or Tommy.'

Vernon tried to make the decision painless: 'The thing is, Tommy, you left us in the lurch and we have been getting on all right with Tom, so I'm going to say we stay as we are now.' Tommy accepted the decision and the two singers left together, as they lived in neighbouring streets in Treforest.

Tommy Pitman recalls, 'We weren't going to fight about a thing like that. We walked back together and chatted about different things. I said, "I paid for half of this sound system and you are coming in for nout." He said, "OK, I'll sort you out." Ha! I never got nothing. When we parted, I said, "I'll see you. All the best."'

In fact, Pitman wasn't too dejected. He had already had an offer to join a group called The Strollers, which Jeff and Colin from The Senators had formed. They were a smarter-looking band, more Shadows than Jerry Lee, and Tommy, who liked to wear an Italian suit on stage, thought they were a better match for him. He recalls with a glint of good humour, 'It wasn't too long before I was in Butlins for a season with them. So I thought then I had the best of the deal, obviously.'

The Senators were Vernon's group. He made the key decisions and was the driving force. Tom was just the singer, but Vernon was in no doubt about his ability. Although they would later have their differences, Vernon acknowledges, 'Right from when he joined, he was as good a singer as I have ever performed with. His voice was so pure.'

The first thing Vernon had to do was find their new frontman a suitable name. Tommy or Tom Woodward didn't sound rock 'n' roll enough in the days of Billy Fury, Adam Faith and Johnny Kidd and the Pirates. They decided to go to the Upper Boat Inn on the Taff River in Pontypridd for a few pints to try to come up with some ideas – they had none, despite the brain-lubricating beer.

Vernon then thought of looking in the telephone book for a name, and nipped across to a nearby phone box to have a quick search for inspiration. The problem with a Welsh phone book was that it contained page after page of people named Jones. Tommy Jones? That would never do, but his finger stopped at S when he reached Scott. Tommy Scott had definite possibilities.

Tom was enthusiastic when he returned to the table, as were the rest of the band, so Vernon went ahead and had some cards printed that read 'The Senators with Twisting Tommy Scott'. It didn't take them long to drop the 'Twisting' part, although Tom was a master of that popular dance.

Keith Davies remembers helping Tom with his Tommy Scott signature, so he would be ready to sign autographs should he be asked. Originally, Tom wrote his name in a very small and spindly fashion. Keith told him, "'You can't write it like that. It looks like you're signing the dole, like." And I showed him, "Do a big S like this, and then put two big lines across the ts." He tried it and said, "Like that?" and I said, "Yeah, like that.'"

A new name was the first step in smoothing out Tom's rough edges to make him more acceptable to a paying audience. The next meant binning the beloved Teddy boy suit. It was the end of a long era, but Tom was persuaded to move on to black leather and a stage outfit that Elvis or Gene Vincent might wear.

One of Tom's notable characteristics throughout his career is that he is amenable to change and suggestion. He doesn't let ego get in the way of what he considers good sense. He accepts things and gets on with it. He wanted to look good, but what mattered most to him was the music he was going to sing. The biggest influence he had within the group was on their repertoire.

First and foremost, he wanted Jerry Lee Lewis. As Keith Davies remembers, the rest of the band would be mischievous about that: 'He was just Jerry Lee Lewis orientated all the time. He would introduce a song by saying, "We would like to sing a song now by Mister Jerry Lee Lewis," and we would all look surprised and go, "Jerry Lee Lewis???"'

Tom took the gentle ribbing in good spirit and was never less than dedicated. At their weekly rehearsals, they used to take it in turns to suggest a number to perform during their week-long round of gigs.

Keith recalls, 'He would say something like, "I want to do a song called 'Bama Lama Bama Loo'" and I would say, "Christ, what's that?" It was usually something I had never heard of. Then it would be my turn and I would say I wanted to do "The Young Ones" by Cliff Richard, and Tom hated his music – he just didn't like it. Every time I used to do the intro, you could see his face going. It was a soppy tune for him to sing!'

Tom had to grit his teeth and learn some of the more anaemic chart songs, because that was what their audience wanted. 'He used to feel a prat doing it, but they were in the charts and people used to sing them.'

Tom was doing his homework though. Most Saturday afternoons, Vernon would go around to the house in Cliff Terrace, say hello to Linda and young Mark and then join Tom upstairs in his mother-in-law's lounge and listen to records on his old portable record player. Tom and Vernon weren't interested in rugby or football or social injustice – just music. They would spend hours talking about it.

Jerry Lee Lewis, of course, featured a lot in Tom's expanding record collection. 'Listen to the drums on this,' he would say enthusiastically, as he put yet another of The Killer's tracks on the turntable.

By a quirk of fate, soon after he joined The Senators, Tom noticed that his hero was performing a concert at the Sophia Gardens in Cardiff as part of his comeback. Tom had been disappointed four years earlier, when Jerry Lee, then twenty-two, cancelled his concert in Cardiff after revelations about his marriage hit the front pages. He had arrived in Britain for a six-week tour in May 1958, when journalists spotted a young girl in his entourage called Myra, who he said was fifteen and his third wife. That was bad enough, but she turned out to be his first cousin once removed and was only thirteen. Their union was a product of the hillbilly mentality prevalent in the Deep South. His management pulled Jerry Lee out of that tour after only three concerts. Tom recalled, 'When the public found out about it, there was uproar and he got sent out of the country.'

Tom managed to get tickets in the front row for his hero's return and would later reveal that it was his favourite musical performance ever. Jerry Lee did all his favourites, including show-stopping versions of 'High School Confidential' and an encore of 'Good Golly, Miss Molly'. One critic described his act as 'far and away the most exciting thing I have ever seen on a British stage'. Tom was mesmerised and would use that performance as a template for his own.

The night was made even more memorable when he spotted Jerry Lee's car leaving, followed him in a taxi and jumped out to ask for his autograph when they stopped at a red light. The fact that Jerry Lee was happy to oblige under these slightly bizarre circumstances made a lasting impression on Tom. He has never underestimated the importance of fans and always made time for them when he became famous.

While Tom continued to be obsessed with Jerry Lee's music, he did absorb the influence of other singers – chiefly great black artists with distinctive and soulful voices, including Solomon Burke, Ray Charles and, in particular, the rich tones of Brook Benton. The American singer had a breakthrough hit with 'It's Just a Matter of Time' in 1959. Tom would listen intently to the way he used the whole range of his voice to carry a song. Play a Brook Benton song and you can easily imagine Tom singing it. Vernon admits that Tom had a much broader knowledge of music than the rest of the band and listening to records at his house was a musical education.

Tom was always keen to find new material, however. One day, after a rehearsal at the Y, he noticed that Keith was carrying a new record by Johnny Kidd and the Pirates called 'A Shot of Rhythm and Blues'. Keith told him that it was fabulous, so they went to Cliff Terrace to listen. Tom loved it. '"Leave this with me," he said. "I've got to learn the words and we'll do it next time." So I left it there and I never saw it again from that day to this.'

Tom improved dramatically as a performer with The Senators. He was more confident and didn't just stand and sing. They used to do a version of the UK number one 'The Twist', by Chubby Checker, in which Tom would twist over to Keith and the guitarist would twist back to him. They were only messing about, but the crowd always loved it.

They had regular work and a supportive following. During these early days, they had no formal manager, but Horace Turner, the father of the drummer, Alva, helped them for the sheer enjoyment of it. He took no commission for sorting out their fees, bookings and regular work. On Tuesday nights, they played the Empress Ballroom in Abercynon; Wednesday, they rehearsed from 7 p.m. until 10 p.m., so they could make the pub for a beer before closing; Thursday, they travelled to Caerphilly for their favourite night of the week at the Bedwas Working Men's Club, popularly known as the Green Fly; and Friday, they still had their usual alcohol-free night at the YMCA in Pontypridd. Many other local venues formed an orderly queue to sign them up when it became clear that they could fill the place. They played often at the Memorial Hall in Newbridge, known to everyone as the Memo, the Cwm Welfare Club in Beddau and the Regent Ballroom in Hopkinstown, on the west side of Pontypridd.

The band was being paid between £12 and £15 a night, which left them with £2 or £3 each after petrol and other expenses. Tom acquired a reputation for never putting his hand in his pocket to buy a drink. Vernon recalls with a smile, 'The only way he would buy a drink would be if you turned him upside down and shook him.' Keith also confirms, 'I can't remember too many times when he bought me a pint, put it that way. Nothing comes to mind.'

The reality of Tom's situation was that he was the odd man out, because he had a wife and son at home and had to hand most of his wages over to Linda. He was still signing on the dole every week for his twelve shillings and sixpence. From time to time, he would take on a manual job, but, as Gill Beazer remembers, 'He never really worked.'

On 26 May 1962, Tom had his first mention as a singer in the *Pontypridd Observer*. A young reporter called Gerry Greenberg had seen them rehearsing at the Wheatsheaf one evening and, because he was keen to be involved in the local music scene, decided to write about them. He recalls, 'I thought he was a good singer, but back then I had nothing much to judge him against in terms of stars. He was a local singer and it was difficult to compare him to big stars.' The paper published a small picture of the band on page three, with a caption that read: 'The Pontypridd group who are making quite a name for themselves in modern music. Their soloist is popular Tommy Scott, Keith Davies on rhythm guitar, Alva Turner on drums, Vernon Hopkins on bass guitar and Mike Roberts on lead guitar.'

Three days later, Tom and The Senators appeared on television for the first time, on a BBC Wales show called *Donald Peers Presents* – not the catchiest of titles by today's standards. Peers was a self-made man from the small mining town of Ammanford. He ran away from home at sixteen and became one of the most popular singers in the country. His signature song, 'In a Shady Nook by a Babbling Brook', was perfect for a singalong at the Wood Road on a Saturday night.

The TV show gave unknown local acts three minutes in the spotlight. Tom was firmly told that he had to tone down the gyrations for polite television. He chose to sing 'That Lucky Old Sun' – another Vaughn Monroe hit he had loved growing up. The producers were impressed and asked him to come back on a future show.

Tom bought a new eight-guinea suit to wear; that was a lot of money then. Keith Davies recalls, 'I thought he was going to sing "Sixteen Tons", but of all the songs they could have chosen for him to do, they decided on a Cliff Richard song, 'I'm Lookin' Out the Window'. At least he had the suit, which he had been measured for and everything, but the wardrobe mistress said, "You are not dressing in a suit." So she gave him a pair of jeans, a red shirt and a tartan dicky bow tie. He looked like Rupert Bear. And he said, "I'm not wearing that." So they came to a compromise and he wore the jeans with a red open-necked shirt.

'I shall never forget him trying to keep a straight face as he sang "I'm Lookin' Out the Window" to a window made of plastic. And what you couldn't see on TV was a man up a stepladder with a watering can, pouring the "rain" down the window. It was hilarious. I was laughing so much Tom told me that if I carried on like that, I was going to have to bugger off.'

Tom didn't add 'I'm Lookin' Out the Window' to The Senators' set list, but many of the songs, like 'Sixteen Tons', which he performed with them around the clubs of South Wales, would later feature on Tom's albums. They used to open with the Ben E. King soul classic 'Spanish Harlem', which had been a hit in the UK charts in the summer of 1962 for Jimmy Justice and was another Tom would record in the future. The song let sceptical audiences know that they weren't going to perform rock 'n' roll exclusively.

One song he introduced to the set list was the powerful Sophie Tucker lament 'My Yiddishe Momme', which his father had taught him when he was a little boy and became a crowd favourite during his later live performances. On one memorable evening at the Wood Road, he sang 'My Yiddishe Momme' a cappella to his mother Freda. She loved the song and was in heaven when her son sang it for her.

Tom was very methodical about learning a new song. He played a disc over and over on the turntable until he had mastered the lyrics, then put his own phrasing on it in time for the Wednesday night rehearsal.

The greater exposure that 1962 brought led to the formation of The Senators' own concert party. They were the headline act of an evening's entertainment that was like a small-scale summer season at a seaside resort. They had a piano player, a girl singer and a comedian called Bryn Phillips, who was known as Bryn the Fish, because he had a fish round in Abercynon and smelled of haddock.

Tom's stage presence was evolving more by luck than design. He would use a series of hand gestures to make sure the band was in perfect synch with him. Many of his powerful arm movements and body gyrations were code for the band and just as much for their benefit as for the watching audience. Quietly, The Senators were becoming less of a band in their own right and more Tom's backing group. Gerry Greenberg remembers, 'He was on a pedestal without anybody saying anything really.'

Gerry recalls watching them regularly at the New Inn in Taff Street. 'Tom would sit downstairs having a drink while the band got the show going upstairs.'

Tom didn't practise or warm up properly. His voice was nurtured on a diet of beer, cigarettes and curry. Young hopefuls starting off in music then weren't particularly aware that you needed to care for your voice. As Vernon observes, 'That was something opera singers did.'

On one occasion, Vernon suggested Tom should have a singing lesson with Brenda, the music teacher who lived next door to him in Rhydyfelin, to see if there was any advice he should be following. Tom dutifully agreed and popped round. At first Vernon could hear the familiar sound of la-la-la voices running up and down scales, and then it went dead quiet.

Eventually, Tom came back, red-faced and flustered. 'You'll never bloody guess, Vern. She sat on my chest.'

# 7

# THE GREEN FLY BOYS

Tommy Woodward and Vernon Hopkins were kindred spirits united by a love of music and a desire to find a better life away from the terraces of the Valleys. They were also two young men, only a year apart in age, who enjoyed the company of women and wanted some adventure in their lives. Vernon, tall and dark, was probably the best looking of the two, but he acknowledges that Tom was better at talking to girls.

Linda came to a gig only occasionally, when she could leave Mark with her mother for the night. Most evenings, the lads would try their luck with the few girls hanging around to meet the band, but Vernon admits that their success rate was pretty close to zero. One of the band might get lucky every six weeks or so, which was hardly something to brag about to The Rolling Stones.

Vernon and Tom did manage to pick up a couple of air hostesses after a Saturday night gig in Ystrad Mynach, five miles from Pontypridd. They were so busy getting steamy with the girls in the car park that the others drove off, leaving them to make the long walk home. That would have been no problem if it hadn't started to rain heavily. Fortunately, they found a shed to shelter under for the night. They managed to keep the girls warm until everyone fell asleep contentedly.

In the morning, the sun was shining and it would have been a lovely day, except that they were all covered from head to toe in pigeon shit. They had spent the night underneath a dovecote, but hadn't noticed in the throes of drunken passion. The boys found it much funnier than the girls, who kicked them both very firmly in the shins as a thank you. The walk of shame back home was not a happy one, especially as nobody stopped to give them a lift.

Clearly, Tom wasn't being faithful to Linda and, if the stories are to be believed, he has never been. She knew that. She heard the gossip. She felt uncomfortable seeing other women chatting up her husband and certainly didn't want the knowledge of his philandering brought to her doorstep. Despite their success with the air hostesses, the Senators weren't girl magnets, much as they would like to have been.

If there weren't enough fast women around in the Valleys, then perhaps Tom would have better luck with a fast car. Vernon was astonished when Tom, who hadn't even passed his test, turned up outside the house in a sparkling new scarlet Ford Corsair. It wasn't his. The car belonged to his brother-in-law, Tony Thorne, who was married to Linda's younger sister Roslyn.

He shouted, 'Hop in, Vern. We're off to Barry Island!' They spent an hour or two sitting on the beach and eating ice cream. Vern told Tom that he was desperate to get away from Ponty; Tom was in whole-hearted agreement. They drove back happily, until Tom was pulled over by the police a few hundred yards from Tony's house. The car had been reported stolen that morning. He had no insurance, as well as no driver's licence. The matter inevitably reached the magistrates' court and ended in a fine.

The escapade prompted Vernon to invest in a car of his own. His old Morris was nothing like the flash Corsair, but did come in useful occasionally, transporting the band to gigs. By late summer of 1962, the group had become friendly with a young engineer called Chris Ellis, who used to come and watch them at the Green Fly and would lend an expert hand if a piece of the equipment wasn't working properly. He soon volunteered to be their roadie, and was responsible for setting up the gear at concerts and driving the van. He remained an integral part of the Tom Jones machine for more than ten years.

Tom was always the last to be picked up when they were travelling to a gig. He was never ready on time. One of the group would run over and bang on the grill with their heel and Linda would let them in. They would chat to Tom while he shaved in a small, cracked mirror that he had used for years. Then they would set off, all of them filled with anticipation, except for Tom. He would get in the back, lie down and fall fast asleep. He was a very deep sleeper. Vernon recalls, 'Tom just used to lie there, out for the count. We always had a hell of a job waking him up when we arrived.'

The Green Fly continued to be the focus for events, both good and bad, in the story of The Senators. On one night, three of his old Teddy boy mates decided to drive over to watch Tom perform. The evening went well, the beer was flowing and Tom decided to catch a lift back with his friends. On the way, they were involved in a nasty collision, which left them all injured. Roy Nicholl had a broken jaw, Johnny Cleaves had a serious head injury and Dai Shepherd needed thirty-six stitches. Tom escaped with a bang on his forehead that gave him concussion and forced the cancellation of several gigs. They were all very lucky.

The band, and Tom in particular, were getting progressively more desperate for something to happen. They were stuck in a provincial rut. Most Tuesdays after collecting his dole money, Tom would drift into the *Pontypridd Observer* and chat to Gerry Greenberg. He was forever trying to persuade the reporter to include a mention of the band in his pop column 'Teen Beat'. Gerry did profile Tom in the column, in which readers learned that Tom had green eyes and that his ambition was to perform with Jerry Lee Lewis; his principal dislike was sarcastic people. It was good exposure, but publicity in the local paper wasn't going to be enough to get them noticed in London.

On one occasion Tom arrived at Gerry's office with a badly cut mouth and swollen cheeks. Gerry recalls, 'He was in a mess. He was struggling to speak, so I asked him, "What happened to you?" And he said the band were over at the Green Fly when they were jumped on by a gang. One of them jumped on him from behind and put his hands in his mouth and ripped it apart. I said, "God, that must have been painful, because you look in a right state."

The Senators gave the impression of being a rough pub band, bashing out a series of rock 'n' roll standards from the fifties. Out front, Tom cut an intimidating figure in a leather jacket. Behind him, the rest of the band incongruously wore blue blazers and white trousers. They were exciting, but they weren't current. The Beatles had their first top ten hit, 'Love Me Do', in October 1962 and music was never the same again. The boys from Pontypridd were in danger of being left behind.

After another night at the Green Fly, they were approached by two ambitious young songwriters, Raymond Godfrey and John Glastonbury, who told them they had enjoyed their performance.

They were seeking an up-and-coming band to showcase their songs. None of the band, according to Vernon, was particularly impressed by the duo, who looked like students and, for some reason, called themselves Myron and Byron: 'They didn't fit in at all. They were a square peg in a round hole. Byron was all right, quite affable, but Myron – I hated him. He was really slimy. Tom didn't like him at all.'

Raymond Godfrey later said that he and John Glastonbury were really only interested in Tom, as he was the one with the obvious talent. This was the first indication that outsiders listening to the band would concentrate on the singer.

The Senators could go on playing local gigs for years to come, but here were two people talking seriously and enthusiastically about London for the first time. Myron and Byron told the boys they wanted them to make a demo of their songs, which they would take to record publishers and producers in the capital. It was a start.

Alva Turner decided he didn't like the way things were going, so he left. Fortunately, they managed to recruit a new drummer right away – a seventeen-year-old Pontypridd shoe salesman called Chris Rees. He changed his name to Chris Slade and would go on to become one of the best-known rock drummers of the past forty years. After he left Tom in 1970, he played with, among others, Manfred Mann's Earth Band in the seventies, AC/DC in the nineties and Asia in the noughties. Keith Davies was also having doubts about continuing as a guitarist with the group and left abruptly after a gig one night. He remained as part of the set-up, however, travelling to venues with them and helping with the equipment. He was happier without the pressure of playing every night. He was also in love and, now aged eighteen, planning to marry soon.

He spent the night before his wedding in the front room of the house in Glyndwr Avenue, talking with Tom and Vernon and getting very drunk. Tom turned to him after more than a few beers and said, 'Don't be a bloody idiot now, Keith. Do yourself a favour. Get up to Treforest Station now. There is a milk train that goes out at six. Get on it and don't bloody get off.' Keith ignored that advice and celebrated his golden wedding in 2013. He was in such a state on his wedding day, however, that he can't remember anything about it.

He and Tom didn't always get on so well. One Christmas Eve, after a couple of shows, the band were having a few beers in the Labour Club in Treharris. Vernon started playing 'Moonlight Sonata', while Tom messed around on the keys. Keith, a little drunk, unintentionally closed the lid on Tom's hands. The next thing he knew, he was up against the wall and Tom had to be calmed down by the others. Later, while Keith was putting the gear back in the van, Tom came to apologise.

Keith recalls, 'He said, "I'm sorry," and me, like a big kid, said, "Fuck off." And I turned back to carry on with what I was doing. The next thing I knew, I had this hand on the back of my collar and I went flying out the back of the van. I always remember it was a lovely night and I was looking up at the stars, and he gave me a little dig with his foot. Cut my mouth and all that nonsense.'

The atmosphere was terrible for a short while, until one night before leaving Cliff Terrace, Tom asked simply, 'You all right?' He also went out and bought Keith a new white shirt to replace the one that had been damaged in the spat. That brief altercation stands out as the only time there was any trouble between Tom and the band.

Before Myron and Byron could take the sound of The Senators – and Tom – to London, however, they needed to make the demo. After much investigation, the duo decided that the perfect place would be the toilets in the YMCA. Tom already liked to sing there while he was having a pee because the acoustics were so good. They recorded four tracks, written by Myron and Byron, reel to reel on an eight-track portable stereo.

Meanwhile, Myron and Byron started taking on more responsibility for the band, eventually signing them to a management contract. They found them gigs that were out of their comfort zone. They were booked as a support act to Billy J. Kramer and the Dakotas at the Grand Pavilion in Porthcawl. Kramer was one of the 'Mersey sound' acts that sprang up in the wake of The Beatles' success and was, for a while, hugely successful. He was managed by Brian Epstein and took a succession of Lennon and McCartney songs into the charts. Billy J. was a heart-throb in the old mould – more Cliff Richard than Mick Jagger, and definitely not Tom Jones.

The Senators raised their game that night and were rapturously received by the Welsh crowd before the headline act closed the show to less than enthusiastic applause. The crowd started chanting for Tom and the boys to come back on, which, after being approached by the management, they were happy to do. They played for another half-hour. Vernon recalls, 'We converted a lot of Dakotas fans to Senator fans that night.'

At the end of a memorable night, Billy J. Kramer was still a star, however, and Tommy Woodward, aka Tommy Scott, wasn't. He kept telling the people at the dole office in Pontypridd that things were definitely moving for him at last. The officials at the Labour Exchange, as Jobcentres were called then, were sceptical about the whole thing. They thought Tom was too smartly dressed for the average unemployed person and guessed the band was more successful than he was letting on.

A dry assessment from a supervisor at the employment office in 1963 reveals: 'He does not want shift work but I believe the reason for his not liking shifts is because he is a member of a vocal group, which is supposedly an amateur affair. From the adverts one sees in the local press, however, it seems that this group had a good thing going.

'From the way he is able to dress, it would seem that Mr Woodward's little hobby is highly lucrative and this would account for his non-enthusiasm in securing employment. Consider and submit as soon as possible to anything which wouldn't dirty his fingernails! Nothing on offer at present.'

Godfrey and Glastonbury tried their luck in London, hawking their demo without success, until they managed to attract the attention of one of the best-known men in pop. His name was Joe Meek and he was a nightmare. His legendary status now owes much to the dreadful circumstances of his death rather than his achievements during his lifetime, although he was by far the most successful figure that Tom had come across. He was a maverick tortured by his sexuality at a time when sex between men was illegal in the UK; it remained so until 1967.

Meek was an innovative producer with an unmistakable style – not as instantly recognisable as Phil Spector perhaps, but one who put his stamp on popular music in the early sixties. Sadly for him, he went out of fashion almost as quickly as he came in. Many of the studio techniques that are taken for granted today, however, were first introduced by the tone-deaf Meek in his home studio in a flat above a handbag shop in the Holloway Road, North London.

His first major hit was the summer of 1961 smash 'Johnny Remember Me' by the actor John Leyton, a lament for a dead lover that featured Meek's trademark eerie electronic sound.

When the song was played on the panel show *Juke Box Jury*, Spike Milligan dismissed it as 'son of "Ghost Riders in the Sky"'. The track did have the galloping beat that Tom had liked so much in the latter – he could have drummed 'Johnny Remember Me' on the desk at school.

Meek's reputation as the UK's foremost independent producer was firmly established by the success of 'Telstar' by The Tornados in December 1962. The instrumental was one of the first British records to top the *Billboard* charts in the US and sold an estimated five million copies worldwide. The *New Musical Express* (*NME*), which named Meek the most influential producer ever, commented, 'It was unlike anything anyone had heard before, packed full of claviolines, bizarre distortions and weird sonic effects, all achieved in Meek's home recording studio above a shop.'

Meek clearly thought he heard something in Tom's voice, because he lost no time in signing a one-year production agreement with Myron and Byron. The Senators made the first of several seven-hour journeys to London to record in Joe's flat. When they got there, they didn't know where to look when they were greeted by Meek's sometime lover Heinz, the singer and bassist with The Tornados, sprawled naked on the bed. The boys were happy to indulge in some blokish humour about keeping their backs to the walls, but they hadn't come into contact with anyone as blatant as Meek.

The producer had very close ties with Decca, who would press and distribute his recordings. The idea was that The Senators would lay down some tracks in his home and he would take it from there. They recorded seven, including a song called 'Lonely Joe', which Meek had written and hoped might make a single, 'I Was a Fool', written by Myron and Byron, two others called 'Little Lonely One' and 'That's What We'll Do', finishing off with some Jerry Lee Lewis to keep Tom happy. One they particularly liked was 'Chills and Fever', a strong bluesy track released in 1960 by Ronnie Love and his Orchestra.

Tom got the message that Joe was at least as interested in his crotch as his tonsils when the producer asked him to stay behind for a word after their first photo session. He asked Tom to show him his stage moves, which, of course, involved a lot of sexy gyrating. He then made a lunge for Tom's lunchbox. Tom dashed out of the flat, down the stairs and into the van, where the boys were waiting patiently. He explained his haste, 'The bloody bastard made a grab for my balls, Vern!'

Tom talked light-heartedly about his experience with Joe on *The Merv Griffin Show* in the US in 1979: 'He was homosexual. It was a bad experience for me, coming from Wales; there's no such thing, or we don't like to think there is, anyway.'

The band persevered, however, and made another seven-hour trip to London. When Tom failed to sing one number just as Joe requested, the mercurial Meek stormed in, pointed a gun at Tom and fired. Apparently it was a starting pistol, but nobody knew that at the time.

This was clearly not a match made in heaven. During the following months, Meek lost interest in the boys from Wales. His biographer, John Repsch, said that part of the problem was Decca's interest in P. J. Proby, who was just starting out. Meek also apparently didn't much care for Myron and Byron or the musical abilities of the band. Once again, it was Tom who was sparking all the interest.

Things ended badly with Joe Meek. The deal with Decca failed to materialise and Meek tore up his contract in front of Myron and Byron and threw it in the bin. An angry Tom was so incensed by Meek's treatment of the band that he and Chris Ellis charged over to the producer's flat to confront him and demanded to know why he had been stringing them along when he clearly had done very little. Tom told Vernon afterwards, 'He thought I was going to kill him! It was pitiful, so we left him to it.' On the way out, they looked for their recordings, but had no luck – an omission that would turn out to be costly later.

Joe Meek never recaptured his early success and, despite another number one hit with 'Have I the Right' by The Honeycombs, he was declared bankrupt. In February 1967, he shot dead his landlady, Mrs Violet Shenton, who, on occasion, had made tea for Tom and the boys. He then turned the shotgun, which belonged to Heinz, on himself.

Tom had come within touching distance of a breakthrough in London. He had better luck with someone who would become even more notorious than Joe Meek. He was helped by the DJ Jimmy Savile, whom he met at the now closed Aaland Hotel in Bloomsbury. Myron and Byron had found out that Savile habitually stayed there when broadcasting in London, so they took a room, while Tom and Chris Ellis slept in the car. The intention was to hand Savile a tape of the band and hope he would pass it on to a record company.

One morning, frustrated after a bad night's sleep, Tom stormed in to find out what exactly his managers were doing to make contact with the DJ. He was banging on their door, when Savile poked his head out of his room to find out what all the noise was about. Tom explained he was in a pop group from Wales and asked if Jimmy could give them some advice. The conversation was brief, but that evening Tom and Chris went back, knocked on his door and poured out the whole sad story of their London disappointment. Savile promised to do something with the tape.

He recalled the encounter in his autobiography. He described Tom and Chris being 'earnest and solemn of face'. He remembered several discussions in which they told him of their progress and he suggested a course of action: 'It started things going the right way and the caterpillar of Tommy Scott and The Senators turned into the world-beater winged wonder of our own Tom Jones.' The egotistical Savile didn't claim to be responsible for Tom's success, but he did say 'when a top man has time to talk or eat with new arrivals, it gives a tremendous boost to the morale of the beginners'.

By some means, the demo tape ended up at Decca and was eventually discovered by a young producer there called Peter Sullivan. He was so impressed by what he heard that he made a special trip to Wales to hear Tom sing. He thought Tom had a voice that was entirely different to the lightweight lead singers of the time. At a later date, Peter would be an important figure in the musical world of Tom Jones, but for the moment he felt Tom wasn't ready.

The man who would have the greatest influence on his career had yet to meet Tommy Woodward.

# PART TWO

## TOM JONES

# 8

# THE BLACK HOLE

Gordon Mills was not a man to mince his words. When he first caught sight of Tommy Woodward at the Lewis Merthyr Club in Porth one Sunday lunchtime, he declared, 'Who's that scruffy bastard?' Gordon was like that: one moment he could be completely charming, the next ruthless and rude. Keith Davies called him 'Mister Moody Mills'. He was, however, a hugely charismatic man who demanded your attention.

Gordon was visiting his mother for the weekend and had been taken to the club by two old school friends from the Rhondda Valley, South Wales: Gordon Jones, whom everyone called Gog, and Johnny Bennett, a club singer who had become a fan of Tom's voice. Tom wasn't singing that lunchtime, but Gordon was introduced to him – as Tommy Scott – and they sat with the rest of The Senators, watching a bad comedian try to entertain everyone.

Gordon was with his beautiful blonde wife, Jo Waring, a London model who was expecting their first child. At one point, the comedian told a risqué joke that led to Gordon waving a warning finger, as if to say, 'There are ladies present' and 'Don't do it again'. Perhaps he was a man who shared Tom's old-fashioned mixture of chivalry and chauvinism where women were concerned.

Johnny persuaded Gordon to come and hear the band play that evening at the Top Hat Club in Cwmtillery, a mining village twenty miles north of Pontypridd and basically in the middle of nowhere. Tom observed drily, 'It sounded posh, but it wasn't.' The notorious Mandy Rice-Davies, a central figure in the Profumo scandal, had launched a singing career and was supposed to be the night's big act, but she had laryngitis, so Tommy Scott and The Senators moved up to the top of the bill.

Johnny made a point of telling the boys that this was *the* Gordon Mills down from London and he was coming specially to see them. The more accurate representation of the event was that Gordon was a minor figure on the London recording scene desperate to find an act that could provide his breakthrough into management.

Gordon was brought up in the Valleys, but had been born in Madras (Chennai), India, where his father, Bill, was stationed as an army sergeant. His father worked as a carpenter when he left the service and returned to South Wales. Gordon inherited his dark, brooding good looks from his Anglo-Indian mother, Lorna. He was approaching his twenty-ninth birthday, five years older than Tom, when they met for the first time.

While he would achieve fame as one of the great pop managers, Gordon was first a talented musician and songwriter. He didn't have a good enough voice to offer him an escape from Tonypandy, a mining town just seven miles from where Tom was brought up in Treforest. Gordon was, however, a superb player of the harmonica — a musical instrument that could be enjoyed when there was little money for expensive keyboards and guitars. His friend and fellow musician from those days, Albert Blinkhorn, who taught him 'Chattanooga Choo Choo', observed that his talent was matched by the strength of his character and his powers of persuasion: 'He could tell you a thing was black and, even if you knew damn well it was white, Gordon would convince you it was black.'

Gordon did his two years of national service when he was seventeen and found Tonypandy even more claustrophobic on his return. He got a job as a bus conductor, but, more important, came runner-up in the British Harmonica Championship, staged at the Royal Albert Hall. He pawned his radio to afford his fare to London, but it was worth it, because that success fuelled his dreams of becoming a wealthy man.

Gordon had to face exactly the same dilemma that he would later present to Tom – give up the life he knew and move to London or stay in Wales and always wonder what might have been. His friend Albert encouraged him to 'take a gamble', which was something Gordon, a keen poker player, was always prepared to do.

He landed a job playing variety shows with Morton Fraser's Harmonica Gang, before striking out with two other members of the troupe and forming a pop act called The Viscounts. They had some minor chart success over the next few years, including their version of 'Who Put the Bomp (In the Bomp, Bomp, Bomp)', which was an anaemic doo-wop song and not one that Tom would have enjoyed performing. Gordon took the lead vocal, despite never having done more than sing in the bath. The Viscounts were much in demand as part of the all-star tours that were fashionable then, and appeared on the same bill as The Beatles and Billy J. Kramer and the Dakotas.

At a gig in Leicester, Gordon met a struggling singer called Gerry Dorsey, who was at the bottom of the bill. The two became

firm friends, discovering in the process that they were both originally from Madras and had Anglo-Indian mothers. A few years
later, when Gordon had become Gerry's manager and renamed
him Engelbert Humperdinck, his career path would inevitably
become entwined with Tom's. By a strange quirk of fate, after
appearing at a charity concert in Manchester, Gerry felt ill and a
subsequent X-ray revealed he had TB. He was in a sanatorium
for six months and needed a further six to convalesce.

Back in London, Gordon and Gerry decided to share a grotty
flat together in West Kensington, eventually moving into a place
in Cleveland Square known affectionately as the Rock 'n' Roll
House, because it was full of musicians hoping for a break. They
had turned up to a party there to celebrate the twenty-first
birthday of the singer Terry Dene, when Gordon met another
resident, the elegant Jo Waring, for the first time. She was
Rhodesian, had been a Bluebell Girl in Paris and was working
as a fashion model in the capital. For a while, she was almost as
influential in Tom's career as Gordon was.

Jo was instantly attracted to the tall, softly spoken harmonica
player, and they soon moved into their own place together in
Campden Hill Towers, a flat Tom would come to know well. Jo
recalled: 'Gordon had something about him. You felt sure that he
was sure about his life. He was a positive man and I loved him
completely.'

As a token of that love, she saved enough from her modelling
work to buy Gordon a piano. He was delighted, because it meant
he could start composing songs. He couldn't read music, but he
could pick out catchy melodies, and Jo would chip in with
possible lyrics. One composition 'I'll Never Get Over You'
became a top ten hit for Johnny Kidd and the Pirates and found
its way onto The Senators' set list. A couple of months before he

met Tom, he had success with another, called 'I'm the Lonely One', which was a hit for Cliff Richard and The Shadows. Tom may not have liked Cliff's recording, but it made Gordon current, and therefore more impressive. Ironically, Tom recorded the song as 'The Lonely One' and it became a B-side of one of his hits, 'I'm Coming Home', in 1967. He made sure it didn't sound anything like Cliff's version.

When Gordon and Jo married, Gerry Dorsey was best man. Gordon returned the favour at Gerry's wedding to his long-standing girlfriend, a secretary called Pat Healy, in April 1964. Pat, whom Gerry called Popea, was already pregnant with their first daughter. Two other important figures in the Tom Jones story acted as ushers. They were the songwriters Barry Mason and Les Reed. As a wedding present, Gordon and Jo paid for the new Mr and Mrs Dorsey's honeymoon in Paris.

A month later, Jo Mills was a big hit when she travelled with her husband to South Wales. 'She was very nice and sociable,' remembers Keith Davies. The couple gave him a lift in their flashy Ford Zephyr to the Top Hat, because there wasn't enough room in the van. 'I went to get in the back and she said, "Come and sit in the front, love. I'm Jo and this is Gordon." I didn't have a clue who they were.'

The Top Hat wasn't a big club and the place was packed. Everyone had forgotten that it was a members-only working men's club and, at first, the doorman refused to let Gordon and Jo in, which was embarrassing. Tom had to leave the dressing room, seek out a committee member and ask permission, pleading that Gordon had come from London specifically to listen to him.

Eventually, with Gordon and a pregnant Jo uncomfortably crowded in by the bar, the gig began with Tom singing 'I'll

Never Get Over You' in a rather blatant attempt to please Mills. He continued with the normal set, starting with a powerful rendition of 'Spanish Harlem'. At the interval, Keith was getting the usual tray of drinks for the boys, when Gordon started chatting to him: 'He said, "I would love to have that boy under my belt. Love to have him."'

Keith couldn't wait to tell Tom what Gordon had said, but he recalls that Tom was rather cool and said that he would have to speak to Myron and Byron about it. Gordon was also careful not to reveal his hand that night, especially as both Myron and Byron were in the audience. Vernon Hopkins remembers that he pretended he was more interested in Bryn the Fish's voice than Tom's.

In fact, Gordon was hooked halfway through the opening number: 'I realised I had never seen anything like him before. He was an uncut diamond and needed a lot of polishing. From that moment on, I decided I wanted to manage him.'

Tom was more agitated about that night than he let on. He had been so close to a breakthrough with Joe Meek, then the meetings with Jimmy Savile and Peter Sullivan. His ambition was like a slumbering bear waking up. He didn't want another opportunity to slip through his fingers and was therefore very keen to impress Gordon. Linda had put in a rare appearance at the gig, but apparently had one drink too many and wasn't helping.

Gordon revealed his true feelings to his wife when they were driving back to London. Jo never forgot the journey: 'Suddenly Gordon pulled the car over. I wondered what the matter was and he said, "I have got to do something with him", and I just said, "How wonderful." The rest of the journey was just us excitedly making plans. It was a wonderful journey.' Tom explained it succinctly: 'He said he saw something in me that he didn't have – that he would like to have had.'

Gordon made several trips to Wales to try to persuade Tom and the band that they needed to sign with him and move to London. One worry Tom had, especially after his experience with Joe Meek, surfaced when the two of them went to a coffee bar in Pontypridd. He told the story on *The Merv Griffin Show* in 1979: 'Gordon said, "Now if I become your manager, you know I will be in control and you must listen to me" and he put his hand on my leg. So I said, "Before you go any further, you're not one of these queer fellows, are you?"'

Tom had a robust attitude to homosexuality. You shared a pint with a man and a bed with a woman. Later, when he was established as one of the world's leading entertainers, he said, 'I don't mind being treated as a sex object as long as it's by females.'

Eventually, like a persistent double-glazing salesman, Gordon wore Tom and the band down and they agreed a harsh contract that promised him 50 per cent of their future earnings. He also managed to dispense with Myron and Byron by offering what would prove to be a very sweet deal of 5 per cent of future earnings. That was not his best bit of business.

Vernon Hopkins was enthusiastic for the move and told Tom he thought he should give it a shot. Chris Slade and Dai Cooper, who had replaced Keith Davies on guitar, were happy to move, but Mike Roberts didn't want to leave his job with the BBC, so they had to recruit a new guitarist, Mickey Gee, who worked for a local brewery.

Tom, unlike the others, wasn't a single man and couldn't make the decision on his own. One can only speculate what would have happened to the career of Tom Jones if he and Linda had added to their family – he might never have made it to London at all. But they had discovered that Linda was unable to have another child. Margaret observes, 'I think she would have loved more children. Tom would have loved a daughter, I think.'

Linda, as always, gave her husband her blessing, which, in effect, made his mind up for him. Her decision to let him go was immensely brave. She couldn't just pop to London for an afternoon when she felt like it – there was no Severn Bridge or M4 motorway in June 1964.

Just after his twenty-fourth birthday, Tommy Woodward enjoyed a beer or two with his best mates in the White Hart, before kissing his wife and child goodbye. He joined the other four Senators in their old Morris van and bid Treforest farewell.

Tom took one look at the basement flat at 6 Clydesdale Road, in Notting Hill, and declared, 'This place is like the Black Hole of Calcutta.' They certainly hadn't signed a contract with Disney that would guarantee a cushy life and the best of everything. This was a grade-A dump – dark, damp and smelling of mice. Naked light bulbs hung from the ceiling, two small gas fires provided token heating and the five lads shared two bedrooms – three in one, two in the other. Tom shared with Vernon and Dai Cooper. The well-kept miners' cottages he'd left behind were like palaces compared to his new living quarters.

Spin doctors might have called the area 'bohemian', but the reality was that it was poor and underprivileged. When the sun went down, the drug-pushers and prostitutes gathered on the street outside. The hookers would pop in for a cup of tea and a cigarette when they needed a break from shivering in the cold night air. Today you need £1 million to live in the neighbourhood, but The Senators were surviving on the £1 a day that

TOP: Tom came from a close and loving family. Smartly turned out, aged nine, at a family wedding. L to R (adults): his dapper father Thomas senior, cousin Emrys, his wife Betty, sister Sheila, cousin Dorothy, proud mother Freda. L to R (children): cousin Jean, the twins Ada and Margaret, and Tommy Woodward himself.

MIDDLE: His mother and father pose outside 44 Laura Street with a new luxury car, one of the early trappings of their son's success.

BOTTOM LEFT: Even as a boy, Tom had a natural charm in front of the camera.

TOP: Tom has kept in touch with his boyhood pals. Brian Blackler, who lived a hundred yards away, remains a loyal friend and has visited him in the US.

BOTTOM LEFT: As a teenager, Gill Beazer was Tom's companion when he played local gigs and he would sing to her in the audience.

BOTTOM RIGHT: The girls loved Tom's energy right from the start with The Senators. The group's founder, Vernon Hopkins, an important figure in the singer's early career, plays bass behind him.

TOP LEFT: Tom and his wife Linda went home to Wales for an old-fashioned Christmas in 1967. He called it one of his happiest-ever times.

TOP RIGHT: Tom and Linda pictured in their fashionable kitchen. She wasn't mentioned in his early publicity, but it soon became widely known that he was married. He was always happy to pose with the love of his life, although she later became camera-shy.

BOTTOM: Tom and Linda had come a long way from the basement flat in Cliff Terrace when they moved into their new grand mansion in July 1967.

LEFT: Tom discovered the finer things in life under the guidance of his legendary manager Gordon Mills, swapping his favourite Woodbines for the best cigars.

BELOW: Tom, Gordon and Engelbert Humperdinck knew they had made it when they had Rolls-Royces parked in the driveway. Tom's immodest number plate presumably referred to his voice.

*Tom with two of the key figures in his career.*

TOP: Composer Les Reed was responsible for many of the great songs of the sixties, including the music for 'It's Not Unusual' and 'Delilah'.

BOTTOM: Lloyd Greenfield, a New York lawyer, was Gordon's right-hand man in the US and a popular figure at Tom's side for more than thirty years.

*Tom wasn't always successful where
beautiful women were concerned.*

Sandie Shaw shared a laugh with Tom, but turned down an invitation to his famous caravan when she appeared on *This Is Tom Jones*.

The Scottish singer Lulu managed to avoid falling for his 'animal magnetism' and confessed he frightened the life out of her.

Tom's television show (1969–71) gave him the chance to appear with the greats of popular music. He sang 'Sunny' with the legendary Ella Fitzgerald, who ignored his hairy chest.

Tom said Aretha Franklin was the only singer he ever felt could match his vocal power.

Stevie Wonder was a favourite guest on several of Tom's shows over the years. In this medley, they performed a fantastic duet of 'It's Not Unusual'.

When the veteran entertainer Sammy Davis, Jr appeared on the show, Tom was proud to introduce him as 'my pal'.

Tom formed a great friendship with Elvis Presley when they were both appearing in Las Vegas. They would often get together after their shows. Sometimes, as here, The King did not want to have his picture taken.

Jerry Lee Lewis was the single biggest musical influence in Tom's life, so it was a huge thrill to sing with him.

Frank Sinatra was another Las Vegas regular who got on well with Tom. Sinatra's singing career lasted sixty years and he advised Tom to treat his voice more kindly.

Gordon paid them as an allowance. Vernon still remembers cleaning his teeth with salt because they couldn't afford tooth-paste – and they were always hungry.

The highlight during these tough times was when Linda clambered into the passenger seat of Chris Ellis's Mini and they drove up to London for the weekend, surrounded by tins of baked beans, so the boys would have something to eat in the week ahead. On these occasions, Jo insisted that Linda and Tom stay at their flat at 97 Campden Hill Towers. She couldn't bear the thought of Linda slumming it in the Black Hole.

Every so often, half starving, they would target a restaurant, usually an Indian one, eat enough for days ahead and then, at the appropriate time, make a bolt for the door – usually with Tom leading the way. There was no mention of their dire circumstances when a cheerful piece appeared in the *Pontypridd Observer* at the end of July 1964. The enthusiastic article, written by Gerry Greenberg, featured Tom lying, 'We are having a great time.'

The week before the newspaper appeared, the group had made their professional debut in London as the supporting act for The Rolling Stones at the Beat City Club in Oxford Street. The Stones were already arguably the biggest band in the country after The Beatles. Their latest single, 'It's All Over Now', had become their first UK number one earlier in the month, so it wasn't a surprise hundreds of fans were queuing round the block to get in.

Six hundred people, mainly girls, were herded into the club. Sixty, all girls, were overcome by the heat and the excitement and had to be carried out. Bill Wyman remembered the night in his autobiography *Stone Alone*: 'It was that hot, you felt you were melting.' Stewards tried to cool the bands down by throwing buckets of water over them, which had the unexpected effect of turning Tom's white cotton trousers completely see-through, revealing more than expected. They were the same pair of tight trousers that had first caught the attention of Joe Meek, and left nothing to the imagination.

After they had performed a forty-five-minute set, the band went to collapse in the dressing room they were sharing with the Stones. Mick Jagger, a middle-class grammar school boy, took one look at the wet-through Tom and cheekily declared, 'Christ, it must be hot out there. Look at him, and he's only the compère.' Tom ignored him. By all accounts, he was unimpressed by the Stones' sulky pouting and didn't think they would last two minutes down the Bucket of Blood.

After the gig, Gordon learned that there was already a singer in London called Tommy Scott, so finding a new name was now a priority. He always took the credit for thinking of Tom Jones, but the idea originally came from one of the agents he was using to try to find work for the band. He did realise, however, that the name could cash in on the popularity of the bawdy, Oscar-winning film *Tom Jones*, starring Albert Finney. He didn't know at the time that Tom's mother's maiden name was Jones and it should have been an obvious choice.

Tom Jones and The Senators sounded unexciting, so Gordon changed the group's name to The Playboys in time for the release of their first single. He had revived the interest of Peter Sullivan at Decca, convincing Peter that he was smoothing out some of the rough edges to make Tom more acceptable to a mainstream audience.

One of the problems Gordon had was that Tom came across as a singing bricklayer in a pop world seemingly overrun by pretty boys with soppy smiles. Number one in the charts soon after Tom's debut single 'Chills and Fever' was released in late August 1964 was the anaemic 'I'm into Something Good' by Herman's Hermits. Their lead singer was sixteen-year-old Peter Noone, who had a patent on toothy grins. Tom Jones, aged twenty-four, singing his brand of tight, funky blues, was his polar opposite.

Depressingly, 'Chills and Fever' was a complete flop, which it didn't deserve. Tom did his best to turn it into a hit, giving a sensational live performance on the BBC2 show *The Beat Room*, the station's first pop programme. He moved, he thrust, he growled, but the studio audience clearly thought they were attending a tea dance at the vicarage. They were arguably the dullest bunch of pullover-wearing youngsters ever assembled in a television studio. Tom loved the song, though, and revived it nearly fifty years later for one of his tours.

Despite everyone's best efforts, 'Chills and Fever' was met with such indifference that it only made number five in the Pontypridd chart compiled by Freddie Feys' record shop. Gerry Greenberg wasn't surprised: 'I never thought it would be a big hit, because it wasn't different enough.' It was back to the drawing board for Tom and Gordon. For the former, that also meant an extended stay in the Black Hole.

The failure was also a blow to Linda, who was struggling to cope in Treforest. There was so little money. Her friend Vimy Pitman says, 'She was worried about the future. It was very hard for her.'

Tom asked Gordon if he could spare a couple of extra pounds for him to send home to Linda, but Gordon, too, was struggling to survive now that motherhood had forced Jo to give up her modelling work. He'd even sold his wristwatch and his beloved car to keep afloat. He had to tell Tom that there was nothing he could do. Tom felt that he had failed miserably as a provider for his family. It was his role as the man of the house. He had grown up watching his weary father proudly put down his wage packet on the kitchen table. He desperately needed to do the same.

Deflated and humiliated, Tom walked round to Notting Hill Gate Tube station and stood on the platform. What was the point of carrying on? He was so down that he seriously thought of suicide. He could end it all in front of the train that was due any minute. He recalled, 'I thought "I'll jump."' He told *Melody Maker* he 'felt at the lowest point of despair'.

He dragged himself back to the Black Hole, where Vernon found him trembling. Tom told him he had nearly topped himself and needed a sympathetic pep talk to reassure him that now was not the time to give up. He still had a wife and son who needed him. It was out of character for a man normally so easy-going, but illustrates how low he was feeling. It was, he confessed, 'the only time in my life I have thought about ending it all'. He was a more sensitive man than people realised.

Tom pulled himself together, sold his leather jacket and bought a train ticket home to ask his wife if he should give up the dream. Linda said no – she would get a job.

Tom popped in to see his cousin Margaret and asked if she could help Linda obtain a job at the sewing factory on the industrial estate, where she worked evening shifts. Margaret had married and had two young sons, so she would stay at home, while her husband, Graham Sugar, worked during the day. She recalls, 'Tom said, "Can you ask for Linda?" and I said I would do my best. I had only just started there myself, but I went into the office and said that my cousin was away trying to make a name for himself and his wife really needed a job. They said there wasn't a position for her. But I kept going in and I could have lost my job, but eventually they took her on.'

Linda hadn't worked since before Mark was born, when she was a fifteen-year-old school-leaver. She and Margaret would set off together, leaving Graham to look after Mark, as well as his own two children, until they came home.

Margaret remembers, 'Her job was making nylon stockings. The next time Tom was home, he came over and said, "Margaret, I can't thank you enough." He was so relieved.'

She loved her cousin and was pleased to do it for him. When her youngest son, Craig, was born, Tom had come to see them. Freda had helped with the home birth, and Tom couldn't wait to see the newborn. He bounded up the stairs, booming, 'Let's have a look at this boy.' Margaret adds: 'He put his hand in his pocket and pulled out a sixpence and put the piece of silver in my baby's hand. He said, "It's for good luck." Tom is a big softie where family is concerned.'

Perhaps someone put a sixpence in Tom's own hand, because, at last, his luck was about to change for the better.

# 9

# IT'S NOT UNUSUAL

After the disappointment of 'Chills and Fever', Gordon knew that he had to steer Tom away from the blues – in more ways than one. 'If I'd left Tom alone, he'd probably have gone on singing the blues for the rest of time. I know he was disappointed when we started on records away from the blues feel, but he eventually realised that it was primarily a matter of getting through to an audience.'

Gordon managed to find the band some gigs outside London to bring in a few much needed extra pounds. For one, at the Top Rank Cinema in Slough, he invited his good mate Les Reed to join him, so he could take a look at Tom and give his opinion.

Les can laugh about it now: 'I was horrified when I saw the main man. He was wearing an open silk shirt, showing his hairy chest, with a massive medallion around his neck. His trousers were so tight, I was worried about him every time he moved! Around his waist was tied a rabbit's foot and his boots defied description. They were massive! I thought, "I ain't gonna like this guy." But when he opened his mouth to sing a Wilson Pickett song and a couple of Jerry Lee Lewis numbers, I was totally hooked!'

Les Reed would be one of the most significant figures in the early career of Tom Jones. He had known Gordon since 1959, when The Viscounts shared a bill with the John Barry Seven. Les was the pianist with the group formed by the man who would become one of the most acclaimed film composers in the world and later wrote the enduring James Bond signature tune.

Les, who was brought up in the Home Counties, was a properly trained musician. He had been immersed in the world of entertainment as a child, when his father ran a semi-professional troupe of dancers, singers and accordion players. He had started playing the piano at five and passed all his London College of Music exams by fourteen. After national service, he played piano in London nightclubs, before an obligatory summer season at Butlins led to an introduction to John Barry.

He spent three years with the Seven, touring up and down the country, before he left in 1962 to concentrate on writing and arranging and forming his own group, the Les Reed Combo. They were much in demand on BBC Radio as the resident band backing famous guest artists, including Jim Reeves and Jerry Lee Lewis, on shows like *Mark Time*, *On the Scene* and *Country Club*.

Tom had no idea when he met Les for the first time that the Combo had backed Jerry Lee and that Les had conducted the sessions. He also didn't know that Adam Faith was best man at his wedding or that Les had played piano on many of the singer's chart hits, including 'Poor Me' and 'What Do You Want?'

One day, Gordon asked Les if he fancied writing a song or two together, so they met up at the flat in Campden Hill Towers and composed 'In the Deep of Night' for a promising girl singer from the North-East called Dodi West. The track was not a hit, but might well have been if it had been recorded by Sandie

Shaw or Cilla Black. They were keen to try again when they next had a good idea.

Les believes their songwriting partnership worked very well: 'Gordon was not a trained musician, but had a way with lyrics that was very much in keeping with meaningful songs of the day. We gelled together because I provided melodies and chords, which were a weak point in his writing abilities.'

One of the oldest clichés in the pop handbook is that it only takes one song. Tom needed to be patient while Gordon tried to find the right track for his next record. Gordon certainly didn't think his latest composition was the one. He had just been tickling the keys of the piano at home one evening, when he came across a pleasing little melody. Jo liked it as well and suggested that he could call the tune 'It's Not Unusual'.

The offering was very thin when Gordon next met up with Les. He sang him a few bars and said he was hoping it would be a song for Sandie Shaw, who had burst on to the pop scene with her debut record '(There's) Always Something There to Remind Me' in October 1964. The melody wasn't the one that would rank among the most famous of all time, but Les liked the title, 'It's Not Unusual', and some of the other lyrics that Gordon had sketched out, so they started working on it.

Five days later, they had completed the song and chose Tom to make the demo. Gordon sang it for him in the car one day and he was keen to be involved. It takes a leap of imagination to think a track recorded by the booming-voiced masculine man from the Valleys was suitable for the whimsical Miss Shaw, whose trademark was going barefoot when she appeared on television.

Tom duly showed up at Regent Sounds in Denmark Street, Soho, to record. Les was there on piano and had recruited some of the best-known session musicians to help: on drums, Mitch Mitchell, who would find fame in the Jimi Hendrix Experience, well-known London session musician Eric Ford played bass, Peter Lee Stirling, guitar, and Gordon banged a tambourine. Stirling changed his name to Daniel Boone and had a number of hits in the early seventies as a singer-songwriter.

Les recalls, 'Tom sang the song well. The following day, the three of us took the demo disc to Sandie's manager, Evie Taylor. We were kept waiting, as Evie was interviewing another act called Des Lane, The Penny Whistle Man. Finally, she led us into her office, complaining that Des Lane was an important act and we had made her cut short her meeting. She heard about eight bars of the song, said, "It'll never be a hit" and showed us the door.'

Evie was known as the 'Queen Bee of Show Business', a female firebrand of an agent in a male-dominated business. She had managed both the John Barry Seven and Adam Faith, so Les knew what she was like. He observes, 'She could not only have secured agency for Tom, but also future publishing on our songs, but she was more concerned about Des Lane. I think she turned down a lot of money that day!'

On the Tube journey home, Tom pleaded with the others to let him record and release the song. He had realised its potential and how much it suited him: 'You can't say what ingredients go into a hit song. You only know when you hear it. It hits you. "It's Not Unusual" was a good song but commercial as well. It had everything in it that I wanted.'

Later, in the pub, Tom wouldn't let it drop. Gordon remarked that he had a face as long as a fiddle. When he asked him what was wrong, Tom announced, 'I want that song.' He felt so strongly about it that he threatened to go back to Wales permanently if he didn't get the chance to record it.

In a way, Evie was right. This wasn't a number for Sandie Shaw once you had heard Tom Jones singing it. She did check with her artist, however, to see what she thought. Sandie listened to it and declared, 'This is going to be a big song. This is his song.'

Fortunately for the career of Tom Jones, Les and Gordon agreed, and the following day the three of them trooped over to the Decca offices on the Embankment to meet the company's veteran founder, Sir Edward Lewis, managing director Bill Townsley and Peter Sullivan. Nervously, they played them Tom's demo. Les recalls, 'They all absolutely loved the song *and* the artist and we concluded a deal for Tom and Decca that very day.'

In the music business, there is nothing unusual about a performer's group taking a back seat while a track is recorded, but the signs were already there that Tom wasn't a member of a group. The Playboys, who were now called The Squires because of yet another name clash, were from the outset perceived as nothing more than Tom's backing band for live performances.

The Squires was a clever name for the group. Gordon was again echoing the *Tom Jones* movie, because Squire Weston, played by the Welsh actor Hugh Griffith, was arguably the most memorable character in the film.

Les Reed explains the situation: 'The Squires were an ideal group to back him up in the early days, but Tom was deemed from the very beginning to be a solo singer. There is no doubt about that.'

'It's Not Unusual' was recorded at the Decca Studios in West Hampstead. Tom, though a recording novice, was completely professional and patient – essential ingredients in what can be a laborious and drawn-out process. 'He was a gentleman in the studio,' says Les. 'He would take both criticism and advice from

Gordon and me, but, really, he was so adept at styling a song that we rarely criticised him.'

The initial recording was not a success, however. Les went for a light Tamla Motown-style arrangement, using vibraphones and bells and rhythm guitars that might have suited an early record by The Supremes or Mary Wells. Tom's voice didn't flow with the music. He was singing well enough, but the overall effect was nothing special.

Decca weren't happy. Peter Sullivan realised something had to be done. He told Tom, 'You've got a big voice. Nice is not enough. You are not nice!' He told Les, 'This score is far too Sandie Shaw. You need a bigger sound. Tom needs brass behind him.'

Les went back to the drawing board to come up with the arrangement that became so well known, an instant classic, using some of the brass section and woodwind players from the renowned Ted Heath Orchestra. Tom, so legend has it, sang his dynamic vocal while standing in a studio cupboard to achieve the best acoustics. The result was thrilling.

Frustratingly, Decca decided to postpone the single until after Christmas. The record company was releasing 'Little Red Rooster' by The Rolling Stones in November and didn't want the two records to be in competition with one another. In any case, there was no point in taking on The Beatles, whose single 'I Feel Fine' was set to dominate the festive charts.

Armed with the new single, Tom went home to spend his last Christmas in Treforest. Gordon had to send everyone back to Wales, because basically he had run out of money and was £1,000 in debt. You could buy a house for £3,000 in 1964, so this was a considerable sum. 'It's Not Unusual' needed to be a hit or his whole financial pack of cards was going to collapse. To add to his private anguish, Jo was in hospital with complications during a second pregnancy. Tom was so broke, he confessed, 'My dad had to lend me a few quid to buy presents. It's the worst Christmas I've ever spent.'

Tom invited Gerry Greenberg over for breakfast at the house in Cliff Terrace to listen to the new song. Linda offered him a boiled egg, while an excited Tom put the track on the turntable. Gerry had been closely connected with Tom's career from the outset and Tommy, as he still called him, valued his opinion: 'I listened to it. I thought, "This hasn't got much of a chance." But I turned to him and I said, "Brilliant – definitely going to be number one in Pontypridd."' Gerry wasn't alone in his opinion. The *NME* gave it the briefest of reviews, describing the song as a 'catchy tune', but not chart material.

'It's Not Unusual' was, in fact, a very unusual song in an era dominated by guitar-led groups. It was a perfect two minutes of Motown dance music, combined with old-fashioned big-band swing. Both Tom and the song seemed too grown up for the teenagers swooning before George Harrison and Paul McCartney. When Tom performed it, the smooth sexuality of the song was complemented perfectly by his pelvic thrusting. The BBC was reluctant to give it airtime when it was finally released at the end of January 1965, but the popular disc jockey Alan Freeman played the track on his late evening Radio Luxembourg show, which was great publicity.

Tom never forgot sitting in a pub one night and watching some regulars, who were playing darts, put his single on the jukebox practically on repeat. They were asking, 'Who the hell is this Tom Jones bloke?' and the barmaid, who was casually washing glasses, glanced up, nodded at Tom and said, 'That's him there.'

At this point, Gordon decided it was time for the first press release announcing the new singing sensation to the world. Tom, naively, went along with it, barely giving the fact that it was a pack of lies a second thought. It was to have a profound effect on the rest of Linda Woodward's life, because Gordon told Tom that he couldn't appear to be married.

The shameful statement read: 'He's Tom Jones, he's twenty-two, single and a miner.' He was, in reality, Tommy Woodward, aged twenty-four, married with a young son and the nearest he had ever been to a mine was washing his dad's back. The stories that gave credence to this spin also said he was six feet tall, which added two inches to his real height.

It has long been accepted in the world of movies and music that you can tell your audience what you like and it doesn't matter if it's a lie. Conning the fans is allowed, for some reason. None of the members of Take That had girlfriends when they started out, we were told, but of course they all did. Kylie Minogue and Jason Donovan were practically living together when they were denying that they were boyfriend and girl-friend. John Lennon kept his marriage and young son secret on the orders of his manager when The Beatles began, so at least there was a famous precedent for erasing Linda from Tom's CV.

Linda was kept out of the way in Treforest with Mark, who was nearly eight. She was still making nylon stockings in the factory. Just after 'It's Not Unusual' was released, she was walking with Margaret Sugar through the centre of Pontypridd, when they heard the record playing in Freddie Feys' record shop. She turned to her companion and confided, like an excited schoolgirl, 'Oh Margaret, he will soon be on *Top of the Pops*!'

An appearance on the iconic pop programme was a landmark in any performer's career. Tom performed 'It's Not Unusual' on 11 February 1965 and it proved to be just the spur to propel the song to the top. Gordon had decided that Tom should wear all white, including his shoes, to try to counteract suggestions that his pelvic performance was too overtly sexual for sensitive teenage girls. Vernon Hopkins wryly observed that Tom looked more like a commercial for Persil washing powder than the hottest singer in the land.

Inevitably, news that Tom was actually a married man of twenty-four with a young son soon appeared in the newspapers. The argument in favour of the deception was that it drew in female fans and once they were hooked it didn't matter whether he was married or not. That was small consolation to Linda.

Tom was apologetic to the *Daily Mirror*, calling it his 'big lie'. He explained, 'It's never been a secret back home in Wales that I was married. But when I came to London, it was felt it was best if my wife and son were "dispensed with". When I came to London, I was told to say I was single. I knew that sooner or later the secret would come out.' His contrition appeared in the newspaper one day before he celebrated his eighth wedding anniversary.

Mark was quoted for the first time in the papers, saying that he wanted to be a drummer when he grew up. He added, 'I'm glad that everybody knows Tom Jones is my daddy.' Linda, too, said it was a great relief: 'I found it very difficult to keep the secret. I am glad all that business is over and done with.'

Jo Mills realised that the damage had already been done, however: 'I think from the very beginning Linda was made to feel as if she mustn't exist in his life. It's very sad, because she is a lovely person, very warm, and if only she'd got that confidence initially, she would have been very different, I'm sure. She always stayed very much in the background.'

A few years later, when Tom was one of the most famous singers in the world, Linda commented, 'I never felt good enough to be Tom's wife.'

This was the age of The Beatles, when singles routinely sold in vast quantities. 'It's Not Unusual' shifted more than 800,000 copies in four weeks. The track entered the charts at number twenty-one, before rising to the top on 11 March 1965. While Tom's debut was one of the fifty biggest sellers of the decade, it wasn't even the biggest of the year – that accolade belonged to 'Tears', sung by the comedian Ken Dodd, with total eventual sales of more than 1.5 million.

The chart was announced on Thursdays, when there was a rundown on *Top of the Pops*. Back in Wales, when he came up to the surface, Tom's father was given the news by one of his mates, who told him, 'Your Tom's got to number one.' He promptly went home to invite all his friends and family round to celebrate.

The man himself was sitting in Gordon's flat with a glass of champagne in his hand, with Gordon, Jo, Les Reed, The Squires, Peter Sullivan and everyone else who had a vested interest in his success. Les remembers a telling exchange between Tom and his manager at the party: 'Gordon almost pinned him to the wall and said, "You talk to no one. I do all the talking; you don't even talk to Les."'

Things would never be the same for Tom or any of his family. His life was like a record on a turntable when the speed changed from a sedate 33 rpm to a rapid 78 rpm. It was a whirlwind. When he returned home to Wales with Gordon, he barely had a moment to see his parents because of the demands on his time. That didn't stop Freda reportedly telling him, 'You may be a big shot up in London, but down in Pontypridd you wipe your shoes when you come in, you're good to your wife and you take your turn bringing in the coal.'

Part of the success of 'It's Not Unusual' was down to the notorious trouser-splitting antics of P. J. Proby. He was on tour with Cilla Black, Tommy Roe and other groups, including The Fourmost and Sounds Incorporated. For a time, the Texan, whose real name was Jim Smith, was the most talked-about singer in the UK, and had enjoyed three top ten hits before Tom came along – then his velvet trousers started splitting on stage. Once was considered an accident, but when it happened again at the Croydon ABC, it was the final straw for the tour's promoters and he was banned from all ABC Cinemas.

Tom Jones and The Squires were ushered in to take his place, not as the headline act – that would be Cilla – but as the one that had the hit record at the time. They did nineteen dates in three weeks, criss-crossing the country from Newcastle to Exeter, from Edinburgh to Cardiff. The publicity for 'It's Not Unusual' was priceless.

The press tried to build a rivalry between Tom and Proby, ignoring the fact that they shared the same record label and were therefore giving both record sales the oxygen of publicity. Tom fanned the flames of competition, telling Keith Altham in the *NME* that he didn't like Proby, whom he nicknamed P. J. Probably, as an artist: 'I like his voice and like his sound – but not his style.' Tom resented claims that he was copying the American: 'I am what I am. I have never tried to be what is popularly conceived as a modern sex symbol. Take a look at these sideburns and the curly hair – brushed back. Do you see any sign of the idol à la fringe and velvet pants? I was singing the same kind of songs, dressed as I am now, when Proby was still in America. I don't copy anyone – least of all Proby.'

The trouser-splitting may now seem more like it belonged in a *Carry On* film or a Benny Hill sketch, but in the mid-sixties, the moral majority, led by campaigner Mary Whitehouse, had a sanctimonious power. Proby later claimed in an interview that Gordon Mills had offered the promoter Joe Collins, father of Joan and Jackie, a great deal of money to throw the American off the tour and replace him with Tom. He said that money had changed hands.

Proby maintained that they were looking for an excuse to sack him, and the fuss that Mary Whitehouse kicked up after his performance at the Croydon ABC gave them just cause. It may or may not be true that Gordon tried to bring some influence to bear on the situation, but all the major protagonists in the decision are long dead. When the dust cleared, Tom was in, at £600 per week, and P. J. Proby was out. Later that month, Proby released a timely, extravagant ballad called 'I Apologise', which just missed out on the top ten when Tom was riding high in the charts.

For a while, Tom had to put up with Proby fans holding up pictures of their idol while he was performing, but that didn't last long. Instead, he finished the tour practically headlining. It had been a meteoric rise.

The realisation that he was truly famous hit him one night while he was in the pub between shows in Southampton with Cilla Black and some of the groups from the tour, and he was dimly aware that a bunch of girls was gathering outside. He was unconcerned, believing they were there for the others, so he innocently wandered into the crowd, only to be torn practically limb from limb as they tried to grab a souvenir. His new black raincoat was in shreds.

He chuckled, 'These females wanted a piece of me, yet the week before they wouldn't buy me a glass of bloody bitter.'

# 10

# PUSSYCAT

The line-up for the *NME* Poll Winners Concert at the beginning of April 1965 was one of the greatest ever assembled and would have graced Live Aid: The Moody Blues, The Seekers and Herman's Hermits were some of the acts in the first half, which ended with The Rolling Stones singing 'The Last Time' and 'Everybody Needs Somebody to Love'. Cilla Black, Dusty Springfield and The Animals kept the excitement levels high in the second half, before The Beatles closed the show with 'Ticket to Ride' and 'Long Tall Sally'.

Tom, dressed in a bright red shirt and tight black trousers, was on between Van Morrison's group, Them, and sixties' favourites The Searchers. Backed by The Squires and his new brass section, he opened with 'Little by Little', before launching into 'It's Not Unusual', which brought a crescendo of screams from the mainly female audience. He closed with what would be his new single, 'Once Upon a Time'. Alan Smith's review in the *NME* called Tom's performance a 'real highlight of the show'. He added, 'He more than proved himself as one of the best visual performers in the pop business', which was high praise, considering three months before he was barely known.

Tom had already come into contact with The Beatles, or more precisely John Lennon, on the pop show *Thank Your Lucky Stars*. In the afternoon at the studios in Birmingham, Tom and Gordon were watching the rehearsals from the audience's seats. John, who was the first of The Beatles out on stage, plugged in his guitar, looked up and started singing 'It's not an elephant, It's a unicorn' to the tune of 'It's Not Unusual'. He then said into his microphone, 'How are you doing, you Welsh poof?' Tom was unamused and responded, 'Come up here, you Scouse bastard, and I'll show you.'

Gordon had to calm things down quickly, fearing that Tom nutting John Lennon wouldn't be a good career move. 'It's just his sense of humour,' he soothed, although Tom was well aware that the Liverpudlian was taking the piss. If there's one thing that Tom does not enjoy being called, it's a Welsh poof. He muttered to Gordon, 'I'll give him a sense of fucking humour.' Later the two became friends and Tom was able to laugh about it – just.

The follow-up to 'It's Not Unusual' was a strangely lacklustre affair. 'Once Upon a Time' had been written by Gordon and arranged by Les Reed, but it was a pale imitation of Tom's first hit. The lyric was banal – all about Adam and Eve falling in love once upon a time. The *NME* said it was tailor-made for the charts. That proved not to be the case.

Sales weren't helped by Joe Meek finding his original recordings of Tom and releasing 'Little Lonely One' on the Columbia label in direct competition. He observed, 'I believe it will do Tom a lot of good.' Tom didn't see it that way. Privately, he was hopping mad. Publicly, he was more measured: 'I think it's dated and I'd like to disassociate myself from it.'

'Once Upon a Time' flopped, reaching a lowly thirty-two in May. For other artists, this might have marked them as one-hit wonders? The record's release was put back three weeks to allow Tom his first chance of making headway in the US. Chris Hutchins, who would be hired as Tom's publicist later in the year, explained, 'It was very important for Gordon to break America because that was a much bigger market.'

Gordon's role model as he plotted the rise of Tom Jones was Elvis Presley. If there had been an Elvis handbook on how to become the biggest star in the world, then Gordon would have read it every night before bed. Part of the Elvis mythology was that when he appeared on the world-famous *Ed Sullivan Show* for the first time in 1956, he was only filmed from the waist upwards so as not to upset the God-fearing families of Middle America. That didn't actually happen until Elvis's third appearance, when he was singing a gospel song called 'Peace in the Valley'. The publicity the apparent censorship brought was worth gold to the star's blossoming career.

The other key aspect of appearing on *The Ed Sullivan Show* was that it bridged the gap between the rock 'n' roll generation and their parents – families watched the programme together. Presley's legendary manager, Colonel Tom Parker, credited the success of the more mainstream ballad 'Love Me Tender' to his client's performance on the TV show.

The Beatles had set a trend in February 1964, at the height of Beatlemania, with a triumphant appearance on the show. More than 40 per cent of the country had watched them. As a result, other British acts were keen to follow their lead. A guest spot on *The Ed Sullivan Show* was just what Tom needed to crack America. Gordon knew, as every half-decent manager would, that the show equalled dollar signs. He negotiated a deal for Tom to appear on the programme five times over the next year.

Gordon was helped in the US by a New York-born attorney called Lloyd Greenfield, one of the most astute and popular members of Team Tom for the next thirty years. He came across as an abrasive personality until he got to know you. Gordon trusted him to pick his way through the minefield of American legal contracts. He also had the task of telling radio DJs prior to Tom's television debut that he was not a black artist, as so many thought.

Tom would have preferred to take The Squires with him when he and Gordon flew to New York for his debut appearance on the show on 2 May 1965. He felt comfortable with the group, but he was told he needed to use American musicians on this occasion. For Tom, it was the first time he had flown. For Gordon, it was particularly stressful because of his fear of flying. He always bit his fingernails, but now they were gnawed to the quick.

Tom wasn't the most controversial act that night – he was preceded by The Rolling Stones. Sullivan had vowed never to have them on his show again after the group's screaming fans had drowned him out the previous October. He relented, persuaded by their popularity. They sang 'The Last Time', which had succeeded 'It's Not Unusual' as number one in the UK.

Sullivan realised that British acts were pulling in an audience, so Tom was joining a list of guests that included the Dave Clark Five and the host's personal favourite, Herman's Hermits. He was warned, though, to tone down his sexiest moves or else the producers would cut to his face. He did his best, swaying from side to side rather than thrusting backwards and forwards. Gordon was delighted, because it was the same sort of censorship that Elvis had experienced.

Sullivan was sufficiently pleased to have Tom back a month later, when he was allowed to do two numbers. He opened the show with 'It's Not Unusual', which had made the top ten on the *Billboard* chart. His hair was now in a ponytail and he rather resembled a posh Ted on a night out. He wore a tight-fitting shiny black suit with a cropped jacket and black Cuban-heeled winklepickers. Unable to do much with his bottom half, he snapped his fingers to the beat, which became rather irritating after the first minute or so. He still oozed a knowing sex appeal that augured well for the future.

Later, he closed the show with 'Whatcha' Gonna Do When Your Baby Leaves You', an old fifties song by the black American blues singer Chuck Willis, which was much more in keeping with his preferred music. Tom had dancers for the first time; he seemed entirely at ease with this 'putting on a show' aspect and moved effortlessly around the stage.

One additional outcome of his appearances on *The Ed Sullivan Show* was that he was revealed to be white. That came as a surprise to the American audience, which naturally thought that his big, brash voice belonged to a black man. Elvis himself thought that Tom was black when he first heard him.

Tom had recorded 'Whatcha' Gonna Do' for his first album, *Along Came Jones*, which had been released in the UK the previous week. The vinyl LP had sixteen tracks and was generally well received by the critics. *Record Mirror* gave it four stars and commented that side one had 'loud vocal work and loud backing'. This contrasted with side two, which emphasised strings, allowing the ballads and the blues to come through.

The album was almost a collection of singles, in that each number was a classic two-minute pop song. Tom was able to include some old favourites from his Pontypridd days, including 'Spanish Harlem', 'Memphis, Tennessee', 'Some Other Guy' and an up-tempo version of the 'Skye Boat Song', which shouldn't have worked but did. The *NME* said Tom sounded 'remarkably coloured'. His voice almost had a James Brown quality, especially on 'I Need Your Loving'. Disappointingly, *Along Came Jones* just failed to make the top ten in the UK, perhaps an indication that Tom was spending too much time in the US.

Gordon was already thinking ahead. He wanted to position Tom next to big, popular movies to give him stature as an important artist. Elvis had continually proved that a film theme tune was a surefire hit, and in the UK artists like Shirley Bassey obtained massive exposure from recording the latest James Bond song. When Gordon learned that Burt Bacharach would be in London working on the soundtrack of a new movie called *What's New Pussycat?*, he pushed for Tom to sing the title song. Tom had already recorded one Bacharach number: the B-side of 'It's Not Unusual' was the dull 'To Wait for Love'.

Tom went round to the luxury flat the composer was renting in Belgravia and listened intently while Burt played the theme. Tom loathed 'What's New Pussycat?' from the first time he heard it. He confessed, 'I thought it was a joke.' When he is asked which is the least favourite of all his songs, the Burt Bacharach/Hal David novelty record is the one that first pops into his mind. He told the *NME*, 'I don't like it at all. It's just not me.'

He was sensible enough to be polite about it and asked Burt to leave it with him for a day or two, so that he could 'live' with the song. He told Gordon his true feelings and was promptly informed he was doing it and that was final.

Bacharach had a reputation for being a hard man to please and, reading between the lines, he gave Tom a tough time in the studio: 'He really takes command of the situation – in a quiet way. He is really intense and he conducts the orchestra like he is really living the music.' Tom had to do a lot of takes, which was something he wasn't used to. 'It was the hardest recording session I have ever done,' he said.

The man who intensely disliked Cliff Richard's music was never going to enjoy singing 'Pussycat, Pussycat, I love you, Yes I do! You and your pussycat nose.' But Gordon was right – the song was a massive summer hit in the US and the UK. The song is like Marmite: either you love it or you hate it. More people, it seemed, loved it, and Bacharach and David were even nominated for an Academy Award the following year.

Tom's attitude hasn't really changed over the years, although grudgingly he now describes it as a 'fun song', a comedy record for a comedy film. The intention was to widen his exposure and it succeeded in that aim, helped by the popularity of the movie. The film starred Peter O'Toole, Peter Sellers and Woody Allen and became a sixties kitsch classic.

For the rest of 1965, Tom criss-crossed the ocean, as Gordon set about conquering both countries. Tom ended up spending four months of his breakthrough year in the US. He disliked touring by bus and the endless nights trying to get comfortable, while he and the other artists on the package tour, including Sonny and Cher and The Turtles, were ferried thousands of miles around the country.

He hated the racism they encountered in the Deep South, where he couldn't be seen talking to The Shirelles, the popular black girl group on the bill. At one hotel, he was chatting to the lead singer, Shirley Owens, in the lobby, when she suddenly marched off. Later, she told him that people were staring at them. She told him, 'We were touching. You can't do that in the South. They wouldn't only hang me. They would hang you as well. "Nigger-lover" they would call you.'

113

Tom, who had spent most of his life in the sheltered streets of Treforest, couldn't believe what he was seeing and hearing. When another black singer, Mel Carter, was arrested during a fight at a truck stop, Tom tried to intervene, but was told in no uncertain terms to butt out by a cop who brandished a gun and called him 'boy'. He told *MOJO* magazine, 'I thought, "My mother's going to pick up the paper and read 'Tom Jones shot in Mississippi'." Jesus, these people are mad.'

In October, Tom was back on safer ground when he appeared again on *The Ed Sullivan Show*, singing 'What's New Pussycat?' and another single called 'With These Hands', a powerful and emotional song.

Tom was pushing himself hard and a month-long tour of Australia the following March seemed to take its toll on his voice. On his return, he went to see a specialist, who told him he needed to have his tonsils out. This was a big deal for a professional singer and Tom was whisked into the London Clinic for the operation. It was a success, but the surgeon was concerned about the level of bruising on his vocal chords and Tom was strongly advised to change his habits. That included giving up Woodbines, which he was still smoking, and cutting down on the beer and spirits.

Gordon stepped in to tell him to try cigars, because he wouldn't have to inhale those, and to start drinking champagne, as this would be kinder on his voice. Tom recalled, 'I always smoked Woodbines and drank beer. My manager said one day I'd be smoking cigars and drinking champagne. I said, "I love Woodbines and I love beer and that's that." So what am I doing today? Drinking champagne and smoking cigars. Times change.'

After a period of rest, Tom was back singing as strongly as ever. In a bizarre postscript, his tonsils went missing from the clinic. If it had happened today, they would probably have been put up for sale on eBay.

Elvis Presley really liked 'It's Not Unusual'; he loved 'With These Hands'. He was filming yet another of his conveyor-belt films, *Paradise, Hawaiian Style*, at Paramount Studios in LA, when the call came in from his manager's office asking if it would be possible for a singer called Tom Jones to come by and say hello. Elvis readily said it was OK.

Tom was in Hollywood to see Burt Bacharach and sign a deal to sing a new film theme tune. He was thrilled to be meeting Elvis, one of his heroes, although not quite so impressed to hear him duet with a child actress on a song from the movie called 'Datin'', which began 'Datin' is a game that grown-ups play' and went downhill from there.

More impressively, when Elvis spotted Tom, he strolled over, arms outstretched, singing 'With These Hands'. It was the start of a genuine friendship that lasted until Elvis's death in 1977. At the first meeting, Tom was suitably gushing. One of the so-called 'Memphis Mafia', Marty Lacker, recalled that Tom told Elvis how much he had been influenced by him, loved what he did and what it meant to meet him. Marty said that Tom had a look of awe on his face and seemed genuinely surprised when Elvis, truthfully, told him how much he liked his album.

Elvis asked him if all people sang like that in Wales. Tom replied, 'Well, not exactly, but Welsh people have strong voices; that is where I get my strength from. My volume is where I come from.'

Chris Hutchins explained Tom's gift and why Elvis loved his voice: 'If you listen to "With These Hands", the passion he put into that song. He wasn't long out of Wales and you realised that this man really felt it. That's the secret of his success, in my opinion – a genuine passion for the words he was singing. That was what got him the admiration of Sinatra and Presley. He poured this passion in, but he had it to pour in the first place.'

That was the drawback of 'Pussycat' – not even Tom could inject passion into such a fanciful lyric. Chris recalls, 'He thought it was ridiculous. That was a stupid song, but it was a monster hit for him.'

While in America, Tom was determined to watch a perform-ance by Chuck Jackson, one of his favourite black singers, who was headlining a show at the Apollo Theater in Harlem, but he had no idea how to get there. By chance, the silky-voiced Dionne Warwick came to his rescue. They had met earlier in the year, when they had both appeared on *Ready Steady Go!* in Manchester and become instant friends, although nothing more.

On this cold evening, she had just been to a recording session and was driving from Midtown, down Broadway, when she saw Tom shivering on a corner. He was hopelessly lost and told her he was on his way to the Apollo to see Chuck. Dionne told him to hop in and she would take him over to Harlem.

They arrived backstage just before Chuck was due to go on. Everybody knew and liked the elegant Dionne, so Chuck was happy to chat to Tom. He decided to give the audience a surprise and so, during his act, he invited Tom on stage to take a bow, and announced that he was the man who sang 'It's Not Unusual'. You could have heard a pin drop. None of the exclusively black audience could believe that this white man, with, to their ears, a funny *English* accent, was the voice on that track. Chuck invited Tom to sing a few bars, whereupon he launched into 'What'd I Say' and brought the house down. 'To my amazement, they loved it,' he said. 'I was very relieved.'

At least when his American schedule allowed Tom to come back to London, he knew that Linda and Mark were waiting for him. One of the first consequences of the success of 'It's Not Unusual' was Tom moved into Gordon's flat in Notting Hill. It was only temporary, but set the precedent that he was the star and The Squires were employees.

Over time, the bitterness felt by some of the group's members would grow. Vernon Hopkins felt betrayed by someone he considered to be a good friend. They did have a raise, but it was peanuts, considering how much money Tom was earning. They were still driving an old van, when Tom sped up in a new white Volvo sports car, having only just passed his driving test.

Gordon was a big part of The Squires' growing disillusionment. He was quite obviously a control freak and liked to get his own way. He micro-managed Tom and had a fearsome temper. Tom, on the other hand, as Chris Hutchins points out, 'hated confrontation', and didn't want to say no to Gordon. He left it to Gordon to deal with his old bandmates, which is probably why they were treated unkindly. Chris observes, 'Tom was always going to be a solo star long before he got into The Squires – or The Senators as they were originally called – and I don't think they understood that. They thought they were like The Beatles and they weren't.'

Living in decent accommodation made it easier for Tom to give interviews. Having Linda around painted a cosy domestic scene. *Rave* magazine called her a 'lovely girl', as she made tea for everyone. Gordon's three Siamese cats – Winnie, Mu and Elvis – added to the impression of domestic bliss, although the one named after Presley would jump on Tom's shoulders and tear his sweaters to ribbons.

Tom and Linda needed to find another place to live, if only to escape from the cats. Gordon had told Tom right at the start that he should put his money into 'bricks and mortar', and it was advice he meant to follow. He paid £8,000 for a house called Rose Bank in Manygate Lane, Shepperton – the first home his family could call their own. Many friends believe Linda would have had a happier life if she had stayed in Pontypridd, but that opinion is delivered with the benefit of hindsight. For now, she was entirely happy to be with her husband.

Linda, as would always be the case, was in charge of decorating. Many of the rooms were full of the souvenirs Tom had brought back from overseas, including a growing collection of weaponry he had started in Spain, when he played some dates there as part of a European tour. His son's bedroom was covered with sporting pennants that Tom had found for him. Linda was keen to have an open-plan living space and plenty of glass to maximise the views towards the river – perhaps the effect of spending too many years in a basement with little natural light. Tom's contribution was to keep an eye on the builders who carried out the improvements. When he went over to see how work was progressing, he was quick to point out a mistake with the stairs, which didn't endear him to them.

While they were excited about the move, it soon became apparent that the three-bedroom house was too small. Open plan was all very well, but it led to domestic conflict when Mark and Linda were watching TV and Tom wanted to put Jerry Lee Lewis on the record player in another corner of the same room. The garage wasn't big enough to harbour his new silver-grey Rolls-Royce and he fretted about it getting dirty stuck outside all day.

Generally speaking, they were on friendly terms with the neighbours, although relations were a little strained when Tom would stumble in at 4 a.m. and decide that would be the perfect time to play loud music. He would sleep most of the day.

Mark started at a local school and, mostly, they weren't bothered by people, even if they went for a drink in the local pub. It was a different story if Tom went out for a beer in the West End, where there was usually some joker drunkenly insisting that he give them a song. Tom, who was under strict instructions not to overuse his voice, would politely decline, which would inevitably lead to a chorus of 'He can't sing. He just mimes.'

Tom would be 'spitting mad' at the comments: 'When the insults get really nasty, I often want to belt someone across the room. I know I must not do that. No matter how justified you are, it is nearly always the celebrity who comes out as the villain.'

That was one of the few drawbacks of becoming a star. Another was trying to work out who was and who was not a friend: 'People are nice to you, but you don't know if they are your friend. When you are not famous, you know who your friends are because they are your friends. But now you can't tell.'

Perhaps that explains why Tom was so keen to have his immediate family near him, despite spending so much time away. Even at this early stage of his success, he had learned to keep his professional and home lives entirely separate.

## 11

# GREEN, GREEN GRASS

---

Tom's career was almost terminated in June 1966, when he smashed his swanky new red Jaguar into the central barrier while speeding down Park Lane. He had spent the evening in the Cromwellian Club, a favourite haunt, with Tony Cartwright, a new member of Gordon's team, Vernon Hopkins and Chris Ellis, who had now moved from Wales to be Tom's full-time driver and general factotum.

It was, Vernon recalls, a great place for pulling girls, and Tony and Tom managed to latch on to two air hostesses. Tom decided to drive Tony and the girls to the Bag o' Nails pub in the West End. As he whizzed down Park Lane in the sports car, one of the young ladies told him to make a hard right turn and take a slip road across the central reservation. He couldn't make it at 50 miles an hour and crashed into a wall.

Vernon, who was following in his Ford, remembered that there was blood everywhere – most of it coming from Tom's head. According to Vernon, the two men decided to run off after making sure the girls were all right. They didn't get very far, as both police and ambulance raced up, blue lights flashing. They took one look at Tom's bleeding head and bundled him off to hospital, where he needed fourteen stitches for a gash above his left eye and was kept in overnight in case he was suffering from concussion.

The incident could have been much worse. Breathalyser tests for anyone involved in a road accident hadn't been introduced, so, provided you could walk in a reasonably straight line, there was no problem. In those pre-paparazzi days, the incident went unphotographed and unreported.

Tom didn't get away totally scot-free, however. He awoke the next day, with a head full of hammers, to find his mother Freda looming over him, demanding to know what he thought he was playing at. She wasn't impressed when he complained that his head was killing him.

He told the *Radio Times*, 'She said, "You better watch yourself. You're drinking too much – get hold of yourself. This stops right now." She stopped me right there and then. I was getting out of hand and I knew it.'

His parents had finally been persuaded to move from Treforest. They wanted to be closer to their son and his family. When he moved into a bigger property in Sunbury-on-Thames, he had told them he was giving them the house in Manygate Lane, which was at least twice the size of their former terrace in Laura Street.

His father observed, 'When he handed over his old house to us, it was all done without any kind of show. He just said to us how he knew we'd always liked the place and so it was ours to keep.'

As soon as he started making good money, Tom was determined to persuade Tom senior to retire. He hated that his father was 'flogging his insides out' in a pit while he was enjoying himself. As Chris Hutchins observes, 'He was always good to his family and they loved him for it.'

Tom senior still had eight years to go before retirement, but Tom told him to work out what he would earn in that time and promised to match it. He had been a miner for more than forty years, so he deserved his comfortable retirement and, finally, was happy to leave the pit. Tom bought his father a large and stately white Ford Granada, so his parents could travel home to Treforest whenever they wished. Tom senior needed to learn to drive to take advantage of the gift, but, unlike his son, decided to pass his test before he got behind the wheel of a car. In a rare interview, he said, 'The mining life, with all the comradeship, was fine for me, but I was much happier that Tom made up his own mind what to do with his life.'

Despite his mother's rebuke about his lifestyle, Tom didn't stop going to the Cromwellian Club; he just made sure that Chris Ellis or another of the team was driving him. One night, he was struggling with a cold, when he was passed an inhaler that he thought was Vicks Sinex. One sniff blew his head off: 'The bloody thing was full of amyl nitrate. Bloody hell! It was like being on a roller-coaster.'

His enjoyment of the high life in London was concealing the fact that he badly needed another big hit in the UK. Six successive singles had barely caused a ripple, while other leading acts of the day seemed to top the charts at will. His power-packed version of 'Thunderball' for the James Bond movie of that name was particularly disappointing, managing only number thirty-five. Tom had put so much into the recording. He almost passed out when he hit the sustained last note, and had to hold on to the studio wall to stop himself from falling over.

He still loved listening to a wide range of music and eventually found inspiration in his vinyl collection at home. He had brought an album back from New York called *Country Songs for*

*City Folk*, released the previous year by his old favourite, Jerry Lee Lewis, who was moving away from rock 'n' roll. On it was a deceptively simple track called 'Green, Green Grass of Home'.

The song was written in 1964 by the gloriously named Nashville songwriter Claude 'Curly' Putnam, Jr, and told of a man on death row dreaming of his home town. The story was one that moved Tom: 'Some numbers are so personal that they can hardly fail. Immediately there is a bond between the singer, the lyrics and the audience.'

The drama of the song lay in the words, which revealed the singer's true circumstance only at the end. Some people never realised that it was the reminiscence of a man who was about to be hanged. Tom admitted that he thought of the song each time he went back to Pontypridd.

Gordon usually chose Tom's songs, but on this occasion he agreed that it had possibilities. Neither of them was prepared for Les Reed's magical touch, however. He explained, 'Tom desperately wanted me to copy note by note the country arrangement that the Jerry Lee recording contained. But I managed to convince him that there was only one Jerry Lee Lewis and we needed to come up with a different version of the song.

'I did add my country piano to the big strings and choir, but I don't think Tom was wholly convinced we had it right until it went to number one!'

For once the *NME* was exactly right. Under the headline 'Tom Jones Is Superb', the review said, 'A gently swaying country-flavoured rockaballad with an easily hummable melody – a splendid and subdued performance by Tom – whose personality and individuality shine like a beacon.' After the exuberance of 'What's New Pussycat?' and 'Thunderball', Tom was displaying the benefit of restraint, reining in his obvious power to give his performance more light and shade.

The music press weren't the only ones predicting success. Jerry Lee Lewis himself was in the UK on tour and told Tom that he would love to hear what he had done with the song. Tom played it for him in his hotel room in London and recalled, 'He was knocked out with it and said, "You've done something different here. The arrangement is great. It sounds like a number one to me."'

The song's release came as the nation was stunned by the Aberfan disaster on 21 October 1966, when a giant slag heap, which threateningly overlooked the small mining village, collapsed and slid down the mountainside and flattened the local school. The death toll reached 144. Of that number, 116 were children. The tragedy cast a melancholy mood, perfectly captured by 'Green, Green Grass of Home', sung by a Welshman brought up just six miles away. The song topped the charts for seven weeks and became his only Christmas number one. With sales of more than 1.2 million, it was his biggest-ever single in the UK.

Elvis loved it. He felt, as fans did, the raw emotion of a man dreaming of his home and his mama and papa while on death row. He was driving his customised tour bus home to Memphis with his 'Mafia', when a well-known local disc jockey, George Klein, played the track. Elvis was so moved, he immediately stopped so he could listen properly. One of his bodyguards, Sonny West, recalled, 'I never saw him so emotionally into a song before, and when it ended he wiped his eyes and shouted, "Call George and tell him to play it again."'

He stopped at the next payphone and insisted one of his entourage call the radio station. He stopped again and again to request the song, until he had driven the 40 miles home to

Graceland, his famous house. He even offered to buy the station just so he could hear it once more. Marty Lacker said, 'Elvis wanted to hear it because he was just wallowing in how blue it made him feel. He was crying a little.'

Ironically, his most famous bodyguard, Red West, had heard the track on the Jerry Lee Lewis album, just as Tom had done, and recommended it to his boss. Elvis told him it was pretty good, but nothing came of it. He was astonished to learn that Tom Jones had turned it into this classic record.

The song touched a sentimental nerve in older audiences. Tom had never reached young teenagers in the way The Beatles or The Rolling Stones had. The Beatles took their loyal fans with them when they moved on from 'She Loves You' and their Cavern Club roots to embrace the philosophies of the Maharishi Yogi and an expanding drug culture. Their millions of devotees weren't suddenly going to change allegiance to Tom. Like Elvis had done, he needed to attract more mature women.

Every night needed to be hen-party night. Tom wasn't going to get that with the current coverage he was receiving in the newspapers. Since the initial debacle over his age and marital status, his publicity had been all over the place. Chris Hutchins was an ambitious writer on the *NME* when he glanced through a leading woman's magazine one day and saw a picture of Tom and Linda in the kitchen at their Shepperton home: 'Tom was wearing an apron and doing the washing up. And I thought, "Would Colonel Tom Parker, Elvis's manager, let his man do that?"'

Chris had a point. The *NME* had carried a feature on Tom, in which he was pictured bringing in the milk, doing the laundry, shaving, watching television and fast asleep in bed. Fans wanted to escape with a star – they didn't want to be reminded of the drudgery at home. The article observed that Tom was a 'quietly amiable person', which, while accurate, wasn't the description of a sex god.

Chris had studied Elvis and his manager during the previous few years and believed that Tom was Britain's answer to The King. He didn't realise at this stage how closely that mirrored the opinion of Tom's manager. He called Gordon and they met at the Ivy restaurant in the West End. Gordon brought Tom and listened to the pitch.

'I told him that I wanted to go into PR and that I would like to work on Tom because there is plenty to be done, to be frank. "Right, you've got it," said Gordon. Tom was tired, probably after a late night at the Cromwellian, and looked like he didn't want to be there. He nodded meekly and I realised this was a man I could work with. There was no arrogance.'

The lunch was the first meeting in a ten-year association between Tom and the man he called Chrissie. The next day Chris cancelled all the interviews in Tom's diary. He wanted to control the publicity.

The next time Chris saw Tom was on Boxing Day in South Wales, when he had the idea that Tom should receive a silver disc down a mine. Neither Chris nor Tom had been down a mine before, but the photographers watched as they gingerly followed Tom's father below the surface. This was more like it. Only real men went down a mine – there were no aprons at the coalface. Tom senior was never quite sure how to take his son's PR, and was unable to work out why he needed someone to speak for him.

Tom was enjoying an old-style family Christmas, although some things had changed. He drove down in the Rolls with Linda's present packed in the boot – a full-length fur coat. He joined everyone down at the Wood Road, where he discovered that the club had elected him honorary president. He had a 'smashing' time, so different from the depressing visit home two years before.

Chris was most impressed by how natural Tom was in his home environment. He met Tom's sister Sheila, who was lovely company, and her husband Ken, who was bald and once gave everyone the biggest laugh of the year when he turned up in a badly fitting wig. 'I can name some stars who were embarrassed by their family because they were ordinary people who said ordinary silly things.' But not Tom: 'He was very comfortable. His mother was fabulous. She was a loving woman. They were all very proud of him.'

Chris was always looking for an offbeat story that reflected his charge's masculinity. When Tom spent most of his time in the US, it became more important to find the right picture on his trips to the UK. One day, when Tom was home, Chris rang a local photographer called David Stein and invited him round to take photographs at Gordon's house. He had moved into a mansion on St George's Hill, Weybridge, and sentimentally called it Little Rhondda. The grounds were big enough for him to fulfil a lifelong dream and install a small zoo.

David arrived and asked, 'What's the picture?'

Chris answered, 'Tom, in Gordon's tiger cage with the tiger.'

Understandably, Tom wasn't keen. 'He looked at the tigers and said, "No way." And Gordon said, "They'll be all right." So we went to the cage and Tom said, "You go in first if you're so keen." Gordon went in first, then called me in and I went into this cage full of Siberian tigers. Next, Tom nervously came over and went in. Then we called David Stein and the tiger leapt on his shoulders and pushed him into a corner. I shall never forget the zookeeper saying, "David has purple trousers on – he doesn't like purple!" We laughed about that for months afterwards – the tiger who didn't like purple.'

The album *Green, Green Grass of Home* reached number three in March 1967. Tom was beginning to mature into an artist who could, quite literally, sing anything. He included Ponty numbers like 'Riders in the Sky' and 'Sixteen Tons', as well as the title track and the follow-up, 'Detroit City'. Tucked away on side two was a little-known song called 'All I Get from You Are Heartaches', which perfectly captured the essence of Tom Jones: a vocal range that began smokily deep and soared to a perfectly pitched falsetto note – a very rare occurrence in one of his songs. The passion was evident.

This was arguably his golden age as a recording artist – certainly in the first half of his career. In July 1967, he released a track that he has often said is his favourite among all his recordings, the unforgettable 'I'll Never Fall in Love Again'. Tom still loves the song that was co-written by Lonnie Donegan, a very popular name from the fifties, who was the 'King of Skiffle' and topped the charts in 1960 with 'My Old Man's a Dustman'.

He told Tom that he had a song that 'he could sing the pants off'. They met at Lonnie's house in Virginia Water, near Ascot. Tom immediately thought it was 'a wonderful song' and has never changed his opinion. Lonnie was completely right. 'I'll Never Fall in Love Again' was the first of three great power ballads that Tom released in a row, all of which reached number two in the charts. He sang the hell out of them.

The second of the trio was 'I'm Coming Home', another emotional song that he could have dedicated to Linda – 'I am coming home to your loving heart.' Les Reed and songwriting partner Barry Mason wrote it especially for Tom, knowing that he was the only singer who could do the song full justice.

For the recording at Decca Studio Number 2 in West Hampstead, Tom was keen to stand in the string section, which, as Les recalls, was unheard of, because of sound separation problems. 'We agreed he could try. On the first go, he sang with such emotion that the whole orchestra, including myself, had tears in our eyes. It was an incredible performance.

'Eventually the engineer's voice came through – "That was terrific, Les … Are you ready to do a take?" Poor Tom collapsed in frustration.'

Chris joined Tom in New York after New Year's 1968. One night, an executive with London Records, Lenny Marcel, took Tom to the Copacabana, the Upper East Side club widely referred to as 'the Copa'. The singer Jack Jones and his famous father, Allan Jones, were both on the bill and the latter made a facetious remark about Tom: 'We've got a hit-maker in the audience tonight. Tom Jones from England. Let's find out if he can sing.' So they called him on stage and Tom turned to Tony Cartwright and asked, 'What can I sing? They won't know any of my stuff.' Tony suggested he perform the one song he always did a cappella – 'My Yiddishe Momme'. He sang his heart out. Chris Hutchins remembers, 'He tore the place apart.'

Tom so impressed that night that Gordon was soon negotiating a two week residency at the club. This was the chance for Tom to try out a new image for the more mature market that Gordon was hoping to reach. He didn't pack the leather trousers. Instead, he wore a black tuxedo and a large black bow tie. His clothes were as tight as ever, but they were classy.

The Squires were flown over for his opening night and rehearsed extensively with the club's orchestra. Tom came across like a youthful and exuberant Sinatra, as he muscled his way through 'What's New Pussycat?', 'I Can't Stop Loving You', 'It's Not Unusual' and standards including 'I Believe' and 'Hello Young Lovers'. The highlight for many was a passionate rendition of 'Danny Boy' that reduced his audience to tears. Afterwards, Tom was elated and declared, 'I'm so happy.'

That feeling wore off quite quickly when the reality of three shows a night in the smoke-filled, candle-heavy atmosphere of the club reduced its charms and put his voice under considerable strain. The Copa was a supper club for organised crime run by a legendary figure called Jules Podell. He never actually saw a show himself, preferring to spend the evenings in the kitchen, perched on a chair by the cash register. Tom's last show was at 3 a.m., when he sang for an hour and a quarter. The schedule was the first sign of his Dracula lifestyle. For the next thirty years, he worked and played at night and slept through the day.

The headline act was the hired help; the people who mattered were sitting at the tables. Each night, the first thing Tom did when he arrived at the club was seek out his host and say, 'Good evening, Mr Podell.' It was a mark of respect. The tiny stage was so close to the tables that Tom was practically sitting with the clientele.

On one memorable occasion, he was so infuriated by one female guest's incessant high-pitched prattle during his rendition of 'Danny Boy' that he jumped off the stage, thrust a microphone under her nose and suggested she finish the song. Luckily, she wasn't the wife or mistress of an important gangster.

The club probably had space for little more than 150, but they were the cream of the New York underworld. Chris Ellis, who travelled with Tom, told the author Robin Eggar, 'If the police had raided the place they'd have cleaned up New York in three seconds flat.'

One evening, a 'button man' came over to where Tom was drinking at a table. Tom, who had been told he needed to stand up for himself, had no idea who he was and said, 'What the fuck do you want?'

The gangster replied, 'Stand up. I want to see how big you are.'

Tom noticed he was being kicked under the table by his worried companions when he said, 'I'll show you how big I am.'

Sonny Franzese, one of the bosses and a ruthless killer, laughed and walked away, while Tom's friends had nervous breakdowns.

The following year, Sonny came up to Tom when he was appearing in Las Vegas and said, 'You're the kid who told me to fuck off!'

Tom smiled and responded, 'I am. And who wants to know?'

In the America of the 1960s, playing the Copa was a sign that you were a serious name in the music business. Frank Sinatra, Sammy Davis, Jr, Dean Martin and Jerry Lewis had appeared there often, but so had more modern acts, including Marvin Gaye, The Temptations and The Supremes, and the great female artists Peggy Lee and Ella Fitzgerald were always popular.

Tom's spell at the Copa included an incident that had a life-changing effect on his career and how Tom Jones would be perceived for the next twenty years. Tom was sweating, because the heat in the club was stifling and, as usual, he was putting his heart into his performance. The audience at their tables were handing him their napkins for him to mop up the sweat. He recalled, 'All of a sudden, this woman stands up, lifts up her skirt and whips off her knickers. She gives them to me to wipe my forehead.' Tom entered into the spirit by accepting them and commenting, 'Don't catch cold.'

An entertainment columnist in the audience wrote about it and called Tom a 'panty magnet'. Knickers became an unavoidable addition to a Tom Jones concert from that moment on. Over the years, he would grow to hate the ritual, because it reduced the attention given to his voice. He didn't care about pants, but he was devoted to the music.

Moving from the Copa to a Las Vegas show was a natural progression. He was such a hit in New York that he attracted the attention of the rich and powerful of Las Vegas. Tom might have appeared there earlier than 1968 if Gordon had accepted offers for him to be a lounge act after *The Ed Sullivan Show* appearances. The money was attractive, but Jo strongly advised against it, because she had been to Vegas as a Bluebell Girl and knew how difficult it was to make the jump from lounge act to headliner.

In March, Tom transferred to the Flamingo Hotel, which wasn't in the best of health and certainly wasn't on a par with Caesars Palace. He was about to change that.

The underwear followed him to Vegas either by accident or design. Gordon was delighted, because it guaranteed some easy publicity. Chris Hutchins was ready with some sparkling one-liners for when Tom picked up one of the many pairs of lacy panties hurled in his direction. He would wipe his face and then declare mischievously, 'I know this woman …', which would be greeted by a roar from the now almost exclusively female audience.

The more intimate surroundings of first the Copa and then Vegas put a greater emphasis on Tom's interaction with the audience — something that didn't come naturally to him. He would have preferred to belt out song after song. Tom had a good memory for detail and was excellent at telling funny stories, but he wasn't so adept at banter. He understood he needed to make the audience feel wanted, however.

The hotel was determined to make Tom the hottest ticket in town before he began. They needed to, because they had agreed to pay Tom a million dollars for three residences over an eighteen-month period. It was a considerable coup for Gordon and Lloyd, who took care of things for Tom Jones from day to day. The point of the entertainment was to bring punters into the hotel so they would gamble at the casino. The Flamingo's publicity director, Nick Naff, devised 'Tom Jones Fever' as the hook for his campaign, which began by placing bottles of pills around the hotel labelled 'Tom Jones Fever Pills'. They were guaranteed not to cure you, but could make the 'fever' more tolerable. Radio commercials leading up to his opening night gave daily updates on the Tom Jones Fever temperature, as if it were a wacky weather forecast. Astutely, Naff even placed an ambulance at the back of the showroom, in case any of the audience were overwhelmed by the fever. It was masterful.

The Flamingo wasn't the biggest hotel on the strip and only 500 people could watch Tom at each of his two-nightly shows. The result was that, from the very beginning, there was always a long line of hopeful women queuing for a ticket. Most of them had a pair of knickers ready in their handbags.

# 12

# A LOVE SUPREME

If the eyewitnesses are to be believed, Tom had a voracious sexual appetite, unequalled in the world of entertainment, and all achieved without the aid of drugs – just a liberal dose of his now favourite Dom Pérignon champagne, a cigar or two that he didn't inhale and a direct approach that worked most of the time.

Over the years, Tom's libido has become a joke subject, which ignores the fact that he is married to a devoted wife. Sometimes the humour is unintentional. A television interview early in his career featured a voice-over that declared with old-fashioned solemnity: 'For the successful pop singer, a grinding succession of one-night stands is the routine.' It would seem that was the case with Tom.

The moment Tom shut the front door behind him, he was a single man. When he opened it again and announced he was home, he was married. Perhaps Gill Beazer was right and he just wanted the company of women and didn't much like the pros-pect of spending a night alone.

The dilemma for Tom was that his publicity was promoting his status as a sex symbol, which once again pushed Linda into the background. From the first time he first wiped his brow with a pair of white knickers, he had a reputation that needed to be fed.

Considering the legend, he has managed to avoid a string of kiss and tells. With a few notable exceptions, he has bedded hundreds of women and yet could count on the fingers of one hand the number who have sold him down the river.

Occasionally, he met someone who meant something more. The first of the few was Mary Wilson, a founder member of The Supremes. They met in January 1968, when he knocked at her dressing-room door at the Bal Paree in Munich, where the Bambi Awards, the German equivalent of the Oscars, were being held. By coincidence, Tom had just recorded the group's classic 'You Keep Me Hanging On' for his next album, *13 Smash Hits*.

The introduction was engineered by the agent Norman Weiss after Tom mentioned he would love to meet her. Norman had booked The Supremes to perform at the ceremony. The glamorous Diana Ross was the undisputed lead singer of the famous girl group, but it was her sultry and more curvaceous bandmate who had caught Tom's eye.

It really was love at first sight for Mary. Norman had mentioned Tom to her enough for her to take an interest. If Google had existed then, she could have typed Tom's name into the search engine and quickly established that he was married. Instead, she had no idea and was 'giddy as a schoolgirl' at the prospect of meeting him, after she realised how good looking he was and how well he sang.

The spark between them was there right from the outset. In the mid-sixties, The Supremes were more famous internationally than Tom Jones, so Mary wasn't some star-struck fan dazzled by a smooth celebrity. She described him tenderly in her autobiography, *Dreamgirl: My Life as a Supreme*. He was like no man she had ever met. 'We talked, we cuddled, then we kissed, and by the time the evening had ended I knew I was in love.' Mary was impressed that they would spend hours just talking. Tom may have been a man's man, but he never lost his empathy with women.

Poignantly, Mary reveals that she believed she had found true love at last. She was single, unattached and struggling to come to terms with the death of Florence Ballard, another founder member of The Supremes, and the fact that the group had been taken over by Diana Ross. She was ready to fall in love.

The most telling aspect of their affair was that it was completely indiscreet. Right from the start, Mary would fly into the town where Tom was performing. She arrived in New York during his week at the Copa and got in the habit of dressing down and donning a pair of de rigueur celebrity sunglasses, but the couple were too famous to fool many people. They enjoyed the little private jokes that lovers do. If Tom rang and she was unable to answer, he would leave a message that Jimi Hendrix had called. She knew it was Mister Jones, even if her entourage thought she had hooked up with the famous guitarist.

As she remembers fondly in her book, she would fly to Vegas when he was playing the Flamingo and sit in the audience. He would quite openly sing songs just for her. One evening, he sang 'Green, Green Grass of Home' and, without pause, swung straight into 'That Old Black Magic'.

Faced with such romantic gestures, it becomes easier to excuse her failure to break it off when she discovered Tom was married. She may have felt like a fool, but it was too late. Instead, she flew to London, checked into the Mayfair Hotel and invited Tom over for the evening. He left the next morning. It was a routine they would follow many times when he was in the UK.

He would send over his new Rolls-Royce to pick her up. He now had two – a Phantom and a Silver Shadow. He would take her to pubs and then, more daringly, to some of the more fashionable restaurants in the West End, like Mr Chow. This was a celebrity Mecca in the sixties and not a place to go if you wanted to keep an affair quiet.

They may have been called the Swinging Sixties, but a man cheating on his wife with a beautiful black woman was still a move unlikely to win Tom any popularity polls back in the United States. There he was a relative newcomer, albeit a hugely successful one.

Despite his obvious affection for Mary, he wasn't stringing her along. He liked being with her, but never suggested it was anything more than a fling. Mary was left under no illusion where she stood in relation to Linda during her trip to visit Tom in Bournemouth. He was appearing in a summer season at the seaside town's Winter Gardens in June 1968. A line appeared in the gossip column in *Disc* magazine that Mary Wilson was back in the UK and she had come to see Tom Jones.

Linda, who liked to read the music papers, immediately phoned Chris Hutchins and asked, 'How do I get to Bournemouth? Will you get me a minicab?' When Chris asked her why, she replied, 'I've just read this and I'm going down there to sort him out.'

Chris organised a car for Linda, who has never learned to drive, then phoned Tom and said, 'Just get her out. Linda is coming down.' Tom's wife was a genuinely nice, quiet woman, except when she felt her position threatened – then she was a tigress.

Chris remembers, 'He told me later that he flew around the place with Chris Ellis. They got Mary out and they went around and they removed every trace of her. And Linda came in and said, "Where is that woman, where is she?" And Tom said, "I don't know what you're talking about." And she said, "Mary Wilson, she's been here." And he said, "No, she hasn't."

'But Linda carried on checking the wardrobes, everything, looking for any trace of the woman having been there. Finally, she opened the oven, the one place the boys had forgotten. Now Mary Wilson was a great cook and she had prepared a meal the previous evening, which they hadn't yet eaten. And so there's this fabulous meal there, and Linda says, "Oh yeah! And who cooked this?" And Tom said, quick as a flash, "Chris Ellis." And Chris Ellis couldn't do beans on toast. But Tom said, "He's been taking cooking lessons."

'Well, he finally owns up and they went to bed and he told me next day that they were lying there and they had just made love and Linda started crying, and he said, "What's the matter, Linda?" And she said, "When I think that bitch has been lying on these sheets …"'

After this drama, Mary's days as Tom's mistress were numbered. She was struggling to come to terms with the inevitable and admits in her book that she even began phoning him at home, only to hang up quickly if a woman's voice answered.

In November 1969, Mary was hosting a lavish party at her Hollywood home. Tom arrived and suggested they have some privacy in her bedroom. He told her, 'I don't think this is fair to you. There is no future for us and I think we should end this affair now.'

Mary dissolved into tears, still hoping that he might change his mind, but in her heart she finally understood that it would always be Linda. She revealed in her book she was able to achieve closure when Tom brought his wife backstage after a Supremes concert and introduced her. Mary thought she was 'very nice'.

Tom occupies a special place in her heart, but later, after she'd married and experienced infidelity herself, she poignantly recognised the 'pain and humiliation' that Linda had gone through. Linda gave some insight into her life as Mrs Tom Jones in a rare interview with the *Daily Mirror* at the height of the Mary Wilson affair. She made no mention of the Supreme when she declared that she was sure of Tom because 'I always know he is coming home'.

She hinted it was difficult coming to terms with the gorgeous women that surrounded her husband on a daily basis. Her self-confidence was so low that she would never answer the front door without first putting on her make-up. She had to endure letters from Tom's female fans declaring how much they wanted to go to bed with her husband – those were the polite ones. She clearly was still deeply in love: 'I feel alive when he comes in through the door whatever the time of day or night it is.'

The front door, in 1969, was the entrance to the most impressive house in the exclusive St George's Hill, Weybridge. Tor Point, as they called it, was a twenty-room mansion that Tom had bought the previous year, a palatial prison for someone who didn't own a car. If you wanted to brag about having made it in show business, then this was the address to seek. Cliff Richard, John Lennon and George Harrison lived nearby, and it wouldn't be long before Gordon's stable of stars joined them.

Gordon lived half a mile away. Engelbert was also close, after he purchased a house in the area that one of those TV property programmes would have called an 'opportunity to increase value'. He spent a fortune – close to £30,000 – on renovations.

A famous photo from these extravagant times shows the three men perched on their matching Rolls-Royces in the driveway of Gordon's home. They are wearing expensive suits and ties and sporting the slightly smug expressions of men who know they have made it. Today, in these harsh times of recession, it would be the height of crass vulgarity, but then it was simply a statement of 'look at me' success. The picture revealed that the number plate on Tom's Roller was the immodest TJ BIG.

Tor Point was the jewel in this exclusive crown. Set in five acres of woodland and nestling behind an impressive set of electronic security gates with a Welsh dragon crest, visitors from Pontypridd thought they were arriving at Buckingham Palace. The house had prime position, overlooking the renowned St George's Hill Golf Course, although Tom never showed the slightest interest in taking up the game.

His sporting interests were well served at Tor Point, however. He could swim every day in a 25-metre pool with another Welsh dragon emblazoned on the bottom in red mosaic tiles. A squash court, a tennis court, a sauna and a gym made up his state-of-the-art fitness centre, which he had built at a cost of £250,000 at the end of the driveway. It was like having your personal health club in the garden. Since Tom now had a much higher profile in the US, he was more aware of the need to keep trim. He had noticed that his trousers were feeling tighter, while his chin was worryingly close to a double.

If he didn't fancy using these facilities, he could enjoy a run around the golf course in the company of the family's newly acquired black Labrador, unimaginatively called Blackie. Tom loved the dog that was always so pleased to see him when he came home. It was a sad day a few years later when he was run over.

Chris Hutchins once asked Tom, to test his mettle, when the last time he had cried was. Tom answered, 'When Blackie died,' and his eyes welled up with tears at the memory.

Linda had been in charge of the interior decoration and design of the house, and no expense had been spared. The television programme *Through the Keyhole* would have focused on the large glass cabinets brimming with Tom's gold and silver discs and his Grammy Award for Best New Artist in 1966. The camera could have dwelled on his expanding collection of military memorabilia, including pistols, swords and a suit of armour. The few bookcases contained beautiful-looking books, but they were false-fronted and behind the expensive façade there was nothing to read. Pride of place in Tom's study was a gold-leaf telephone with a mahogany base – the height of opulence. As the writer Robin Eggar perceptively commented, 'Linda liked the money but not the fame.' She would have been happier if they had won the pools and nobody knew who they were.

She turned Tor Point into a beautiful home that they were both very proud to have. Upstairs, on the top floor, she allowed her husband his own play area. They installed a home cinema with sixteen seats. Next door to that was an enormous snooker room with a jukebox and Tom's very own bar, a real beer barrel and an endless supply of chilled Dom Pérignon.

The house was by no means a masculine paradise, however. Linda filled the rooms with brightly coloured fruit bowls and vases always full of freshly cut flowers from the gardens. Despite Tom's wealth, Linda preferred to do her share of the cleaning – even though she had a cleaner – and all of the cooking herself. It was how she spent her days, waiting for the next time her husband came home.

When he was there, he was a man who liked hearty food. As well as lamb curry, he liked nothing better than to sit down with his wife and son and enjoy a home-cooked fillet steak with his favourite vegetables, which unusually happened to be sprouts.

The house was always immaculate, ready at any time for guests to be received. Chris Hutchins used to call round occasionally to collect a photograph or to tell Linda something important. He recalls one particular day that stuck in his memory: 'It was a huge house, but she was doing the dusting. And as she dusted, she had one of Tom's albums on the record player and she was dancing and singing along to it. She was a fan. Of course she was. All of us were, including Gordon. We were all fans of Tom Jones.'

Tor Point truly was a Hollywood mansion in a leafy enclave 20 miles from Central London. It was a place made for grand and glamorous parties – except, in the seven years they lived there, the Joneses never had a single one.

At least Linda could enjoy visits from family who travelled up from Wales. She couldn't persuade her mother Vi to leave her home in Cliff Terrace and move permanently. She was a frequent visitor, but Vi continued to work at John's Café, next to the White Hart pub. Despite a strong admiration for Tom's talent, she was never happy about stories involving her son-in-law's indiscretions.

Tom's parents were only five miles away in Shepperton. They were even closer when he bought them a new house in Weybridge. His sister Sheila and her husband Ken moved into the lodge at Tor Point and Tom gave his brother-in-law the job of looking after the extensive grounds. He liked to keep his family close and that never changed.

Linda did have friends, of course, and while he was young, she was looking after her son, who was enrolled at an expensive school in Shepperton. Jo Mills was only just up the road, but she was a very different type of woman and, in any case, she had an expanding family. She was sociable and socially adept, and enjoyed throwing extravagant showbiz parties.

Tom would associate with celebrities away from home, but, as a couple, Tom and Linda weren't part of a show-business set. The most famous person ever to come to Tor Point was probably Michael Jackson, but at the time he was only a boy and Tom had invited him to shoot a video in the grounds. Michael turned up and spent half a day driving a little go-kart about the place while being filmed.

Tom, when he was at home, was just the same as Linda. He preferred to go out to be sociable. He liked nothing better than to hold court in an old-fashioned boozer. Once, just before Christmas, Linda was worried because she didn't know where he was and he had been missing for two days and two nights. She phoned Chris Hutchins, who told her he would try to discover what had happened. He found Tom in the local pub in Weybridge. Chris walked in and Tom looked up at him, smiled and said, 'Hello, Chrissie. Have a drink.'

Linda chose to stay at home when she had the money to do anything she pleased. Tom was about to sign a television deal that would make him a multi-millionaire. She didn't choose to do what some other women with wealthy husbands do. She could have travelled the world with her husband, or by herself. She could have started a charity or a foundation. She might have started a fashion and design business or found an artistic pursuit that enriched her life, but she drank champagne and dusted. It may or may not be coincidence that she became more reclusive after Tom's affair with Mary Wilson became public and she had to deal with that humiliation.

Ironically, the third great Tom Jones song of the sixties was about infidelity. Thankfully, none of Tom's affairs ended as badly as 'Delilah', the dramatic ballad that perfectly showcased his powerful voice.

Les Reed and Barry Mason wrote it and, surprisingly, they didn't compose the song with Tom in mind. He was second choice – just as he had been to Sandie Shaw when 'It's Not Unusual' was written. They wrote it for P. J. Proby. Les, who admired the Texan's individual approach, had been hired as producer for his album, called *Believe It or Not*. Les joined forces with Barry to write a number of songs for inclusion, but he recalls, 'From the very beginning, on hearing the song, P. J. absolutely hated it. After a long and heavy day at the Wessex Sound Studios, we finally came to record his voice onto the track of "Delilah". He was so against the song, he ended up singing it like Bob Dylan! Eventually, as his producer, I gave up on the song and we released an eleven-track album instead of twelve. I played "Delilah" to Gordon and Tom the following day … and the rest is history.'

Tom had to answer some critics who thought the song glorified murder. He told the *NME*: 'Of course "Delilah" has violence. It's a song about a man who sees his girl being unfaithful and who kills her in the heat of the moment. It's been known before. It's not a song that glorifies murder. The whole point of it is that I'm sorry for what I've done.'

As usual, a little controversy was good for sales and 'Delilah' reached number two in the singles chart. The album of the same name was Tom's first UK number one in August 1968. The song is one of his best loved, but also remained controversial because of its violent subject matter. There were even calls for it to be banned after Tom sang it before the Wales rugby international against England in 1999, more than thirty years later. It became an unofficial anthem of the Welsh team, with the crowd cheerily singing, 'I felt the knife in my hand …'

The lyricist Barry Mason summed it up: 'Nobody listens to the lyrics.'

13

# THIS IS TOM JONES

Tom continued to badger Gordon to let him have his nose fixed and his teeth done. His manager had always resisted, telling him he wanted him to look natural. Tom's rugged masculinity was part of his appeal. Gordon changed his opinion, however, when the dollar signs began to appear in front of their eyes. The rough and ready rocker didn't suit the image of a Vegas headliner or a budding movie star.

Gordon now told him, 'You are a star and you must look like a star.' Tom was booked into a clinic in London for what was called an operation to repair some nasal cartilage. He soon grew tired of that subterfuge and has subsequently been happy to talk about his cosmetic surgery. The large, misshapen hooter he so hated was remodelled, his teeth were whitened and capped, and his long face became more rounded under his chin. He has never been afraid to top up his cosmetic treatments to continue to keep the years at bay. The procedure worked, because Tom emerged looking much more traditionally handsome.

The movie star Tom was the one that Lew Grade first saw at the London Palladium. Lord Grade, as he would later become, was a legendary figure in television history. He was born Lovat

Winogradsky in the Ukraine, but his family moved to London when he was thirteen, and he had become Lew Grade by the time he was crowned Charleston Champion of the World in 1926. He later billed himself as 'The Dancer with the Humorous Feet' before deciding that his future was as an agent and impresario.

Tom likes a cigar, but Lew Grade must have been born with a large Montecristo in his mouth. He was the archetypal cigar-chomping TV tycoon. His great talent lay in spotting potential and exploiting a gap in the market. After the Second World War, he signed some of the UK's favourite entertainers, including Peter Sellers, Harry Secombe and Tony Hancock, and secured a foothold in the rapidly evolving world of television. His aim was to provide programmes for the 'average working-class family's evening'.

By the time he first saw Tom Jones, he was the renowned boss of ATV (Associated Television). More importantly for Tom and Gordon, he had an eye on the American market and was always on the lookout for shows that could work for both the UK and US audiences.

He recognised Tom's potential when he watched a run-through for *The London Palladium Show*, a hugely popular variety show that ran throughout the sixties: 'It was only a rehearsal and Tom was dressed casually, but he performed as if he was doing his actual performance.'

Lew could see straight away that it was the music that mattered for Tom: 'He was a very attractive sensuous-looking man, but that was incidental. Without the vitality he put into each perform-ance, he would never have been a sex symbol.'

Lew called his American contact, Martin Starger, the vice-president in charge of programming at the ABC network, to invite him to London to see Tom live at the Talk of the Town, the well-known London nightspot, where he was booked for a month's residency. They chose a good night. He gave a rousing rendition of many of his best-known songs from the sixties. Lew Grade observed, 'Even when he sang a ballad, you could feel the rhythm.'

Lew must have been thinking of 'I Can't Stop Loving You', a song made famous by Ray Charles. Tom sang it as if his very life depended on extracting every ounce of emotion from the lyric. He was backed by the Ted Heath Orchestra, demonstrating how quickly he had mastered singing with a big band. It was Sinatra with balls.

Grade and Starger were looking for a charismatic artist who could bring 'variety' to a younger audience. They both believed they had found that man. Lew told *Omnibus* that Martin was 'over the moon' and suggested that they produce a Tom Jones special in the first instance, with a view to commissioning a series if it was a success.

Tom wasn't keen when he heard the plan. He was uncomfortable with the idea of introducing acts, 'Ladies and gentleman, put your hands together for Bob Hope.' He did trust Gordon, however. He accompanied him to meetings in Lew Grade's office, smoked one of their host's fine cigars and sat quietly while the two men conducted a series of tough negotiations. Gordon already had a reputation for being fearless – he needed to be when he had discussions with the Mafia in the US and looked them in the eye.

Lew recalled their third meeting in his autobiography, *Still Dancing*: 'I said, "Gordon, that's my final offer, and I'll tell you what else I'll do. I'll give Tom a box of cigars for every programme he does." Tom, who'd remained silent at these meetings, spoke for the first time. "You've got a deal!" he said.'

It's a good story that doesn't ring true. Gordon made all the decisions. Tom would have known when the enthusiastic poker player was happy with his hand. He had every reason to be pleased. The three-season contract was set to earn Tom £9 million, the highest figure ever paid to a single performer.

Elvis Presley was the first star that Tom asked to be on the series *This Is Tom Jones*. The King was booked but never appeared. Apparently, there was a contractual problem. He had appeared on TV in 1960 in a special programme hosted by Frank Sinatra that welcomed him home from his national service in the army. The show was an opportunity for Elvis, minus sideburns, to show America his new toned-down image for an adult audience. It also gave him the chance to plug his new film, *G.I. Blues*, which co-starred the dancer Juliet Prowse, with whom he'd had a passionate fling during filming.

Elvis told Tom that he had been contracted to make two specials with Sinatra and wasn't allowed to appear on another show until he did. That was the official line, although the critics had been harsh about Elvis's appearance alongside Frank and he may not have been too keen to sing alongside another vocal powerhouse.

Sinatra was probably the only guest who could have matched the prestige of Presley, but he too proved to be beyond reach. When Tom started in Vegas, Frank and The Rat Pack were the kings of the strip. The two men became friendly and Tom has often quoted the piece of valuable advice that Sinatra gave him: 'He said, "Tom, you don't have to hit everything hard. If you keep hammering everything, you're gonna hurt yourself."' Frank encouraged Tom to find his crooner voice and not focus so much on rock 'n' roll.

Juliet Prowse, whose bee-sting lips revealed the widest of Hollywood smiles, did appear on *This Is Tom Jones*, in the pilot show recorded in the autumn of 1968. The guest list was a touch middle of the road for Tom's taste: Juliet, the accomplished harmony group The Fifth Dimension and the French chanteuse Mireille Mathieu. The reaction from the focus groups was very positive and the go-ahead was given for the first series to begin in January 1969.

Tom, by all accounts, tried his luck with Juliet, but was rebuffed. Despite all the headlines concerning his sex life, his success rate with some of the leading female entertainers wasn't spectacular. Dionne Warwick, Sandie Shaw and Lulu were just three who were strike-outs. Lulu wrote in her autobiography that Tom was misled in believing she liked to fool around: 'I think he was disappointed to discover that he was wrong. I was aware of his animal magnetism, but to be truthful he frightened the life out of me.' He was falsely rumoured to have had an affair with Kathy Kirby, who, for a time, was the biggest British female star of the sixties and had toured with Tom. She was even said to have had Tom's baby and was heckled about it by a member of the audience at one of her concerts. It was complete nonsense and Tom managed to laugh it off, although Kathy found the whole thing rather cruel. This sort of gossip has plagued Tom throughout his adult life.

Just as the TV series was getting under way, Tom and Gordon had to go to the High Court in London to contest a claim from his old managers, Raymond Godfrey and John Glastonbury, who were seeking the royalties from their original contract. Eventually, the former managers settled out of court for a figure reported to be £50,000 each. Tom has always been dismissive of Myron and Byron's efforts on his behalf, referring to them as Pinky and Perky. He wouldn't have enjoyed giving them any money.

The resolution of the contract with his old managers seemed to prompt a spring clean by Gordon. He gave Vernon Hopkins a lift back home from the courts and told him The Squires would not be needed for the new television series, because the Americans wanted to bring in musicians who could sight-read and accompany the guests, as well as play for Tom. In the meantime, he suggested the band record a song he had picked out, called 'Games People Play' by Joe South.

They promptly recorded the song at a studio in Barnes, with new guitarist Bill Patterson on lead vocals. Gordon showed up for the session, but, according to Vernon, took little interest and made zero contribution. A few days later, the bassist was looking through the *Daily Mirror* and came across the headline that declared 'Tom Jones and The Squires in amicable split'. It was the first Vernon had heard of it.

The report quoted Tom's management: 'Tom will be spending most of the year making his new television series, any future tours will be with the Ted Heath Orchestra. The Squires have, for some time, wanted to branch out on their own and will soon be releasing a new single.'

The Squires' one and only record didn't even make the charts in Pontypridd. Vernon says it received so little promotion that he's not even sure if it was given a proper release. The probability is that Gordon was looking to avoid any future obligation to the band by sorting out a half-hearted single that was doomed to failure. Its poor showing gave him an excuse to sack them and they had no written contracts. Vernon received three weeks' wages – a grand total of £120. It was especially galling in the light of the settlement paid to the former managers.

The Squires were young men in their twenties. They had seen the world with Tom and enjoyed more than their share of willing young women, but they were still paid a pittance – £40 a week – while Tom was a millionaire. Simply, they didn't fit in with Gordon's vision for Tom's future. He saw his man as a TV star, earning a fortune in Las Vegas and possibly Hollywood.

It was the right time to let them go. Neither Gordon nor Tom has revealed the reason why the boys were apparently treated so badly. Only the group members have given their version of events. Vernon has spoken to Tom just twice since and still has a strong antipathy towards him.

Tom, as we know, hates all forms of confrontation and Gordon was a man who liked to be in total control. Chris Hutchins, who remembers the circumstances well, observes, 'Tom would always say, "Talk to Gordon." He wouldn't negotiate his way out of a paper bag; Gordon had to do all the dirty work. I don't know if it was a sign of his early financial insecurity, but the last thing Tom would ever do is give the band a lot of money. He has never been one to do that.' The harsh truth may be that the band members weren't his close friends; they were just his band.

Gradually the old team was breaking up. Les Reed still wrote songs for Tom, but was concentrating more on other artists. Peter Sullivan left Decca and was no longer responsible for producing his records. He had loved working with Tom, appreciating his natural talent and said dramatically, 'I feel as if my left arm has been cut off.'

Peter gave a fascinating insight into Tom's attitude to the songs he recorded: 'He has to really feel something to sing it well. If Tom was singing a particular song that really wasn't happening, he'd lose interest. He'd get very depressed about it and want to forget all about it.'

The vacancy for a producer for Tom Jones was filled by Gordon, which was not necessarily a good thing, as his golden age as a hit-maker was soon over.

The television series was filmed at Elstree Studios in Hertfordshire. The schedule meant that Tom had to be ready for work early in the morning, at a time when he was usually about to go to bed after a night out. He coped well with the stop–start demands of filming, when a two-minute segment could take half a day.

One morning, the director, Jon Scoffield, wasn't happy with the colour of Tom's white jeans, which he felt didn't blend with the set. Tom had to go to his dressing room, take off his jeans, wait for them to be dyed grey and dried, put them back on and return to the set. The director still wasn't happy, so it was back to the dressing room, slip them off, wait for them to be dyed white again and dried, then put them back on and be ready for filming to start. He had been there all morning and achieved nothing.

Tom wasn't a prima donna. He would sit patiently, sometimes with a glass of champagne, but more often with a mug of tea, and wait to be called. It was, after all, better than working in a glove factory.

One incident brought home how lucky he was. He was being driven to the studios in his Rolls-Royce Phantom after a night out, and wasn't looking forward to the production number, which involved choreography and dancing. He told Larry King, the legendary CNN host: 'I thought, oh my God, I have to go in today and I have got to get made up and do all of this.'

When he stepped out, he spotted a young hod carrier humping bricks up a ladder – exactly the job he had once done on a building site. The lad shouted to him, 'Hey, Tom, you want to help me out with this?' It opened Tom's eyes: 'I thought, "I'm complaining about a production number and this kid is going to be running up and down that ladder all day.'"

Sandie Shaw was a guest on the first show and memorably duetted with Tom on '(I Can't Get No) Satisfaction', which was a Rolling Stones song that was hugely popular at Tom's live show in Las Vegas. He invited her to his luxury caravan for a glass of champagne, but she turned him down, perhaps sensing that he had more on his mind than bubbly.

Tom's success rate in the caravan was very high, however. It was referred to as a caravan, but it was nothing you would take on holiday to Clacton. It was the size of a small apartment with several rooms and was parked out of the way so visitors could come and go unobserved.

Production staff had to knock four times and wait to be called just in case he was 'entertaining'. The TV producer Stewart Morris recalled that if Tom had spotted someone he liked the look of in the audience, Chris Ellis would be despatched to invite her for Dom Pérignon in the caravan. Chris would then stand guard outside the door for the duration of her visit.

Tom's most serious liaison then was with a stunning Californian model called Joyce Ingalls. They had met in Vegas and he had invited her to the UK when he was filming the second season of *This Is Tom Jones*.

Joyce, who was just nineteen, was an archetypal dizzy blonde. She also thought she meant more to Tom than she actually did. He found her entertaining, called her 'Clogs' because of her preferred footwear, and fancied her. The back of his Rolls-Royce, the caravan and the earth all moved when they were together. She appeared to think she was going to be the second Mrs Jones, and practically moved into the caravan. She began to dictate who could and could not gain admittance. One of Tom's entourage at the time observes, 'Joyce was trouble. She was trying to take over from Gordon Mills. She threatened his position because she would say, "You have got to wear this or you have got to wear that." Only Gordon was allowed to do that. Linda would never have tried to do anything like that.' The final straw was when she refused to allow Tom's dresser access to the caravan. It wasn't long before she was packing her bags for her return to the US.

Joyce made a handful of movies, including *Paradise Alley* with Sylvester Stallone in 1978 and *Lethal Weapon 4* alongside Mel Gibson in 1998. She achieved some notoriety in the mid-nineties when she was linked to Sir Anthony Hopkins, whom she met at an AA meeting in Los Angeles. He declared, 'Joyce has given me back a passion and vigour that has been dormant for years.' Tom, it seems, also liked her passion and vigour.

To her credit, Joyce has never talked about her fling with Tom; a series of men close to him have kissed and told about her, though. Tom has always had more trouble with men than women when it comes to providing the media with lurid headlines.

The years between 1968 and 1974 were the ones when he was most indiscreet, but his marriage somehow survived. He even managed to gloss over a misplaced joke about his activities in the caravan from his friend, the Liverpool comic Jimmy Tarbuck, who was guest comedian on one show. Tarby, as he was known, was a member of Tom's circle, because he made him laugh in a court jester sort of way. During the show, a sketch involved a series of lovely girls parading on stage carrying champagne. Tarby had to give them directions to Tom's caravan, which was harmless enough, until he turned to the camera and declared, 'Do you know that caravan of his has had six new sets of tyres and it hasn't moved three feet?' When Linda watched the show with Tom, she didn't get the joke, which was lucky for him – or perhaps she chose not to understand it.

Tom never felt completely at ease with the scripted part of the show, the comedy sketches that were light relief. He would have been happier if every episode consisted only of him singing. The schedule was exacting because each programme had to be recorded twice on subsequent days, first for the English broadcast and secondly for the American transmission. His day off was Monday, so that was Linda's favourite day of the week, because he was home.

The aspect of the show that Tom disliked most was the presence, throughout the recording, of a censor – a woman from the ABC network whose sole job seemed to be to make Tom sanitise things so they would be acceptable to an American audience. Tom had realised that the US wasn't the great land of freedom when he first visited in 1965. Then it was just a case of toning down suggestive movements or altering a song lyric or two; now it was something altogether more depressing. He was singing the timeless 'Somewhere' from *West Side Story* with the elegant black musical star Lesley Uggams, when the censor stepped in. The show's producer Jon Scoffield refused to go on set and relay her concerns. Instead, Gordon ambled out to tell Tom that he needed to look more into the camera and less into Lesley's eyes. It was considered too controversial for a white man to gaze into a black woman's eyes and sing the words 'There's a place for us'.

Tom was furious, especially as the song in the original was sung by a white man and a Puerto Rican girl – a racial divide was the very point of such a poignant heartfelt lyric. Ever the professional, however, Tom agreed to look into the camera more. 'I didn't really do it,' he confessed.

Even worse than that, he was singing the evocative ballad 'Passing Strangers' with the velvet-voiced black singer Nancy Wilson, when Jon Scoffield informed him that there was a problem with clearing copyright on the song and asked if he would mind singing a different one. Jon suggested that perhaps an up-tempo number might work well at that point in the show. So they sang a dynamic duet of 'Ain't No Mountain High Enough'. The following week, when Tom asked him what the problem had been with the licence for 'Passing Strangers', Jon revealed there wasn't one. 'It was the censor,' he admitted, who had thought that the words 'we seem like passing strangers' suggested that white Tom and black Nancy had once been lovers.

Tom has been widely reported to have had flings with both Lesley and Nancy. In fact, his best-known backing singer, Darlene Love, even wrote about the latter in her autobiography *My Name Is Love*. Both Lesley and Nancy have subsequently denied they had affairs with him.

When Tom reminisces on the television series *The Voice* about the many great artists he has sung with, many of them are from this golden three-year period, when his stature in world music grew almost as quickly as his sideburns. Despite the success of the show, Tom had to battle to have musical guests that were acceptable to the American network.

He wanted to sing with musical heroes, the great rock 'n' roll and rhythm and blues artists he so admired, including Jerry Lee Lewis, Ray Charles and Little Richard. The network wanted more middle-of-the-road, mainstream performers. In the end, there was a trade-off between Tom and ABC, which resulted in some curious line-ups that worked brilliantly.

Jerry Lee, for instance, shared a show with Barbara Eden, who at the time was the star of the popular sitcom *I Dream of Jeannie*.

Tom didn't mind. He was in heaven singing with his musical hero at last. She was a guest for a second time in the 1970 season, when she appeared with Wilson Pickett, one of Tom's favourite soul singers. Little Richard was on the same week as the French actress and insipid singer Claudine Longet.

One show that perhaps showed how well this formula could work was the one in which the peerless Aretha Franklin appeared alongside Hollywood great Bob Hope – a television dream team. Even Hope played up Tom's reputation as a sex symbol. In a reference to women's liberation, he joked, 'Tom has his own movement for women and they are watching it very carefully.'

Aretha was the one performer who inspired complete admiration in her host. He had loved her voice ever since he had bought her breakthrough single 'I Never Loved a Man the Way I Loved You' a couple of years earlier, when he was touring the north of England. She is the only singer he has ever thought could match his power.

He was awestruck when they were rehearsing without microphones: 'We were just singing live to one another. The volume that came out … I could so appreciate what the woman has.' Her performance of the Burt Bacharach and Hal David song 'I Say a Little Prayer' is arguably the highlight of the entire three series. She and Tom sang a breathtaking version of 'The Party's Over'. She also sang a few bars of 'It's Not Unusual' in a bossa nova style, accompanying herself on the piano.

The guest list for Tom's show read like an encyclopaedia of music greats: Ella Fitzgerald, Joni Mitchell, Dusty Springfield, Johnny Cash, Janis Joplin, Stevie Wonder and Sammy Davis, Jr were just some of the best. Ella and Tom effortlessly sang the timeless 'Sunny' while seated in rocking chairs. In 1969, Sammy opened season two – the first to be partly shot in Los Angeles – by sending up Tom's performance of 'It's Not Unusual', which began every show. 'You ain't coloured, Tom,' he declared, before giving the song a slow and smoky treatment. Sammy also acted the part of 'Mr Bojangles' while Tom sang. The melancholy ballad would later become Sammy's signature song.

The powerhouse Janis Joplin had a reputation for being prickly, and clearly didn't rate Tom as a singer before she appeared on the show. She changed her mind after they rehearsed their duet of 'Raise Your Hand', a song she had made famous at the Woodstock Festival in 1969. She clearly thought she was going to wipe the floor with Tom, and asked him, 'What key do you sing in?'

Tom responded modestly, 'I just sing', and proceeded to match the great blues-rock singer note for note. After the first run-through, she turned to him, smiled and said, 'You can really sing.' It seemed as if Tom and his glittering line-up of guests all realised they needed to be at the top of their game.

Each show ended with Tom in concert, singing a selection of his own music to an enraptured audience. It gave him the chance to showcase his new material, as well as his old favourites. During the second series, he sang 'Daughter of Darkness', a Les Reed composition, which was a top ten hit in the UK and was number one in the US Easy Listening Chart – a distinction that demonstrated Tom had been successfully positioned as a mainstream entertainer in America. The recording at the Decca studios in London was noteworthy because one of the backing singers was an ambitious singer-songwriter called Elton John.

One number he performed during that series, which wasn't one of his own recordings, could have been one of his greatest-ever hits if the cards had fallen differently. He was in a fashionable club called Scotts of St James in Jermyn Street, when he bumped into Paul McCartney. Tom asked him, 'When are you going to write me a song then, Paul?' The Beatle said he would sort something out and a few days later sent a song round to Tom's house. It was 'The Long and Winding Road'.

Tom was desperate to do it, but it turned out to be a complicated process. Tom explained, 'The one condition was that I could do it, but it had to be my next single. Paul wanted it out straight away. At that time I had a song called "Without Love" that I was going to be releasing. The record company was gearing up towards the release of it. So the timing was terrible, but I asked if we could stop everything and I could do "The Long and Winding Road". They said it would take a lot of time and was impractical, so I ended up not doing it.'

'Without Love' was a top ten hit at the end of 1969, but the song that got away became one of pop's great classics after it appeared on the *Let It Be* album. At the time, The Beatles were going through much internal strife and the song became controversial, with McCartney apparently unhappy with its production. That would explain why he'd offered it to Tom and wanted him to release it quickly. He was probably pleased in the end that Tom couldn't record it, as the track became one of the most popular during McCartney's solo tours.

While his TV show was a resounding success, particularly in the US, not everything that Tom touched turned to gold. He topped the bill at the Royal Variety Performance at the London Palladium in November 1969. Afterwards, the Duke of Edinburgh was introduced to him and enquired, 'What do you gargle with, pebbles?' Tom laughed off the insult when Chris Hutchins asked him about it. He said, 'I forgave him everything when I noticed his shirt collar was frayed.' Tom always took huge care and pride in how he dressed, even as a young man with nothing but pennies in his pocket.

He was less pleased the following day, when the Duke followed up by telling a luncheon for the Small Businesses Association in London, 'It's very difficult to see how it is possible to become immensely valuable by singing what I think are the most hideous songs.' Prince Philip is renowned for his gaffes, but at least he instructed an aide to send Tom a written apology. A year later, he sought Tom out at a Buckingham Palace function and told him he was misquoted.

The seventies began with Tom discovering he had made a profit of more than £1 million without even trying. Acting on the advice of their accountant, Bill Smith, Gordon had formed a company with Tom, Engelbert, Bill and himself as directors. The idea was that it would make them all more tax efficient. They called it MAM, which stood for Management, Agency and Music and gave a quiet acknowledgement of the importance of their mothers. When the company went public, Tom's shares were worth close to £600,000. Within four weeks of being quoted on the stock market, they were worth £1.6 million.

Tom left money matters to Gordon. Gerry Greenberg remembers visiting him in his hotel room in Manchester and being amazed at the amount of cash lying about: 'He was in the shower and I was in the bedroom chatting away to him. I looked around and there seemed to be money everywhere. There were wads of notes just thrown around. I could have taken anything I wanted. He either trusted me implicitly or he didn't give a damn about his money, which I suspected he didn't.'

He was, it seemed, more concerned with embracing the latest fashion – a haircut that covered his ears completely, so he resembled a tea cosy. He also unbuttoned his shirt to reveal a hairy chest and a large silver crucifix, which looked slightly ridiculous when he was in his rocking chair next to Ella Fitzgerald, who was old enough to be his mother.

He sang his biggest hit of the seventies in the third series in January 1971. The lyrics to 'She's a Lady' were scribbled by Paul Anka on the back of an airline menu on a flight from London to New York after he had appeared on Tom's show. Gordon had asked him to write a song, and he came up with this brash and chauvinistic lyric, which he thought suited Tom's personality. Anka, who also wrote 'My Way', dislikes the song more than any he has ever written, even though it made him a fortune.

Today 'She's a Lady' sounds very dated, but it reflected the trend of the early seventies, when disco was beginning to take over the world. The song reached only number thirteen in the UK, but the American audience turned it into his biggest-ever hit in the US, where it reached number two on the *Billboard* chart.

Paul Anka found Tom and Gordon quite hard to handle. He recalled in his autobiography that after one show he was taken out to dinner and then Gordon suggested they move on to a shady private club for some late entertainment. Tom was worried about the cost, because Paul observed he was very 'thrifty'. The 'cabaret' was a large woman engaging in some kinky games with a sheep. The boys had just wanted to see their guest's reaction and have a laugh at his expense.

Just as illuminating was Paul's insight into Gordon, the puppet master: he was 'a bigger star in his own way than either Tom or Engelbert'. He also revealed the reckless gambling streak that Gordon had, betting $25,000 on a game of tennis against him. Gordon lost. Gordon also met his match in Lew Grade, when he thought he had won the negotiations battle over becoming a co–producer on the show. The wily Grade agreed, 'If that is what you want.' Gordon was pleased, until the expenses for the show began to trickle in, with such gems as 'Camera tube … £8,000'. 'How the fuck do I know if they've replaced the camera tube?' complained Gordon, realising that he had been bested.

Thanks to his TV series, Tom began the seventies as the top British entertainer in the world. His American tours were now the biggest ever undertaken by a British performer. Gordon was fond of saying that the audience at home had no idea how big a star Tom was in America and the rest of the world. He estimated wildly that his man had sold 100 million records worldwide by the end of the sixties.

Tom never forgot the contribution that Lew Grade made to his worldwide success. In 1975, he appeared in New York in a special tribute to the impresario, which also starred John Lennon in his last broadcast before he was shot.

The event, *Salute to Lew Grade*, provided Tom with one of his favourite stories, which he never tires of telling. The guest of honour was Lord Mountbatten, who approached Tom afterwards, when he was chatting to Lennon. 'Mr Jones, I want to tell you we are very proud of you,' he declared, perhaps still recalling Prince Philip's gaffe, and marched off. He completely ignored the former Beatle, who proceeded to shout after him, 'Hey, OBE me!' Lennon turned to Tom and declared, 'Do you believe that? The fooker blanked me. I've met the fookin' Queen.'

# 14

# ON TOP OF MISS WORLD

---

Dai Perry was having a pint in the Wheatsheaf when he took a call from his best mate Tom, inviting him to catch a flight to Las Vegas and become his new bodyguard. Dai was going through a messy divorce, so it seemed the perfect antidote. He had all the physical credentials for the job, but he had never learned that tact and diplomacy were just as important as a smack in the face.

When *This Is Tom Jones* came to an end in 1971, beaten in the ratings by *A Man Called Ironside*, Tom's constant touring provoked travelling hysteria. He needed protection from fans intent on tearing the shirt off his back. Dai was the man for that, his eyes darting from side to side, constantly watching for any threat. He was able to step in when things got out of hand at Madison Square Garden in New York, and Tom had his crucifix ripped off and his trousers torn to shreds.

Tom was determined to have his 'butty' Dai with him, even though his manager was never keen on the new arrangement. Gordon recognised that after a few drinks there was a danger of Tom and Dai becoming Treforest Teds once more. The rough edges that he had spent years smoothing were beginning to reappear. Tom was the headline act at Caesars Palace, not the Bucket of Blood. The inherent risk was apparent when Tom visited Madison, Wisconsin, in June 1971. He was enjoying a party with his entourage in his hotel suite, when a local boxer tried to gatecrash the celebration. His entry was barred on three separate occasions by Dai, until the man shouted out that the bodyguard was a 'pumped-up Welsh factory worker' and called Tom a 'coal-mining prick'. Tom saw red and punched him, then Dai punched him and the two of them proceeded to kick him all the way to the elevator. He looked like the victim of a hit-and-run accident and needed hospital treatment.

Chris Hutchins, who wasn't at the party, observes, 'Tom was out of order and I think he regretted it. Tom could handle himself, but he doesn't get into fights. I don't think he has any vengeance in his heart.'

The problem was that Chris and Gordon would use Dai shamelessly to deal with paparazzi they wanted to discourage from taking pictures. They would just send him in to get rid of them without asking any questions first. Chris admits, 'We could have helped him. I felt a bit guilty about Dai. There was no diplomacy about him and we could have taught him that.'

A few months after the Madison fracas, alcohol led to another unsavoury scene – this time on a plane. It was an eventful day. Tom was travelling with Linda in a limo bound for Kennedy Airport in New York, where they were catching a plane home to London. They had already enjoyed a drink or two, when Linda told him she wished he had never become so famous.

'We could have been happy in Pontypridd,' she exclaimed.

Tom pointed to the expensive gold jewellery that she was wearing around her neck and wrists and replied, 'You've not done too badly on it.'

That was enough for Linda, who opened the car window and began hurling her bracelets, rings and necklaces onto the freeway. The habitually thrifty Tom was clearly the worse for wear, because he began to laugh when she couldn't get her £50,000 diamond ring off her finger, later telling friends, 'You had to see the funny side of it.' Linda, too, got a fit of giggles, even though she had thrown away thousands of pounds of jewellery. She may have been a 'lovely woman' most of the time, but she undoubtedly had her moments.

The excitement of the day wasn't over, however. Tom had a drunken row with a woman sitting across from him over the noise he was making listening to music. She threw her coffee over him, and he tossed his brandy over her. The plane's staff came to sort out the commotion, whereupon Dai, who had been asleep, woke up to what he thought was an attack on his boss. He pinned the person he thought was the ringleader to the ground and held him there with his knee on his chest. Dai told him that he was staying put until the plane landed. The man, who was wearing a uniform, exclaimed, 'It's not landing until I get up. I'm the captain.' He was actually a steward, but his quick thinking probably saved him from getting punched. Both Tom and his bodyguard were fortunate that the incident didn't end in prosecution.

Clearly Tom and Dai were a potentially explosive combination. To be fair, considering how many live shows and how much travelling the two did, there were very few incidents. Tom loved having his pal around.

On a rare visit back home to Pontypridd, they had met a vivacious teenager called Kay Tranter at a nightclub in town. She was wearing a striking pair of hot pants and the boys invited her over to join them. She thought Tom was 'stonking', but preferred the larger and more rugged Dai.

She and Dai were invited to Tor Point, which she thought was a 'fantastic' house. Linda was very homely and cooked for everyone. When Kay had a big disaster with a bottle of blonde bleach and a frizzy perm, Linda stepped in and cut her hair. This is the down-to-earth life that Tommy Woodward has when he is not being Tom Jones. For her twenty-first birthday, Tom paid for Kay to fly out and visit Las Vegas and stay with him, Linda and Dai in his suite at Caesars Palace. She met Elvis, Andy Williams and Fats Domino.

Although Kay preferred Dai, Tom was encountering more than his fair share of attractive women. He thought Marjorie Wallace looked perfect. The dazzling blonde beauty queen is the only woman he has ever met who was equally beautiful whichever side of her face you were looking at. Her beauty was symmetrical. Their affair was exhilarating and ultimately very sad.

They met in December 1973, two weeks after she was crowned Miss World at the Royal Albert Hall. Engelbert Humperdinck was on the judging panel that year and was in no doubt that Miss USA was the most appealing of that year's contestants. Subsequently, at the Miss World ball, he and Marjorie enjoyed a snog for the cameras that was a front-page picture the next day, which had been the plan, of course. He had apparently hoped that they might meet up again, but he never had a chance after she met Tom.

She was escorted by Chris Hutchins to see Tom, who was appearing at the London Palladium. They met before the show in his dressing room, and the chemistry was instant. For Tom to entertain *before* he went on stage was very rare and evidence of just how bowled over he was by the shapely and statuesque Miss Wallace. Later, they agreed to move on to Hatchetts nightclub in

Piccadilly, where they were discovered by a less than delighted Engelbert. After much Dom Pérignon had been consumed, they adjourned to Tom's usual suite at the Westbury Hotel.

This liaison became something much more significant than a routine one-night stand. They grew to have great affection for one another. Marji, as she was generally known, stayed in London and enjoyed more rendezvous with Tom during his nights at the Palladium. Inevitably, a paragraph of gossip about them reached the newspapers, and Linda exploded when she read it at Christmas time in Tor Point. She gave her husband a hiding. He recalled on American TV the occasion when she beat him up. He was trying to say sorry and pointed to his chin, inviting her to whack him. She didn't need a second chance: 'She went "Bang!" and then started kicking me.' Dai Perry was with them when this scene of seasonal goodwill unfolded. 'You're on your own, Tom,' he said, still observing the Ponty code of conduct regarding women. Tom just had to take it, and observed, 'That was my Christmas present.'

After New Year, he was visiting Chris Hutchins at his house in Richmond, when he asked for Chris's help. He needed to buy a couple of birthday presents. They repaired to a local jeweller's, where Tom chose an elegant gold and pearl bracelet that cost more than £400. It was for Linda's birthday on 14 January. He then selected a cultured pearl bracelet at just over £200. This was for his new lover's twentieth birthday nine days later. He had to be careful not to get them muddled, which would have turned the episode into a farce.

The following month, Marji and Tom flew out to Barbados, where she was a guest on a BBC show he was filming called *Tom Jones on Happiness Island*. He looked very happy indeed, when they were pictured on the beach tenderly kissing or, more precisely, sucking each other's face. The media immediately got the right end of the stick. Tom sang the love ballad 'Make It with You', which, of course, he already had. It wasn't a romantic get-away for two, however. As well as the television production team, Tom had his Ponty posse in attendance: Dai Perry, showing off his tattooed arms, Chris Ellis and the newest member of his entourage, his son Mark.

During the previous summer, Tom became worried about his son, now a burly sixteen-year-old, who seemed to be moping around. Like his father, he wasn't enjoying his schooldays, and despite his obvious love for his mother, he missed Tom. Over dinner Tom could see how moody he was. He recalled the occasion: 'I've only ever wanted what made him happy. I asked what the matter was and he told me he wanted me to spend more time with him.' Tom had been a wonderful provider for his family, but one thing he had been unable to give his son was more of his presence. That needed to change and the decision was taken for Mark to leave school and go on the road with his father.

Linda wanted her son to be content, so she agreed to the arrangement, even though it would be a big change for her. It was the making of Mark. He was popular and unassuming. Chris Hutchins recalls, 'On the road he was lovely. There was no "my dad is Tom Jones" or anything like that ever. Not a trace of it. He was just like his dad – a nice man.'

Tom was quite strict with him, at least at first. Worried that his son was getting homesick, he allowed him to make a transatlantic call from his dressing room – enormously expensive then – so that a friend could play him the whole radio commentary for a Leeds United match, which was the team he supported.

* * *

The quite obvious affair between Tom and Marji was made even more complicated because she was engaged to a dashing American racing driver called Peter Revson, heir to a billion-dollar fortune. They had got together in May 1973, when he competed in the famous Indianapolis 500 race, which was held in Marji's home town. She was nineteen when she met the thirty-four-year-old playboy in a drugstore, where he was making a pre-race personal appearance. He became a well-known name in Europe after he won that year's British Grand Prix for McLaren.

Her love life became even more tangled when the newspapers printed extracts of what was alleged to be her diary, revealing a brief fling in London with the heart-throb footballer George Best. She reportedly gave her lovers marks out of ten. Tom was a nine, while poor George was a three.

The diary may well have been an urban myth, but it was one controversy too many for Julia Morley, organiser of Miss World, who promptly stripped Marji of her title in March 1974. A statement said she had 'failed to fulfil the basic requirements of the job'. She was clearly a Miss World who was becoming bigger news than the title itself, which was not the point of the annual contest. Two weeks later, Peter Revson was killed, aged thirty-five, in a horrific crash during practice for the South African Grand Prix.

Tom offered a broad shoulder for Marji to cry on during the subsequent days and weeks. They spoke on the phone frequently and were able to sneak in a meeting here and there. That changed when he opened at Caesars Palace in Las Vegas. Tom was being paid £450,000 for five weeks' work. Marji went too, while Linda, as she often preferred to do, stayed at home in the UK. For a brief time, Tom and Marji were to all intents and purposes living together. She stayed at the mansion he had rented and at night the lovers would travel in Tom's limo to the hotel for his shows.

It was only a matter of time before such blatant indiscretion was discovered and, sure enough, Chris Hutchins took a call at his new office in Los Angeles with the news he had been dreading: a paparazzo had taken a picture of Marji sunbathing and looking gorgeous by Tom's pool. By now, it was abundantly clear to everyone that Linda would consider it a public humiliation. She hated that, so Chris had to act fast.

He flew to Las Vegas to confront the couple at Tom's house. When he arrived, Marji was there, wearing a skimpy bikini. He took Tom aside and explained the situation about the picture and the possible consequences regarding Linda and his marriage.

Marji, according to Chris, didn't take kindly to his suggestion that they should be more discreet. 'It's Tom I love, not Linda,' she declared. And she was not impressed by the idea of taking a taxi to the hotel instead of arriving each night in Tom's limousine. It seemed hopeless. Eventually, Tom felt he had no choice if he wanted to save his marriage, which he wholeheartedly did. He told Marji that she had to go. A few hours later, she left Vegas for Indiana, but that wasn't the end of the story.

A couple of weeks later, at Caesars Palace, everyone was excited about a party to celebrate Tom's thirty-fourth birthday, when Chris Hutchins took a call from a hospital in Indianapolis. Tom was about to go on stage. Marji was in a coma, having apparently attempted suicide with sleeping pills she had taken from Tom's bathroom cabinet. He used them only occasionally and hadn't missed the bottle.

She was in a coma for two days and in intensive care for a week. Chris decided not to give Tom the news before he performed. 'When he came off, I told him and he was very upset. It looked at one point as if she might die.'

Marjorie Wallace may have become internationally famous during her brief reign as Miss World, but she was still just a twenty-year-old suburban girl, the daughter of an Indiana businessman, who had lost her fiancé and now her lover. It was too much for her.

The mood back at Caesars Palace was grim, lightened that night by, of all people, the camp and outrageous entertainer Liberace, who had been invited to join Tom's party in the VIP bar. He invented a game for them all to play that night, in which everyone had to be blindfolded and try to identify a series of soft drinks placed in front of them. Much laughter was had as they failed to spot the difference between ginger ale and lemonade. It took all the tension out of a situation that could have been so much worse. Chris even scribbled a statement for Tom to give should the unthinkable happen and Marji not pull through.

Tom has always said, without prompting, that he has only ever loved Linda, but his feelings for Marji were the closest he came to loving someone else. It was the most serious affair he has had.

Chris Hutchins observes, 'It had to end, because it wasn't good for either of them. It was very sad, because they were genuinely fond of each other.

'He would never, ever, ever have left Linda, no matter how much trouble he got into. Linda is the great love of his life, but he did have genuine affection for certain women – because he is a genuine man.'

Later in the year, when Marji had fully recovered, she reportedly met up with Tom in Acapulco, Los Angeles and Bermuda. Subsequently, when her love affair with Tom was truly over, she had a high-profile relationship with tennis champion Jimmy Connors and was seen supporting him at Wimbledon in 1976. The same year, she told *People* magazine that she had not attempted suicide. She explained, 'I was depressed and OD'd on a few too many sleeping pills.' From time to time she has appeared in acting and presenting roles on television, but has kept a low profile for the last thirty years.

She has kept in touch with Tom, however. She was contacted by the *Sunday Mirror* in 2012, when Tom was appointed a judge on *The Voice*, and she was very gracious about him: 'We stayed friends and we are often in touch. I wouldn't want to rehash our relationship as it was so long ago and I have no interest in doing that.

'But it is great to speak to him on the telephone once in a while. I always follow his career and I am really pleased he is going to be coaching up-and-coming singers. He has such a beautiful voice.'

Tom is on very good terms with the women who have been important in his life. Linda, however, did not take the Marji Wallace affair lying down. Whenever she spotted Marji on television, she threw something at the screen.

Dai Perry was finally involved in an incident that was too serious for Tom to ignore. In May 1974, Tom's South American tour had reached Caracas and the airport was heaving with journalists, photographers and fans trying to get a piece of Tom. Dai didn't know if he was coming or going, and when someone ripped off his crucifix, he turned round and lashed out. His signet ring caught a reporter's eyebrow, causing a nasty gash. The ring was a big, heavy piece of bling with a Welsh dragon etched into it. Both he and Tom wore identical ones.

The reporter promptly filed a $65,000 lawsuit and secured a court order against Tom, who was instructed to appear before a judge three days later. Gordon wasn't there, but Lloyd Greenfield was on the phone immediately, asking him what to do. The instruction was brief and to the point: Dai Perry needed to be shipped out on the next plane. He was flown to Miami and from there straight to London.

Tom and the rest of the party set off for the airport as planned, only to be told that they weren't allowed to leave. They were sent back to the Hilton Hotel, where armed guards made sure they stayed put. It was a hostile situation. Chris Hutchins then had the bright idea of sending a cable to Prime Minister Harold Wilson for help. It worked, because the next thing they knew, Lloyd received a call saying that Tom needed to present himself at the judge's office at 6.00 the following morning and bring $9,000 with him in cash. Only Tom went into the chambers.

He later told his entourage all about it. The first thing the judge did was lay a gun on the table. Then he told Tom that neither he nor his people could behave like this in his country. He told him that there was a plane leaving in two hours for Miami. The judge said, 'Be on it or you are going to be arrested.' They had police outriders, with blue lights flashing the whole way, to make sure they made the flight. When they arrived in Florida, the newspaper placards were already out, proclaiming 'HAROLD WILSON GETS TOM JONES OUT OF JAIL', which was a perfect result for Chris. He observes, 'It wasn't Harold, or Tom. It was $9,000.'

All did not end well, however, because Tom had to agree to let Dai go. Chris recalls, 'He was so upset when Dai had to go home. So upset.'

# 15

# THE KING AND I

Tom couldn't believe it when he was told Elvis and his wife Priscilla had been seen in the foyer of the Flamingo. He thought it was a wind-up and said, 'Fuck off!' But it was true – The King and his entourage, the 'Memphis Mafia', had driven from Los Angeles just to see the show. They had been invited by Chris Hutchins, who knew both Colonel Tom Parker and Joe Esposito, Elvis's road manager, and suggested they come over.

Elvis was curious to see how a performer like Tom would be received in Las Vegas, because he was seriously thinking of making a live comeback there himself. His recording career was in the middle of a slump and he needed something to reinvigorate his career – a problem Tom would also face at a later date.

The lighting in the audience was quite dark, so Tom had to peer into the gloom to see if Elvis was really there. He had been primed by Chris, so he knew what to say if he caught sight of the man. Eventually, he realised The King was in the very front row. Halfway through the show, he introduced Elvis, who stood up to take a bow, and the place erupted. It went on for ages and ages, until Tom managed to calm everyone down. Elvis eventually sat back down and Tom said, 'Don't forget I'm the star here tonight.' It was a tongue-in-cheek comment, but took some nerve: Tom was just starting his Vegas adventure, whereas Elvis was the biggest star in the world.

After the concert, Elvis and his gang went backstage to congratulate Tom in his dressing room. The 'Mafia' usually numbered about half a dozen or so of Elvis's oldest friends and yes-men. If Elvis told them at breakfast that scarlet was the new colour, they would all have their cars resprayed by lunch.

Linda was at the Flamingo that evening and she sat and chatted with Priscilla. Tom remembers Elvis saying he wanted to watch him in concert to see how he put together his act. Tom and Elvis talked about music, something they both never tired of doing.

Priscilla Presley believes that Elvis took to Tom because he was a real person – 'someone who was down to earth that you could talk to, that was not on an ego trip'. Tom's show also reminded Elvis how it used to be for him: the adulation of the girls, the applause and the fantastic music. He missed it. He also liked the way Tom didn't take it too seriously. For his part, Tom thought the Presleys were 'a great couple'. He gave Priscilla an autographed photograph for their daughter Lisa-Marie, who was six months old.

The first meeting went so well that Elvis invited Tom to stay at his holiday villa in Hawaii. When he arrived, Priscilla told him that her husband had popped out to buy a couple of guitars so the two of them would have something to goof around with later. After dinner, the two men enjoyed a sing-song, like a couple of enthusiastic schoolboys, belting out 'Blue Suede Shoes', 'Hound Dog' and 'Jailhouse Rock', as well as 'It's Not Unusual' and Elvis's favourite, 'Green, Green Grass of Home'. They jammed together through the night. Tom said simply, 'I'll never forget it as long as I live.'

The two men became genuine friends. Elvis called Tom 'Sockdick', although not often to his face. He thought his pal's impressive bulge must be due to the old trick of sticking some knitwear down the front of his tight trousers. Tom spoke graciously of Elvis to the *Daily Express*: 'I never sat at his feet looking up to him, because we regarded each other as equals. He was much too modest to be comfortable with someone who fawned around him and was never afraid to admit his own vulnerability – always the mark of the truly great.'

They were rivals, as well as friends, when Elvis began a season at the newly opened International Hotel in July 1969, which two years later was renamed the Las Vegas Hilton. Both shows were ruthlessly advertised. On one side of the strip the huge billboards read, 'Elvis Presley is at the International'. On the other side, the hoardings declared, 'Tom Jones is in Town!'

Tom moved briefly to the International too, because its show-room was three times the size of the Flamingo's. In 1971, he finally settled at Caesars Palace. Elvis, meanwhile, stayed loyal to the Hilton, where he lived in the impressive penthouse, which became known as 'Party Central'. The two friends would take it in turns to visit each other's suites.

Elvis was a reality check for Tom – a stark example of a road he would go down if he didn't look after himself. Tom tried to keep in shape. At home in the UK, it was relatively easy, thanks to his fitness complex. On the road or in Vegas, it was more difficult, but he swam and took up squash. In the eighteen months before he opened at the Flamingo, he slimmed down from fifteen to eleven and a half stone. He said goodbye to chips for ever. He never stuffed himself with burgers or other junk food and avoided puddings, preferring a chateaubriand steak for dinner with the finest wines.

Tom didn't drink before a concert, which was particularly important where the desert air was so dry and put a strain on his voice. His shows were a workout in themselves, because Tom finished dripping with sweat and as much as six pounds lighter. After a show, he took a long, thirty-minute shower and then enjoyed a vodka martini or opened a bottle or two of Dom Pérignon while he socialised. His friend and backing singer Darlene Love became so sick of the constant supply of vintage champagne that she loathes bubbly to this day and only has a glass if it is mixed with orange juice.

Elvis, however, struggled with his weight yo-yoing up and down. Early on, he told Tom that he took pills to stop the pounds piling on. The two men would have many discussions about the merits of drink and drugs.

During one conversation, Elvis told him that he had taken every kind of drug imaginable just to keep his 'head together'. Elvis asked him what he took to keep sane and Tom replied simply, 'Nothing, that's why I feel I am sane.' Tom's aversion to drugs is very well known. He told Sylvie Simmons of *MOJO* magazine a funny story of the evening he went to a party in London thrown by Lulu. A rock star sidled up to him and said, 'You want to see what's going on in the kitchen!' Tom, being Tom, immediately thought it might be something involving one or hopefully two women. He was disappointed to see that the great excitement was a pile of white powder on the kitchen table. 'See you later,' he said.

Elvis never took any drugs in front of Tom – he had too much respect for him. Instead, they would be sitting down, listening to records, when Elvis would suddenly disappear into the bedroom and come out a new man. They would listen to a few more records and then the same thing would happen again.

They may have had differing opinions on drugs, but both Elvis and Tom had similar views on gambling. Although they were the bait to draw thousands of punters into the hotel casinos, they never indulged themselves. That example was not followed by their respective managers, who lost fortunes at the gaming tables. Gordon incurred heavy losses playing blackjack. He was rumoured, in one disastrous night, to have lost the whole of Engelbert's fee for a year.

Tom just didn't get the attraction. Why give away so easily what you had worked so hard to earn? One evening at Caesars Palace, Linda came bounding up to him and asked for some money so she and a friend could spend some time at the tables. Tom reached in his pocket and gave her $5. He advised her, 'Don't lose it all at once.'

Tom was intrinsically more sociable than Elvis, who preferred quiet evenings in his suite. He loved gospel music and was prepared to stay up even later than Tom, just singing. Tom would say goodnight and be halfway out the door, when Elvis would start something else and Tom would be obliged to go back in and sing another song.

For the most part, they kept their friendship low-key. Elvis would slip into Caesars Palace with a baseball cap over his distinctive black hair and sit at the back of the room. Disappointingly, Elvis and Tom never sang together in public. Elvis might walk on stage when Tom was performing, but he was under strict contract to another hotel, so he would never join in with a quick chorus of 'Delilah'. Their duets were private moments and Elvis made it clear that they must never be recorded. His manager, Colonel Parker, had told him that he must ensure there were no bootleg recordings, an instruction he followed religiously. Tom was the same where Gordon was concerned: he never forgot what Gordon said.

When they weren't singing, they would talk about music. Elvis once suggested they could do a concert together, with The Beatles as their backing group. They could do their own songs, followed by a few duets and the Fab Four could play all the instruments. Elvis asked, 'Do you think there is a chance we could get them to do it?' Tom, who still laughs about that conversation, responded: 'It would be fantastic.'

The pair were such good friends, they exchanged rings. Elvis gave Tom a splendid black sapphire ring, which annoyingly disappeared from his hotel bathroom one night on tour – along with the young lady who was using it. Tom, in turn, presented Elvis with a tiger's eye ring that he knew he liked.

Elvis, for whom death threats were a way of life, was obsessed with firearms and would make sure he was armed even when he used the toilet. He gave Tom a gun with 'Tom Jones' engraved on the barrel. Tom has never had to fire his gun, although he made sure he knew how to use it. Perversely, Elvis also gave him a book that he'd enjoyed, entitled *The Impersonal Life*, a famous text about self-discovery and leading a spiritual life.

These gestures of friendship continued when Elvis came to the rescue after Tom's famous backing group, The Blossoms, walked out during a Las Vegas concert. Tom had made a stupid joke about the Ku Klux Klan. He was mopping his brow with a handkerchief, which he then made into a mask, Klan style, turned to the girls and said, 'Be out of town by midnight.' The three black singers didn't find it funny and walked straight off stage, leaving Tom wishing the ground would open up and swallow him. Some things you just don't joke about.

He contacted Elvis and asked him if he could help. Elvis immediately put his own backing group, Sweet Inspirations, on a plane to Vegas to cover for the girls. In the end, Tom apologised and The Blossoms agreed to resume their role.

The most famous of The Blossoms was Darlene Love, who had been one of Phil Spector's troupe of artists and appeared on his acclaimed Christmas album. She was a gifted singer and probably should have been a solo artist, but the girls made $2,000 a week opening for Tom and then backing him throughout his concerts. Darlene had a soft spot for her employer, but was another singer who managed to avoid an affair with him.

She hopped into bed with him one night in Las Vegas, but skipped out again quickly before her underwear came off. In her book *My Name Is Love* she amusingly suggests she was on 'a fact-finding mission' to see what all the fuss was about. She made her apologies when she realised that lying next to a 'hairy white man' was a mistake. She wrote, 'Tom was very nice. He didn't try to force me to stay.'

Darlene also gives some insight into the decadent world surrounding Tom Jones. She and one of her bandmates glimpsed what went on at one of Tom's parties while they were on tour in Long Island. She wrote, 'We felt as if we had stumbled into a porno film. Naked men were chasing naked women everywhere.' The action got so steamy on top of a glass-topped table that the whole thing shattered. She observed, 'It was a miracle that, beyond a few nicks and cuts, nobody really got hurt.'

In the small world of Vegas, Tom had signed The Blossoms from under the nose of Elvis, who also sang with them and was keen to make the arrangement permanent. There were no hard feelings.

Elvis was always gracious about Tom. In August 1974, Tom had flown in to Las Vegas to prepare for a new season at Caesars Palace, and went along to see his friend perform at the Hilton. Elvis paused between songs and announced, 'There's somebody I'd like you to meet. To me … he's my favourite singer. He's one of the greatest performers I've ever seen, and the greatest voice, Tom Jones. There he is. He's too much. Tom, you open at Caesars Palace tomorrow night, right? Folks, if you get the chance, go over and see him. He's really something.'

The King had split with Priscilla in 1972, when she left him after she had an affair with her karate instructor. As a result, Elvis spent much more time in Las Vegas, and, with hindsight, it is easy to think their split was the beginning of his fateful downward spiral. He had known Priscilla since she was fourteen and he was a GI stationed in Germany, so she had been the most important part of his life for fourteen years. By the time Elvis was divorced in 1973, Tom had been married for sixteen years. He never had to face being a superstar without knowing that his wife was at home waiting for him.

Not everyone in Vegas was as easygoing as Elvis. Tom finally got to know Jerry Lee Lewis better. It turned out he was unable to match Tom's drinking power, even though he tried. The rock 'n' roll veteran wanted to discuss an idea for a TV special called, amusingly, *Tom & Jerry*. As the evening wore on and the champagne flowed, he became more belligerent, waving a bottle of Dom Pérignon at Tom and calling him a 'motherfucker'. Coincidentally, he had suggested a similar show to Elvis, which would instead be called *The King and The Killer*. Elvis was unimpressed, and later told his bodyguards that Jerry Lee had a lot of talent, but should be locked up in a cage when he wasn't performing.

The only time Elvis and Tom fell out was one evening when Elvis gave an impromptu concert in his suite. He wouldn't stop singing his then current favourite, the Roberta Flack classic 'Killing Me Softly with His Song'. He enlisted his backing group to accompany him each time. After half a dozen encores, everyone was getting a little tired of it, but singing came to an abrupt end when Chris Ellis, anxious for Tom to get some rest, pulled away the piano player's stool and they both tumbled on to the floor. It was meant to be a joke, but Elvis didn't see it that way, and aimed several karate kicks at Chris. The atmosphere between the two camps was fraught for a few days.

Although this incident had nothing to do with it, Chris Ellis's time with Tom was coming to an end. Once again, Tom avoided any confrontation with the man who had been a close member of his team. He had been best man at Chris's 1973 wedding in Las Vegas to his Swedish bride, Eva; Linda was a bridesmaid. But Tom had Mark by his side now and didn't need Chris. He wanted Mark to be more closely involved, in effect to serve an apprenticeship.

Tom and Chris saw each other for the last time in March 1975, when they went out drinking while Tom was rehearsing near Paris. According to Chris, Tom was in a sombre mood, worried about the hit records drying up and wondering what the future might hold. He was unusually quiet and had tears in his eyes. A few weeks later, Chris discovered that Mark had been given his job and he and Tom never spoke again.

This was a period of momentous change in Tom's life. In 1973, he was earning $160,000 a week at Caesars Palace. He was performing all over the world for ten months a year and earning an estimated £5 million, but was incensed that he was paying so much tax to the British government. He was hardly ever at home in the UK, so it seemed ridiculous. He calculated that over the years he had already paid the Inland Revenue more than £7 million. The income tax was an eye-watering 98 per cent on unearned income, 84 per cent on earned income. Tom is pretty easygoing about most things, but not this.

The only sensible course of action was to apply for an American Green Card. This would allow him to work in the US and pay his taxes there, which was much more cost effective. His application would take two years to process, and turned him into a stateless person. He couldn't go back to the UK and could only spend a limited number of days in the US, so as not to risk heavy penalties from the Internal Revenue Service there. When he wasn't performing, he would slip out of the country, often to sail around the Caribbean. Tom felt that he didn't have a proper home at this time.

Eventually, the Green Card came through, and he was able to move to the US permanently. He and Linda found a sumptuous sixteen-room mansion in Bel Air that had belonged to Dean Martin. Unusually in this part of Los Angeles, where every home seemed to be a white Spanish-style villa, this house was red brick, which gave it a more British feel. It would be ludicrous to suggest it reminded Tom of home, but once a pair of Welsh dragons had been added to the electronic gates, there was something of Tor Point about it.

The house was already on various tours of movie stars' homes, so Tom had to have a large wall built to ensure some degree of privacy. His collection of gold and silver discs, his antique weaponry and most of the Tor Point furniture were shipped across, which made it seem more homely to Linda. Pride of place went to the old red phone box that had stood in Laura Street all those years ago. The bright red antique was installed next to the impressive 25ft by 45ft swimming pool – perfect for ringing the house for another chilled bottle of champagne.

The move took Linda even further away from her friends and family, but, in reality, she had been trapped in Tor Point. At least if she were permanently in the States, she might see more of her son. Tom senior and Freda made the move as well, settling into a house less than five minutes away by car, with magnificent views over Los Angeles. Sheila, who was now divorced from Ken, came too, so Tom had all his immediate family close to him. He observed, 'I like having my family around me, because some people don't spend enough time with their families and then it's too late.'

At least he could feel more settled now. Elvis, however, seemed progressively less happy. Tom didn't see him for the last eighteen months of his life, although he tried calling him in Memphis. Elvis became more reclusive before his shocking death, in August 1977, at the age of forty-two. His weight had ballooned dangerously and he was clearly suffering the effects of long-standing drug abuse, although the exact cause of his death continues to be a source of suspicion and conspiracy theories.

Tom said afterwards that he wished Elvis had been able to reach out to his friends. The debate about who was the better singer is one for late night bar-stool arguments. Elvis wasn't the singer he once was by the time he reached his thirties. He released versions of 'Green, Green Grass of Home' and 'I'll Never Fall in Love Again', but they are pale renditions of Tom's definitive performances.

Les Reed sums it up, 'Having worked with both men, I would say that the main singing talent lies with Tom, but Elvis has a drawing power for his millions of fans that cannot be questioned.'

# 16

# THE SLUMP

Gordon Mills was obsessed with the idea of Tom becoming a big film star. He nearly pulled it off, but it probably represents their biggest professional failure. Tom himself dreamed of playing James Bond and, at one time, was being seriously considered for the role. He let it be known that he would be happy to step into Sean Connery's shoes, drinking shaken martinis and unzipping the dresses of beautiful women. Cubby Broccoli, the famous producer of the Bond films, vetoed the idea. Tom said, regretfully, 'He said I was too well known for people to believe it.'

As long ago as 1965, Tom revealed his movie ambitions in a naive way: 'Now that I am fairly established as a singer, I would like to go into films. I think for a singer to keep in the public eye, you should try and widen the scope a little bit, because I think you can make so many records that people start to get used to your voice and your sound. I would like to try and act in some straight roles, if possible – if I can act at all. First of all, I would like to get a small part to try and learn about the film industry and then go on to something bigger.'

These words reflect Gordon's intentions more than those of the boy from Treforest, who just wanted to sing. But if Gordon thought it was the right step, then Tom was happy to go along with it. Gordon had wanted him to follow the path set, not just by Elvis, but also Frank Sinatra and Dean Martin, who were both very accomplished actors. Elvis was in many forgettable films, but Frank had won an Oscar for *From Here to Eternity* and been nominated for his portrayal of a heroin addict in *The Man with the Golden Arm*.

One thing Tom was always sure about: he didn't want to make a movie with dancing girls. He'd had enough conversations with Elvis to realise how much his friend hated these shallow cashing-in exercises.

A promising project, called *The Gospel Singer*, had first been talked about in 1971. Tom and Gordon had acquired the rights to the book by the cult writer Harry Crews, which told the story of a singer/Messiah who can't handle the adulation and is ultimately lynched by his disillusioned followers. It was not a cheery tale.

Armed with this project, Gordon negotiated a three-picture deal with United Artists that was announced in August of that year, but the film was never made. Crews, who died in 2012, believed Tom got cold feet about his character dying. Tom said at the time, 'We may change the ending of the book.' This would have fundamentally altered the sense of the story.

The years dragged on and still nothing happened, even though Tom and Gordon would sit up late in his Las Vegas hotel suite, working on the script, the casting and the production. Tom even took lessons from Elvis on how to speak with a Southern accent. A starting date of May 1975 was mooted, and Charlene Tilton from *Dallas* was rumoured to be the co-star. Tom, approaching his thirty-fifth birthday, was already too old for the role and eventually the project was permanently postponed.

# THE SLUMP

A year later, he was offered the male lead in *The Stud*, written by Jackie Collins and starring her sister Joan. Ostensibly, this was perfect for Tom, but he told the author that there were too many F-words. This may seem rich coming from a man whose conversation is littered with them, but Tom observes miners' rules when it comes to swearing: 'fuck' is fine when used liberally by men at the bar with a pint in their hands, but is not acceptable if a woman walks in.

While the film is quite tame by today's standards, it did feature scenes of drug-taking and bisexuality. Tom observed, 'I wouldn't like my mum and dad to see that sort of film. It's just short of being pornographic.'

Jackie responded, 'It's certainly not porny and I'm flabbergasted that Tom should have any scruples about playing a super lover.'

Such comments provided welcome publicity for the movie, which, even without Tom Jones, ended up making more than $20 million at the box office.

Tom started filming his next project in August 1976 – a thriller curiously titled *Yockowald*, in which he was cast as a hit-man hired by the CIA to hunt a foreign agent in Los Angeles. He liked the role, because he was an anti-hero, but one who still used a gun and chased bad guys. He wasn't a Tom Jones character who breaks into a chorus of 'It's Not Unusual' when he kisses his girlfriend goodbye. He commented, 'This film is going to be a real challenge.' Shooting scenes in downtown LA attracted the attention of the seedier side of the neighbourhood, and Tom was spotted cheerfully signing an autograph for a 230-pound streetwalker between takes.

The production ran out of money after just three weeks, leaving everyone disappointed. Gordon tried to take over the

187

financing, but it proved too problematic. He was getting progressively more anxious about finding his man a movie. It was almost the case that anything would do.

Then along came *Pleasure Cove*, which Tom filmed in July 1978 in California. It was hard to believe that after all the aspirations, his first proper role was in this froth. Filming was relatively quick, so Tom only had to clear his diary for a month. Even for a novice, this was unexacting material. The worst thing about it was sitting around soaking wet for a scene in which he wore the briefest pair of budgie smugglers. When it looked as if he might be drying out, a member of the on-set team would throw a bucket of water over him.

At least, after his experience in television, Tom was used to hanging around, but he didn't enjoy it: 'When I come offstage I feel great. I feel I've really done something. This isn't the same at all. All the hanging about is just wearying.'

Tom played a charming crook called Raymond Gordon and had little to do except smile winningly and show off an impressively hairy chest. He sounded most convincing when he told an attractive undercover cop at the nudist beach, 'I wish you'd take your clothes off.' The idea of the film was that it would lead to a TV series in the *Love Boat* tradition, although Tom wouldn't have been involved in that. After a couple of network showings, it sank without trace and is of interest today only because of Tom's involvement.

In a way, Tom seemed as if he was doing what he said he would do all those years before in the sixties: starting with a small role and then moving upwards. It never happened, sadly. Perhaps he was weighed down by a fear of failure. He was widely acknowledged as one of the best, if not the best, singers in the world, but he really knew nothing about acting, having never even taken part in the school play at the Central School in Treforest. 'I don't want people to say, "He's not such a good actor,"' he admitted honestly.

Gordon had seen the movies as a way of revitalising Tom's flagging recording career. Elvis, for instance, was able to shift millions of records on the back of limp movies like *Blue Hawaii* and *Viva Las Vegas*. Even he might have avoided *Pleasure Cove*, which did nothing to improve things.

Tom's last top ten hit record in the UK had been in 1972. The song was called 'The Young New Mexican Puppeteer' and was a pale shadow of the passionate and powerful songs of the Peter Sullivan and Les Reed era. Tom barely seemed to get out of second gear. His days with Decca were numbered when a succession of singles disappointed, despite reasonable reviews. Inevitably, a greatest hits collection in 1975 heralded a parting of the ways, but, as a consolation, it was his first number one album since *Delilah* in 1968. It also neatly coincided with the tenth anniversary of 'It's Not Unusual'. At least 'The Young New Mexican Puppeteer' wasn't on it; the track had absolutely zero sex appeal. All of Tom's great songs had a sort of stripped-back masculinity, even when he sang of a breaking heart.

Gordon and Tom had already marked their tenth anniversary together. Gordon had called Chris Hutchins into his office in London and told him, 'Remind Tom it's our tenth anniversary coming up.' Chris imagined he wanted to make dinner reservations, but Gordon bluntly told him, 'I want a present.' The PR and his wife trawled around Bond Street until they found a superb pewter mug, which they had engraved 'Ten fabulous years, Tom'. He duly presented it to his manager, who gave him nothing in return. Chris explains, 'That was their role. Gordon thought that Tom owed everything to him.'

189

Not long afterwards, Chris left the Jones camp, deciding that he needed a fresh challenge away from the easy but soulless life in Los Angeles. Looking after Tom had become too repetitive and he missed writing. In his new role, he wrote an exposé of 'The Family', as he called them, which made Gordon, Tom, Engelbert and Gilbert O'Sullivan, the singer-songwriter discovered by Gordon, seem like some sort of pop mafia.

It was strictly business for Chris, although Tom didn't see it that way. He hated the revelations, especially the ones about his sex life, which Linda would loathe if she read them. He said, 'I'd trusted this man. When he left, he wrote me a letter saying how much he treasured my friendship. I kept the letter. Then this happened. At first I thought I'd strangle him if I ever caught up with him. But there's nothing you can do. Just sit it out.'

Both Tom and Gordon hated not being in control of the situation. Ironically, that rested with the man who had so expertly 'controlled' their publicity for the previous ten years. The stories made Chris a hate figure among Tom's fans. That hasn't changed to this day, although privately Chris is very complimentary about Tom Jones, whom he admires enormously: 'He was honest; he was straightforward; he had a great sense of humour and there was no ego.'

The bedrock of Tom's organisation was beginning to crumble. Chris Hutchins, Chris Ellis and Dai Perry were all back in the UK. His acclaimed guitarist, Big Jim Sullivan, left in the mid-seventies after more than five years touring the US with him. Their version of 'Guitar Man' was a highlight of Tom's stage performances during these years. Big Jim was one of the best session guitarists of all time and played on more than a thousand hits over the years, including 'The Young New Mexican

Puppeteer', although that wasn't a career highlight – 'Green, Green Grass of Home' was.

He and Tom had intuitive banter on stage. He wrote to the fan site Tom Jones International before he died in 2012: 'I think I had more experience of life in the five years working with Tom than I did in all the rest of my life put together. The problem was that none of it was to do with music!'

Tom's popular music director, Johnny Spence, died from a heart attack while finishing the score of the *Spiderman* movie in August 1977, the day before Elvis was found dead at Graceland. Gordon, in particular, was devastated by Johnny's death. The pair would go on safari to Africa together, something Tom wasn't bothered about doing. Both Tom and Gordon acted as pallbearers at his funeral. The three men had moved to LA at the same time. Gordon admired Johnny because, while he played hard and enjoyed a drink, he also worked tirelessly to keep Tom at the top, labouring often late into the night to write out all the parts for each musician individually.

Tom was still one of the biggest stars in the world, as Gordon never tired of telling everyone. The problem was that the UK had no idea of his status, because he was never in the country. He no longer had a proper fan club in Britain. Instead, he continued to lead a life of unimaginable luxury, flying around the US in his Boeing 707 plane, which ferried the tour party from city to city. Occasionally, he had to slum it in a chauffeur-driven limousine.

Tom still liked his routine while on tour. He would sleep until after lunch, then start his day with a trip to the hotel spa and gym, have a steak, chicken or prawn dinner, arrive to do his show no more than twenty minutes before he was due on stage and then socialise from midnight until the alarm clocks were going off for most normal people. Tom has never knowingly left a bar or a party until the cleaners switched the lights on. Then it would be time for sex and sleep. If they were flying on the next day, the plane wouldn't take off until the afternoon.

Sex, according to one of his entourage, was very much just letting off steam for Tom. He once declared that he didn't get an erection singing, but that sex was very much part of his performance. He needed a release, and the women who went to be part of the sexually charged show were happy to oblige him afterwards with very little effort on his part.

The super-fans were entirely different, however. They adored Tom, but they didn't want to be part of that particular conveyor-belt. They were ordinary women, from all over the US, who would plan their year so they could see as many Tom Jones concerts as they could. One of these devoted fans, Glenna Stone from Massachusetts, saw him hundreds of times over a fifteen-year period from 1971 to 1986.

She had plenty of opportunity to watch Tom in action. 'Every time we would see somebody go up on that elevator with him to his room, you never saw that girl again.' On one memorable occasion, she and her friend were in the ladies' restroom, when they overheard a young woman say that now she was 'dating a celebrity she would need a whole new wardrobe'. The next day, she left town on the tour bus with the band. An hour or so later, Glenna and her friend drove past her, sitting plaintively on her suitcase by a bus stop.

The girls weren't under age, but they tended to be young women, no older than their early twenties. The super-fans were more mature, often the same age as Tom. Their ambition was not to go to bed with him, but to have a conversation and, if they were lucky, prepare his dressing room with flowers, fruit and

Dom Pérignon champagne. They were familiar faces to Tom, often welcoming him to an hotel lobby in a strange town and occupying the front row at his shows, so he would always know there would be an appreciative audience.

Glenna and her friends relied on Lloyd Greenfield and Tom's son Mark to help them gain insider knowledge about Tom's itinerary and where he would be staying. Lloyd was the key, because he was responsible for making sure everything ran smoothly for Tom. 'He had a gruff persona and liked to make sure he had everything under a tight rein. He was the front man, and made sure Tom didn't have to open his mouth except to be nice. He was so good at what he did,' said Glenna.

She had first met Tom in a Hilton hotel in Cranston, Rhode Island: 'We asked for his autograph, told him we had all his records and all that crap, but he was very personable. He spent a lot of time talking to us. I asked him if there was something he missed that he couldn't get in the US and he replied, "After Eight mints." So I phoned Harrods and got them to send over a case of the mints. From then on, whenever I saw Tom, I was never without a box of After Eight.

'Most of the fans like me would bring him gifts. I was forever combing the record stores for obscure Jerry Lee Lewis records. And he would never just say thank you. He was always very interested in everything — and wanted to know where you'd found something. He knew we weren't interested in jumping into that bed with him — the more genuine we were with him, the more so he was with us.'

While many of the women who continued to flock to his concerts weren't concerned about what he sang to them, both Tom and Gordon were extremely worried about his recording career, not least because an important source of revenue was running dry. He joined EMI from Decca and released 'Say You'll Stay until Tomorrow', which was the start of his country period, the least musically satisfying of his career.

'Say You'll Stay until Tomorrow' went to number one in the US country charts, seducing Gordon into believing that this should be Tom's new direction. He had done plenty of country songs before, but they always had a Jones twist to them. Now, on the PolyGram label, he released album after album of dull material, which won him few new fans and disappointed those who still played the songs from his sixties heyday. Nothing registered in the UK charts.

On the 1982 album *Country*, partly recorded in Nashville, he even posed as a cowboy on the front cover. It seemed he was treading a path towards obscurity, although he was still in huge demand as a cabaret act across the US. He had a five-record deal with PolyGram and each one was a country album.

Tom's touring schedule meant he still spent little time each year at his beautiful home in Bel Air. As a result, Mark was away too, leaving Linda to rattle around in the big house by herself. Gordon had settled in LA for tax reasons, but his marriage to Jo began to decline in the late seventies, as she grew tired of her husband's philandering ways and the amount of time he spent in Las Vegas; she had five children to bring up in the UK. She later explained candidly how difficult it was to maintain a good marriage in the music business: 'It's exciting, but there are lots and lots of times when wives have to be on their own and then it's lonely. And you can't trust them completely because of the situation in show business – people are there for the taking.'

Tom, meanwhile, was disappointed that his father failed to settle in LA. His parents preferred to make their home in the

UK, although they visited twice a year when Tom was at home. Their son remained in tax exile, so it was up to them to travel.

Tom senior found the heat, the freeways and the yes-men a little too hard to take, but he did enjoy meeting some of his celebrity heroes, like Frank Sinatra and Elvis. His favourite was Muhammad Ali, whom Tom had met when he first went to Las Vegas. They became good friends and the great boxer was one of the few celebrities that Tom entertained in his own home. They would spend hours together, talking about their early lives.

In 1980, Tom took his father with him when he visited Ali at his training camp in Deer Lake, Pennsylvania. Ali asked if Tom would like to do a little sparring. 'C'mon, Jones, we'll have some fun,' although it didn't sound too entertaining to Tom. Ali was a good sport, however, and allowed Tom to knock him to the canvas. His former business manager, Gene Kilroy, who had first introduced them in Vegas, took pictures of Tom looking jubilant as Ali pretended to be hurt. Kilroy said, 'Tom's a pretty tough fella. He'd be great in a street fight, I think, and if I could choose anyone to have next to me in a foxhole it'd be Tom – he's a stand-up guy.'

The following autumn, Tom senior was taken ill on a visit to Los Angeles. The many years stuck underground, breathing black coal dust, finally took their toll. He was advised against travelling home, so he spent the last week of his life in bed at Tom's house in Bel Air with his family around him. He died on 10 October 1981, at the age of seventy-one.

Both Freda and Sheila decided they would prefer to live in California, so they buried Tom senior in the Forest Lawn Memorial Park, a few miles from Bel Air, and close enough that Tom's mother could visit her husband's grave whenever she wished. They had been married forty-eight years.

Tom bought a house near his own for his mother and sister, who both loved the climate in California, although Freda was fair skinned and would never soak up the sun. She loved seeing relatives when they visited from Treforest. When Margaret and Graham Sugar called in on holiday, she enjoyed reminiscing. 'I always remember you doing me egg and chips,' she told them.

Sadly, Tom's father missed the big family wedding the following year, when Mark, now twenty-five, married his girlfriend, Donna Paloma, a strong-willed woman from New York, who was five years his senior. She had been the girlfriend of one of Tom's band members, so she had known Mark for a few years before they became romantically involved.

More than 200 guests attended the wedding and reception at the house. Tom sang while the newlyweds took a turn on the dance floor. As a present, he bought them a house a few minutes' drive from his. Once more, he had his close family around him, as he always wanted. He was even happier the following year, when he became a grandfather for the first time in June. Tom was just forty-three when Alexander Woodward was born: 'I have a grandson, when most people would be having a son. So I'm still young enough to enjoy it.'

Soon afterwards he embarked on his first British tour since he had gone into exile. Predictably, it was a sell-out. At the beginning of September 1983, he invited more than a hundred of his Welsh relatives to a reunion party at the splendid Celtic Manor Hotel near Newport. He even laid on a coach to bring fifty or so of his cousins from Pontypridd. Many hadn't seen him for more than ten years. One of the twins, Margaret Sugar, ran up to him, her face wreathed in smiles.

She asked excitedly, 'Which one am I, Tom?'

'Margaret,' he replied.

# PART THREE

---

# SIR TOM

---

# 17

# KISS-OFF

The 1980s weren't kind to Gordon Mills. His marriage to Jo was over, he had lost two of his great acts – Engelbert and Gilbert – Tom's career was stuck in a country music stagnant bog, the MAM organisation was nothing like as healthy as it had been and he was spending too much time chasing his losses in Las Vegas. He had, however, met a beautiful Tahitian-born travel agent called Annie Toomaru, whom he put in charge of organising and liaising with the vast number of Tom Jones fan clubs throughout the US. They planned to marry as soon as his divorce came through.

When he visited the UK in 1986 to sort out the settlement regarding Little Rhondda, Jo Mills noticed that he wasn't looking well. She was so shocked by his appearance that she asked if he was all right. He told her he was fine, but he wasn't. He started to suffer excruciating abdominal pains, and was diagnosed with stomach cancer.

Annie Toomaru slept in his room at the Cedars-Sinai Medical Center in Los Angeles while his condition deteriorated. Jo and his five children flew out to see him when they realised the gravity of his situation. Tom visited him for the last time and they joked half-heartedly about his odds of pulling through. Gordon said he would take fifty–fifty, but, in reality, they were a million to one. Tom, distraught at the fate of his mentor, cried to Gordon's daughter Beverly, 'What am I going to do?' Gordon died the next day, on 29 July 1986. He was fifty-one. It was a little over twenty-two years since he had first met Tommy Woodward, the 'scruffy bastard'.

Gordon was buried in England, next to his father, in Burvale Cemetery, Hersham, in Surrey. Before the funeral, Tom and Beverly walked around the gardens of Little Rhondda, because Tom was intent on finding the right single rose to throw on Gordon's coffin. He wasn't ready to leave for the local St Peter's Church until he had found the bloom he wanted.

He was full of emotion, describing Gordon as 'the finest man I knew' in his eulogy. He continued, 'He took me from nowhere and gave me everything. I owe him so much, it's incalculable.'

Gordon Mills may have been a flawed man, but he was a mercurial and immensely charismatic one. It has become fashionable to blame him for perceived faults in Tom's character or behaviour. That is part of what made him a good manager – he protected his star and made the unpopular decisions.

Gordon liked to be in control and he had an unshakeable belief that he was right. He once cornered Prime Minister Harold Wilson at a party at Chris Hutchins' house in Richmond and demanded to know the latest government thinking on Rhodesia, Jo's native country. Twenty minutes later, he burst into the kitchen, where Chris and Tom had escaped to enjoy a glass of champagne, and declared, 'Throw Wilson out! He just won't listen.'

On another occasion, Gordon was furious with Tom when he came back to the UK after touring extensively in the US.

When Chris demanded to know what the problem was, Gordon said, 'Tom has been back three days and he hasn't phoned me.'

Chris replied, 'But Gordon, he's two minutes up the road.'

Gordon was unimpressed. 'That's not the point,' he shouted. 'He should have called me.'

Gordon and Tom were, quite simply, a double act. There's a wonderful scene in a documentary about Tom in which they are flying over Treforest in a helicopter. Tom said, 'That's the paper mill down there, where I used to work.'

Gordon responded, 'Oh yes, what do they make there, then?'

Tom paused for a split second. 'Paper,' he said, chuckling.

In 2008, a commemorative plaque was unveiled outside his family home at 97 Brithweunydd Road, Trealaw, in the Rhondda. It said, 'Gordon Mills, 1935–86, lived here: Songwriter and manager of Tom Jones'. Jo Mills, who attended the ceremony with her children, said, 'I think Tom would have made something of himself sooner or later, but I doubt it would have been by the direct route he had.' His daughter Tracy commented, 'My dad was an extraordinary man, who was able to see talent for what it was, get tremendously excited about it and then actually act on his own excitement to turn that talent into star quality – a rare gift indeed.'

Les Reed, who had known him even longer than Tom, summed up Gordon's talents: 'He had many hang-ups, was very complicated and intensely sensitive of others who tried to get close to him. But as a manager he was the best there ever was.'

Tom wasn't happy. Nobody seemed to be caring about his voice any more. His shows had become a parody. The audience was more concerned with collecting sweaty souvenirs than in listening to his new repertoire. He knew he had to do it, because that's why they had paid good money to see him, but he needed to change their perception of him.

It wasn't going to happen overnight. At a concert in Bethlehem, Pennsylvania, a woman ran the length of the auditorium to hand him a towel. He dutifully wiped under his arms and patted down the hairs on his chest, before handing it back with a kiss. He had done it thousands of times, but the delirious fan shouted, 'I've been waiting eighteen years for this.'

All Tom could do was make sure that he put his point across in interviews. He told the *Chicago Sun-Times*, 'At first it was a sexy, spontaneous act. Now it's a gimmick. For a long time, the underwear tossing – or the anticipation of underwear tossing – would overwhelm whatever else I was trying to do onstage.

'Reviewers never mentioned my voice, and it's been a constant struggle to overcome that. People were beginning to think I was nothing more than a pair of tight pants and a hairy chest.'

He found it most frustrating when he launched into 'Green, Green Grass of Home', which required the audience to listen closely and quietly. He complained, 'There's always some nutcase woman who thinks "now's my chance" and whoosh. It fucks up the song.'

The difficulty was that he was still being paid a king's ransom to appear in Las Vegas. He was earning $250,000 a week for three months a year – that's $3 million a year, for starters.

Both Gordon and Tom enjoyed money and the lifestyle it could bring. The former believed success and achievement were measured solely by the size of the cheque, the number of rooms in your house and the fleet of luxury cars in the driveway, but Tom wanted more that that. He needed to prove he was still a relevant artist or, at least, that he could become one again.

Gordon was a one-off and there was never going to be another like him in the music business. It turned out that Tom made a very sensible decision when he died. He chose his son to take over. Mark had spent fifteen years learning the business from top to bottom, so it seemed a natural progression for him to become his father's manager. The move would arguably save Tom's career.

For the last few years, Mark had been working as his father's lighting director. He had literally been waiting in the wings, ready with his own ideas. He didn't want Tom to be a leathery supper club act. Mark was only twenty-nine, but by coincidence that was the age at which Gordon turned to management and took over Tom's career in 1964. Tom trusted Gordon with all his heart, and only his family, his own blood, could occupy such a place in his future.

Mark, as his father was about to discover, had very strong opinions. He was like a famous football club's new manager who ditches anything connected with the old regime. His wife Donna was at his right hand as they swept away Gordon's empire. The first to go was Annie Toomaru. She was fired less than two weeks after the funeral by a company accountant.

She has complained bitterly that Tom didn't phone her, but Tom never rings anyone. It was one of his traits most influenced by his late mentor: right from the start Gordon told him, quite forcefully, not to speak to anyone. He never phoned Chris Ellis or Vernon Hopkins, or Gordon's family back home in Britain. In fifty years, he only ever called Les Reed once: 'Gordon was Svengali to Tom, who adhered to everything that he was told not to do. It stuck with Tom and, to this day, he has only lifted the phone to me on one occasion. I was very hurt, considering the number of years working on his behalf. But that's life.' Other than his immediate family, the only person Tom would call on a regular basis was Dai Perry, whom he would ring every week or two to find out what was going on down at the Wheatsheaf.

After Annie was sacked, the second to be shown the door was the PR director, John Moran. He was replaced by Donna, who had worked as the actor Bill Cosby's secretary and promised to do her best to keep the knicker count down. Some of the older musicians were dispensed with, and most of the office staff left within a few months. Just about the only familiar face left at the newly named Tom Jones Enterprises was Lloyd Greenfield. When Lloyd began to wind down his work schedule in the nineties, his place at Tom's side was taken by Don Archell, a former singer from Luton. Silver haired and distinguished looking, he has been at Tom's side ever since.

The super-fans were next. Many, including Glenna Stone, went to fewer concerts or stopped going altogether. 'We felt unwelcome – limited to no access, shutting down of fan clubs, and little acknowledgment from the stage. Unwelcome is the proper term.' They didn't suddenly turn against Tom. They still loved him, but the attraction in following him around the country had gone. It was no fun any more.

Mark and Donna had two initial tasks: first, to change Tom's image, so he was reaching a younger audience; second, to find and release new material and not rely on songs that were twenty years old and being sung by sixties tribute acts. Mark explained to BBC's *Imagine*, 'Some things were just wrong, certain choices of material were not challenging. In an ideal world, the focus of his image will shift about three feet upwards and be on his voice and nothing else.'

It was easy enough to modernise Tom's wardrobe, give him a younger haircut and tighten up a few bags under the eyes and chin, but he needed to be in the charts and he didn't even have a record deal. He wanted a song, but he wasn't on the radar of the popular songwriters. Nobody was sending Tom Jones their latest composition.

Mark eventually came across a new ballad called 'A Boy from Nowhere', which had been written by songwriters Mike Leander and Edward Seago as part of a concept album called *Matador*. Rather like Les Reed, Leander was a much-respected figure in the music business and had worked with The Beatles and The Rolling Stones. Some of his best-known songs are never played these days because they were recorded by the notorious Gary Glitter in the seventies. 'I'm the Leader of the Gang (I Am!)' and 'I Love You Love Me Love' were just two of the biggest-selling songs of the glam-rock period of the early seventies – a fashion that thankfully passed Tom by while he was in his Las Vegas bubble.

'A Boy from Nowhere' was a song that Tom was born to sing. It was a passionate ballad that stretched every vocal chord. It may have lacked the rousing anthemic chorus of 'Delilah', but it matched its intensity.

Rather like 'Green, Green Grass of Home', audiences mistakenly thought the song was Tom's tribute to his own humble origins. *Matador* was based on the inspiring story of the famous bullfighter El Cordobés. He had been born into poverty, but had risen above a life of petty crime and manual labour to become rich and revered doing the one thing he did best. Perhaps the story did resonate with Tom a little after all.

Tom recorded six songs for the concept album, but only 'A Boy from Nowhere' was released in the UK, where it reached number two in April 1987. Its success enabled Mark and Donna to book Tom into a round of interviews and performances in

Britain, including *Top of the Pops* for the first time in fifteen years. By far the most significant was an appearance on the cult chat show *The Last Resort with Jonathan Ross*, then an up-and-coming television host.

Ross clearly admired Tom. In a world where talk-show hosts have to put up with many prima donna celebrities, he liked the easygoing naturalness of Tom. Jonathan loves the story of Mark and Tom flying into Los Angeles and, instead of posing for photographs, heading straight to the bar to sink a few pints before breakfast. It may or may not be true, but it gave the impression of a man who knew what his priorities in life should be.

On *The Last Resort*, guests would sing a number that they weren't usually associated with. Jonathan, who looked about twelve next to Tom, during a rather strained piece of banter, asked him what new material he was putting in his act. Tom told him he liked Prince and was singing 'Kiss', which the studio band just happened to know. This was unexpectedly contemporary for Tom, but Mark had encouraged him to try it.

Tom gave an inspired performance of the hit, with just the right amount of restraint and suggestiveness when he sang the line 'Women not girls rule my world.' The audience were cheering and whistling at the end, proving to the British public that he still had it. Jonathan couldn't resist interrupting to mop Tom's brow with a pair of knickers.

One particular viewer liked what she saw. Anne Dudley, one half of the synth-pop duo The Art of Noise, observed, 'He came out, as cool as you like, in black leather and he seemed to have a fantastic confidence about him, but he didn't take himself so seriously. Tom Jones had fallen off my radar ... I really thought the days when he would make great records were probably in the past.'

The Art of Noise were one of the most fashionable acts around and won a 1986 Grammy Award for their version of 'Peter Gunn', featuring Duane Eddy. They were innovative users of digital sampling technology and not the sort of group you might associate with Tom Jones, but the collaboration worked. These days, sampling has become hackneyed, but not in 1988, when 'Kiss' was released as The Art of Noise, featuring Tom Jones. The single reached number five in the UK and number thirty-one in the US *Billboard* chart. More importantly, it provided a blueprint for keeping Tom at the top for many years to come: put him next to a fashionable act and he appeared current, and he made the other artists look good. It paid off time and time again. 'Kiss' was The Art of Noise's biggest mainstream hit, so the alliance benefited them as much as it did Tom.

He went back to his arduous touring schedule in the US with a new repertoire. His greatest hits were reduced to a medley and his new material, including 'Kiss' and songs from *Matador*, jostled for attention with others from Paul Simon, Billy Idol and Wang Chung.

Touring wasn't the breeze it was in his younger days. Now approaching fifty, Tom needed to take care of himself more. He spent two hours each morning in the gym and made sure he drank a gallon of water a day and not eight pints of champagne. He travelled with humidifiers to prevent his hotel rooms from becoming too dry and harming his voice. He also liked to suck a menthol lozenge and keep it tucked into his cheek for lubrication while he sang.

One of the best lines in Tom's version of 'Kiss' is 'I think I'd better dance now' – he did just that across America. One reviewer noted, 'Ninety per cent of the time Jones rock 'n' rolled like the hottest of male strippers. Ten per cent of the time he looked as if he were leading a geriatric aerobics class.' Patricia Smith, who wrote of his show at the Chicago Theatre, observed, 'When he soared into my personal favourite, the heart-wrenching "I (Who Have Nothing)", I figured the least I could do was show the man my appreciation. It was then I discovered, the hard way, that there's absolutely no way to remove one's underwear in a crowded theatre.' Patricia obviously didn't realise that the panties were newly bought and just out of the wrapping when they were tossed on stage.

'Kiss' didn't lead to a consistent upswing in Tom's recording fortunes. Not every decision was a good one. In April 1989, he released 'Move Closer', an unsubtle sex track that had been a number one hit for Phyllis Nelson four years earlier. The song was released on the hugely successful Jive label. *Melody Maker* thought the version was a 'delight' and 'wicked', oozing lust. It only just sneaked into the top fifty, perhaps because it was overly blatant.

Tom had already moved too close to a young woman in New York called Katherine Berkery, with whom he had a four-day fling in 1987. Katherine was twenty-four, a part-time model and an exotic blend of Korean and American. She had been brought up by adoptive parents in New York. A regular in the fashionable nightclubs of the time, including Studio 54, she had met other celebrities, including Robert De Niro and Kurt Russell, before she got to know Tom in Regine's, on Park Avenue, in October. At the end of the night, she agreed to go back to Tom's luxury suite at the Ritz-Carlton Hotel next to Central Park.

According to Katherine, he kept a tape recorder in a silver briefcase and would get in the mood for their lovemaking by playing his own songs. More importantly, he didn't wear a condom, which apparently was his usual practice. Katherine explained bitterly in the *Mail on Sunday* that she didn't know he was married and thought he was genuinely fond of her.

Six weeks after Tom moved on, Katherine discovered she was pregnant and phoned the offices of Tom Jones Enterprises in Los Angeles, only to be given the brush-off by staff quite used to this sort of mischievous call. She wanted to speak to Tom, but he probably never received any message.

When her son Jonathan was born in Florida in June 1988, she registered the father as Tom Jones. Her baby was younger than Tom's two grandchildren – Mark and Donna had celebrated the birth of their second child, a daughter Emma, the previous September.

Distressed at getting nowhere in obtaining any sort of acknowledgement from Tom, Katherine engaged the services of a top New York divorce attorney called Raoul Felder. He had represented Robin Givens in her divorce from Mike Tyson and had a fearsome reputation.

Tom didn't attend when the paternity case first came before the family court in New York in July 1989. Donna Woodward provided a robust statement for the press on Tom's behalf: 'Mr Jones is disgusted and depressed by these lies. He is the victim of an irresponsible and scurrilous allegation.' Linda reportedly leaned out of the window of their mansion and shouted, 'My husband has completely denied any involvement with this girl. I love him just as much as I ever did and he loves me.'

Tom was ordered by the court to take a blood test, which proved 99.7 per cent certain that Tom was Jonathan's father. A further DNA test increased the probability to 99.9 per cent. During acrimonious proceedings, Tom's lawyers suggested that Katherine was a prostitute – an allegation she vigorously denied. With the paternity tests firmly on her side, Tom lost the case and, in a confidential settlement, was reported to have agreed to pay her £2,000 a month plus other expenses, including school fees. After the case was concluded, Katherine said, 'I'm so glad it's over.'

Tom wouldn't acknowledge his son, however. He refused to speak about it for nearly twenty years. Then, in a radio interview in 2008, he revealed that he felt he had been used: 'It wasn't something I had planned. If I had planned it, I would have done something more than just financially. But it wasn't. I was tricked really. I just fell for it.'

Katherine, who now lives in North Carolina, no longer talks about Tom, although she took further court action in 1996, asking for more money, and reportedly accepted a further $50,000. Jonathan Berkery launched a singing career as Jon Jones and has given several interviews blaming his father for his teenage years, when he became involved in drugs. He told the *Sun*, 'I was one angry kid crying out for a father.'

The media decided it signalled an imminent divorce when Tom bought Linda a house in South Wales. She had been spending more time there, wanting to be with her family after her mother, Vi, died in the summer of 1987. She had forgotten how much she missed her sister Roslyn. Her brother-in-law, Tony Thorne, would look after her new home, Llwynddu House, on the outskirts of Welsh St Donats, a village twelve miles south of Treforest.

Linda, publicly at least, has always been unswerving in her support for Tom over the Berkery affair. She was quoted in the newspapers as saying, 'Tom has told me he was never with her and I believe him absolutely. It is ludicrous to suggest I want a divorce. There will be no divorce. That is for the record. I don't know about any tests. I prefer to take the word of my husband.'

# 18

# YOU CAN LEAVE
# YOUR HAT ON

Making Tom Jones cool didn't happen overnight. 'Kiss' had been a positive and unexpected start, but 'Move Closer' was bordering on cheesy. A musical based on *Matador* finally made it to the West End stage in 1991, but initial discussions about Tom playing the lead came to nothing and the title role was taken by John Barrowman. The production closed after three months. Tom, meanwhile, still had to contend with knickers on stage, despite a plea to fans asking them not to continue the practice. He started to ignore those that were thrown, letting the panties stay on the floor instead of picking them up and wiping the sweat off his face.

His credibility was improved, however, by his association with Van Morrison, who had been a contemporary of Tom's in the sixties, but had managed the leap from pop star to cool, critically acclaimed artist. He had long ago achieved what Tom was now looking to do. They had remained friends from the time, twenty-five years before, when Van was the singer with the Irish band Them and had toured the country with Tom.

Van had called him when they were both in London to talk about a track called 'Carrying a Torch', which he specifically wanted Tom to hear. Van told him, 'I've recorded it myself, but

211

when I listen to it back, it sounds like a Tom Jones record to me.' Tom loved the song, as well as three others that Van had recently written. 'He said if I wanted to record them to go ahead, but I wanted him to be part of it, because he is a very personal song-writer. I wanted him to like them.'

Tom decided to call his new album *Carrying a Torch*. It was his first major recording since he had undergone an operation to remove nodules on his vocal chords. He hadn't been following the advice of Frank Sinatra, all those years ago, to treat his voice more kindly, as closely as he should have done. He had been very worried about the procedure: 'My doctor told me I was doing too many shows back to back – I was doing two a night. I had to have them removed and I was worried that I would lose my voice. I didn't know if I would sing again. And I didn't know if it would change my voice. Thank God, my voice was OK. In fact, I think it took years off it.'

*Carrying a Torch* featured all four of Van's songs, but wasn't the break-out record it perhaps deserved to be, despite some airplay on VH1. *Rolling Stone* magazine thought the title track had the makings of a classic, with a 'stately chorus and shining verses'. Mark, in a rare interview, praised their collaboration: 'The words that Van Morrison writes and the way that Tom Jones can portray them and sing them is a perfect marriage.' Tom was pleased with the songs, but felt that the distribution left something to be desired. Disappointingly, it failed to secure a proper release in the US.

The album did enhance Tom's profile when the BBC's flag-ship arts programme, *Omnibus*, devoted a programme to him. He explained that he wanted to feel he was still competing and wasn't just an 'oldie but goody'. He wanted the public to view *Carrying a Torch* as a contemporary album.

Despite disappointing sales, Mark's long-term plan to make Tom cooler was gradually coming into play. Tom never took himself too seriously, and his ability to have a sense of humour about his image became an asset as he tried to become more relevant to a younger audience. He started accepting fashionable charity work, which ensured maximum coverage for artists while associating them with good causes.

For many, the highlight of the 1991 Comic Relief special was 'The Battle of the Sex Gods' between Tom and Theophilus P. Wildebeeste, the outrageous character created by the comedian Lenny Henry. He was loosely based on the singer Teddy Pendergrass, but had elements of Tom and Barry White thrown into the mix. Tom and Lenny both wore open shirts, revealing hairy chests with huge silver 'T' medallions. Instead of the familiar red nose, they wore a large fluorescent scarlet codpiece. The sing-off was 'Can't Get Enough', the 1974 debut hit for the supergroup Bad Company. Tom rocked the love machine off the stage and Theophilus needed to lie down after doing his back in. Tom still made a pelvic thrust appear easy, although he was looking a bit chunky in his leather trousers.

Comic Relief was popular, but Glastonbury was much cooler. The organisers of the festival were in touch to suggest an appearance at the 1992 event. Tom observed, 'All I need is an invitation.' Nowadays, the Glastonbury Festival is famous for the reinvention of iconic performers. Dolly Parton, for instance, was the star turn for many at the 2014 event. For once, the weather was glorious in 1992, with none of the traditional Glasto mud. Tom was simply billed as a surprise guest on the Pyramid Stage, but everyone knew it was going to be him. He recalled, 'Van Morrison was on before me and he was complaining that the crowd was falling asleep. When I went on, kids seemed to arrive from everywhere and there was a banner that read "Tom Fucking Jones". That was really something.'

The crowd of 70,000 probably were little more than curious to see a man they perceived as a relic from a bygone age, but he effortlessly got them singing along to 'Kiss', 'It's Not Unusual', and his other famous songs – the hallmark of a successful Festival set. He even managed to send himself up with his old 'time to take my jacket off, because it's so hot' routine. Afterwards, he told off a BBC reporter who suggested he brought middle-aged respectability to the event. He said, 'Middle aged but not respectable. I have never thought of myself as respectable.'

Tom's performance proved such a success, he featured in the *Daily Telegraph*'s 2014 list of the 100 best Glastonbury performances ever: 'Tom Jones's first appearance instituted the tradition of a Sunday slot for glitzier old school entertainers and proved in the process that Vegas had taught him to work any crowd with impeccable, likeable charm.'

Comic Relief and Glastonbury were also part of a conscious attempt to reconnect with British audiences, which had been practically ignored by Tom for more than ten years after he moved to the US. It was a good moment to return to TV. *Tom Jones: The Right Time* was a clever idea. It was a six-part series, made by Central Television, which showed off Tom's versatility across every musical genre. It was a brief cruise around the world of music, with Tom steering the ship.

In the first show, entitled pop music, his guests were the alternative rock band EMF, Shakespears Sister and Erasure – all big chart acts that year. This was a million miles from *This Is Tom Jones*. That show may have been pivotal in making his career in the US, but easygoing entertainment with Bob Hope and company was not the direction he wanted to take now. *The Right*

*Time* made its way onto the VH1 channel, something his original series was never likely to do.

When Tom performed EMF's biggest hit 'Unbelievable', one of the band jumped onto his back. He told the *Boston Globe*, 'The first time he did it, I almost threw him into the audience. You're on stage and somebody's on you – the first thing to do is to get him off. I wanted to strangle him. But then I realised it was a good bit of fun. The next take, I was ready for it.'

EMF took an almost childlike delight in appearing with Tom and told him that it was the 'apex' of their career when they heard he had sung their hit in Las Vegas. Their performance together was dynamic and slightly mad, but proved that Tom could sing with the 'kids', as he called them. Crucially, he didn't have an old voice.

Joe Cocker, a guest on his original TV series, joined him on the rhythm and blues episode, but the highlight for many was an entire show devoted to Stevie Wonder – also a memorable guest from more than twenty years ago. Tom called him a 'genius' and Stevie responded by singing snatches from 'What's New Pussycat?', 'It's Not Unusual' and a melancholy verse or two of 'My Mother's Eyes', an old favourite of Tom's. Their duet on 'Superstition' was good, but Tom's rendition of 'Heaven Help Us All' – a Stevie song that perfectly suited Tom's affinity with gospel music – was even better.

Tom probably reached a wider audience with a guest 'appearance' on the hugely popular American cartoon series *The Simpsons*. In the episode entitled 'Marge Gets a Job', Marge takes a job at the power plant, and Mr Burns kidnaps Tom in an evil plot to seduce her. Burns has a change of heart when Homer stands up for his wife. The final scene features a chained-up Tom serenading the couple with 'It's Not Unusual'. The cast thought

Tom was fun to work with; he responded good-naturedly that he found the experience 'incredible'.

Tom moved on from there to guest in an equally popular show, *The Fresh Prince of Bel-Air*, which starred Will Smith before he became one of the world's biggest movie stars. Tom was cast as a guardian angel to Will's best friend, Carlton Banks, played by Alfonso Ribeiro. Carlton's 'Tom dance' to 'It's Not Unusual' and their subsequent duet were highlights of the season.

Tom's image had almost become an anti-image: keep nothing back from the public and be open to any question. He was an accessible star, whether it was in the roles he took or the interviews he gave. The famous shock jock Howard Stern, for instance, wanted to ask Tom about the size of his penis. Howard had plenty to say on the subject, but, thankfully, Tom had nothing to add. Tom's attitude was simple: 'You don't have to have a moody bloody thing going or be aloof. If you have a basic talent and you do it, people can see it and hear it. I don't have to go thinking about my image.'

These guest-starring roles and his adoption of ironic self-effacement were demonstrating that Tom was climbing down from his ivory penthouse in Las Vegas. He seemed forever to be on the brink of a successful comeback. The million-dollar cheques that still found their way into his bank account suggested he wasn't exactly on skid row, though.

The most vital ingredient in any revival, however, remained his voice. The momentum would stall if he began to decline vocally. On tour in the States, the panty count showed signs of slowing down. Tom was now trying to reach young men who were discovering his music for the first time and didn't just remember him as someone their mums used to like.

TOP LEFT: One of the two most significant liaisons Tom has had outside his marriage was with Mary Wilson of The Supremes, pictured with him at a backstage party after he opened at Caesars Palace in April 1971.

TOP RIGHT: The other was with Miss World, Marjorie Wallace, with whom he enjoyed a famous kiss in Barbados in February 1974.

BOTTOM: The whole world knew that Tom and Marji were more than chest good friends.

Tom was worried about the well-being of Marjorie Wallace when he celebrated his thirty-fourth birthday in 1974. Celebrity friends Joan Rivers, Sonny Bono, Dionne Warwick, Debbie Reynolds and Liberace helped to cheer him up.

When a fan kissed Tom Jones, she got her money's worth. This woman received a smacker at a Paris concert in 1979 that she would remember for the rest of her life.

Not every couple gets to have Tom Jones sing at their wedding. His son Mark and Mark's new wife Donna were the lucky bride and groom when they married in March 1982.

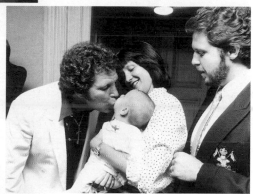

Tom is hugely proud of his family and showed off his new grandson Alexander, with Donna and Mark, when he visited Britain in September 1983. He was a granddad at forty-three.

Tom with Freda Woodward, the mother he adored.

TOP: Tom and his best friend Dai Perry were like brothers, growing up together in the same street in Treforest. Tom was thrilled when his pal became his bodyguard in the 1970s. Dai was someone to share those champagne moments with, as well as keep a watchful eye on things.

BOTTOM: They were still best buddies twenty years later, when Dai visited from his home in South Wales. The boys pose in front of the beautiful Utah landscape on a visit to the Snowbird resort near Salt Lake City in 1993.

Tom made sure he had time for his genuine fans, especially those, like Glenna Stone, who would plan their whole year around his tours. She saw him in concert hundreds of times and would always give him a box of his favourite After Eight mints.

The distinguished-looking Don Archell, a former singer, has been Tom's loyal and well-liked personal assistant for more than twenty years.

After Dai Perry died in 1999, Tom was a great support to his friend's partner, Glynis McKenna, and was pleased to see her when she visited Las Vegas later that year.

Robbie Williams described performing alongside Tom at the 1998 Brits as the best five minutes eleven seconds of his life.

Tom and Cerys Matthews may have been singing 'Baby, It's Cold Outside', but the chemistry between the pair at a concert at the London Docklands Arena in December 1999 was sizzling hot.

*The four faces of Tom ...*

TOP LEFT: The rugged look of the sixties. Everything is a little bit wonky.

TOP RIGHT: New nose and teeth for the Vegas years ... a perfect eighties look.

BOTTOM LEFT: Dye me a river – collecting a Brit Award in 2003.

BOTTOM RIGHT: A silver fox, aged seventy-three, in November 2013.

Cool Alliances: The fashionable artists of the day love being seen with Tom. After singing together at London's 100 Club in May 2012, he left happily hand in hand with fellow judge on *The Voice*, Jessie J.

Going in for the kiss …
New judge on *The Voice*,
Rita Ora, met with Tom's approval
at the show's London launch in
January 2015. That old Welsh
magic is still there.

The critics were beginning to realise that Tom bridged the years in a way that other great stars did not. Michael Saunders summed it up in the *Boston Globe*, when he reviewed Tom's concert at the South Shore Music Circus in August 1993, 'Tom Jones is the music missing link between eras.'

He concluded, 'He capped the night with his cover of Prince's "Kiss", the song that awakened interest among younger listeners. It was authentically definitely funky, and punctuated with a crotch grab far more substantial than Michael Jackson's, and in an entirely different league than Madonna's.'

Tom signed with the Interscope record label to make a new album. Interscope had made its name with urban artists, but was diversifying into other areas of music. Tom was joining Snoop Dogg and Dr Dre on the roster, which again added to his credibility in a younger marketplace.

Tom was desperate for it to be a success. He decided to call the album, somewhat clunkily, *The Lead and How to Swing It*, a play on the familiar expression 'swinging the lead', which was one of his father's favourites and meant to shirk or skive. Tom surrounded himself with some of the best current talent, including The Verve's producer Martin Glover and Teddy Riley, who worked on the Michael Jackson album *Dangerous*. He also involved more established names, like Jeff Lynne from ELO and Trevor Horn, who had been responsible for many of the hits of Frankie Goes to Hollywood and Pet Shop Boys.

The stand-out track was another duet, this time with the critically acclaimed singer-songwriter Tori Amos on the Diane Warren song 'I Wanna Get Back with You', in which her gentle ethereal vocal contrasted effectively with Tom's soulful growl. One critic said, 'Jones sounds like Otis Redding's ghost in a remarkable performance', which would have given him huge pleasure. All the power and passion was still there.

With the benefit of hindsight, this should have been the lead single from the album and not an afterthought released when no one was interested. Instead, 'If I Only Knew', produced by Horn, was strongly sung and a top twenty hit, but ultimately forgettable. Tom Jones rapping was a step too far for many.

Perhaps the album was too conspicuously trendy, because, despite encouraging reviews, the sales were ultimately disappointing. The *Washington Post* noted, a little harshly, 'The album's success may well hinge on whether people young enough to know the meaning of phrases like "chill in the crib" will smile or cringe when they hear Grandpa Jones utter them.' *The Lead and How to Swing It* failed to make the top fifty in the UK, although it was number one in Finland.

Tom still dreamed of that elusive hit album, but all he could do was be patient and continue to be relevant. He sang the plaintive 'Tennessee Waltz' on The Chieftains' album *The Long Black Veil* and hosted the 1995 American Music Awards, alongside Queen Latifah and country star Lorrie Morgan. Best of all, he played a cameo role in Tim Burton's comedy sci-fi movie *Mars Attacks!*

Tom had been performing at the MGM Grand in Las Vegas when the director, a long-time fan, came backstage and asked him to do it. Burton explained, 'You feel as though he'd deal with any situation with the same kind of strength, whether it was a concert or a Martian invasion. He'd just get in there and go for it.'

Tom played himself, singing 'It's Not Unusual', of course, when Martians invade the Las Vegas casino where he is performing. He turns around and suddenly his three backing singers are transformed into little green figures. He has to lead a small group of survivors to safety, flying out from a small airfield near the city. For the closing scene, Tom is on a cliff-top, with an eagle perched on his arm, singing a reprise of 'It's Not Unusual' – then the credits roll. It was very funny, utterly camp and perfectly in keeping with Tom's developing flair for self-parody.

Tom was seriously considering moving back to the UK permanently in the mid-nineties. Mark and Donna made the move in 1995, when they bought a mansion in Henley-on-Thames, so their children could be educated in Britain. Alexander, who had the second name John, like his grandfather and great-grandfather before him, was now twelve and ready for senior school.

While they still owned the house in Welsh St Donats, Linda, conversely, was spending more time in the US. She had tired of life in South Wales, which proved just as monotonous as Los Angeles but with more rain. They eventually sold Llwynddu for £650,000. Many had assumed that the house was a symbol of marriage problems, especially as its purchase seemed to coincide with Tom's paternity case. If there had been any hiccups, they were now resolved.

Occasionally, Linda showed up on tour. In Atlantic City, for instance, she went shopping with a $1,000 bill Tom had given her to buy whatever she wanted that afternoon while he conducted a stream of interviews. Shopping, it seemed, was an acceptable way to spend money; gambling was not.

Tom recorded the follow-up to *The Lead and How to Swing It* at the world-famous Hit Factory studios in Manhattan at the end of 1996. He wanted to move away from the more electro-pop sounds of his first Interscope album and include more musicians in the studio, evoking the live atmosphere for which he was so famous. The sessions were produced by the highly respected musician Steve Jordan, who had begun a long career as the drummer in Stevie Wonder's backing band and subsequently worked with Keith Richards and The Blues Brothers.

Together, he and Tom adapted some twenty songs with a mainly soul feel, including songs by Otis Redding, Wilson Pickett and the George Jones country ballad 'He Stopped Loving Her Today', a song made for a mighty vocal. Tom's interesting take on the latter was that country and soul could be very close, thereby revealing the secret of his classic songs like 'Green, Green Grass of Home' and 'I'll Never Fall in Love Again' – they were basically country songs that he sang as a soul singer. That was his edge.

Excited by the recording sessions, Tom sent twenty songs to the record company with a view to picking the best twelve to go on the as yet untitled album. Interscope didn't like the product, being unable to visualise a market for the material. They couldn't identify a single. It was hugely disappointing and the songs from New York have never been released. Unsurprisingly, Tom left Interscope.

He needed to regroup, continue touring, take part in charity singles like 'Perfect Day' and wait for his next opportunity. He was one of twenty-seven singers who performed on the BBC Children in Need 1997 single 'Perfect Day'. An all-star version of the Lou Reed song, it featured the composer himself, as well as Bono, Elton John, David Bowie and Tammy Wynette. Tom sang the line 'You're going to reap just what you sow' and put more emotion into his segment than the rest of the cast combined.

Tom always seemed to have so many projects on the go that it was impossible to predict which one might trigger new momentum. Appearing on *The Last Resort* had been one such unexpected event. Now it was the turn of a low-budget British film called *The Full Monty*. Anne Dudley, from The Art of Noise, had been commissioned to write the score and she wanted to use the Randy Newman song 'You Can Leave Your Hat On' for the pivotal last scene.

The film tells the story of six unemployed men in Sheffield who decide to cure their financial woes by forming an all-male striptease act. The difference between them and other performers, like the Chippendales, was that they would go 'the full monty' and take every stitch off. The movie ends with the six men stripping off until all they have left on is their hats, which they throw into the air. It is a joyful, uplifting scene.

Originally, Anne was going to use the Joe Cocker version of 'You Can Leave Your Hat On' from 1986, but the director decided it sounded too serious. A more fun, tongue-in-cheek interpretation from Tom Jones would strike exactly the right note.

She phoned Tom and asked him to do it, explaining that she was working with a shoestring budget. The whole film was being made for $3.5 million – petty cash for most movies. Tom recorded the song in an afternoon while he was on tour around the UK.

The film was an astonishing success all over the world, taking more than $250 million at the box office – a producer's dream. As a result, thousands of people left cinemas pretending to be Tom Jones singing 'You Can Leave Your Hat On'. He recalled, 'Who knew that this film would do what it did? It was supposed to be a low-budget, small British film, but it became a world-wide smash, so I was thrilled to be part of it.'

Ironically, considering the number of ill-judged or disappointing forays into acting that Tom has made, here was a film he could have appeared in and he wouldn't have had to play himself. The publicity he received from his association with it was as significant as singing *What's New Pussycat?* had been thirty years previously. While it wasn't the title track, his song was effectively the film's theme tune.

Tom was invited to sing it at the 1998 Brit Awards at Earls Court. More significantly, he was asked to duet with Robbie Williams, who, at the time, was among the coolest young pop acts in the UK. Two months earlier, the song 'Angels' had entered the charts for the first time and transformed Robbie's career.

Robbie Williams was just one of the younger generation of stars who regarded Tom as a musical hero. He used to study old footage from the sixties and seventies of Tom performing his hits and try to copy him. He always loved 'Delilah', believing it to be the all-time best song to get you out of bed on a Sunday morning when suffering from a Saturday night hangover. The only problem for Robbie was that he had supported Port Vale Football Club all his life and 'Delilah' was always the song sung on the terraces by arch-rivals Stoke City.

When Robbie finally appeared on stage with his hero, it was as if they had been singing together for years. Their duet of songs from *The Full Monty* was the best thing to have happened to that tired awards show in years. Robbie pranced about the stage in black leather and Cuban heels – an outfit remarkably similar to the one Tom had worn on *The Last Resort* when he first sang 'Kiss' on TV.

Robbie was having the time of his life. He began with a version of the Cockney Rebel seventies classic 'Make Me Smile (Come Up and See Me)'. Then Tom arrived to sing 'You Can Leave Your Hat On', which featured Robbie dancing like a clockwork toy that had been overwound. It was a tongue-in-cheek tour de force from a master showman. One reviewer described it as a bull being tormented by a mosquito. They finished with 'Land of a Thousand Dances', which Tom had been performing for more than thirty years. He could have sung it in his sleep, but even the record executives sitting smugly at their tables stood up to dance and applaud.

Tom gave Robbie substance and in return Robbie made Tom appear up to the minute. It did wonders for Robbie's confidence when Tom told him he was a great singer. After the show, Robbie declared, 'Those five minutes eleven seconds on stage with Tom Jones were the happiest of my life.' The Brits proved once and for all that Tom Jones really was cool. The night also set in motion the album that would become the most successful of Tom's entire career.

# 19

# MY BEST FRIEND'S FUNERAL

Whenever Tom saw Dai Perry, it was as if they still lived a few doors away from each other. Dai's partner, Glynis McKenna, who always called him Dave, loved watching the two friends enjoy one another's company. 'It would be just like they had seen each other only last night. They would pick up where they had left off. Tom has got a marvellous memory and he dredged names up and Dave would tell him how they were going on. It might be somebody from primary school days and Tom would say, "Do you ever see so and so?" and Dave could tell him the last time he saw them. It was lovely to see them together. A lot of the conversation went over my head because I wasn't around in those days, but it was fascinating listening to them. They were like two schoolboys together.'

The two men kept in close touch after the incident in Caracas. Tom used to phone every week or two from the US and, when he was able to set foot in the UK, he always made sure he visited Dai or invited him to meet up in London. Dai's youngest daughter Gemma remembers, as a little girl, getting up from bed because she heard voices downstairs. She walked down to the lounge and there was Tom Jones sitting on the settee: 'I was just like, "Oh." In those days, it was just like "Oh, him again." Thinking about it now, when I'm older, it was a big thing.'

Tom had bought the house in Lower Alma Terrace for Dai after he married his second wife, Kay. It was just around the corner from Laura Street. Tom has a reputation for being less than generous, but that wasn't the case where his best friends were concerned. He always looked after Dai. When they met up, he would give him a brown envelope containing £500. Nothing was said. It was just a nod between pals, and the right amount not to cause embarrassment.

Tom also paid for Dai's regular trips to the US, where he would spend his holidays in Las Vegas or Los Angeles. In the early days, before they divorced, he took Kay. After his divorce, he travelled with Glynis, who was Brian Blackler's cousin.

Glynis had already met Tom. She had walked into the lounge one day and there were Tom and Mark, sitting with Dai, watching a rugby match on television. It was all so perfectly normal, she never had the chance to be star-struck.

The first time she travelled with Dai to see Tom was in 1993, when they stayed in Las Vegas, where he was appearing at Bally's, which was formerly the MGM Grand Hotel and Casino. Tom played fourteen nights there, before they moved on to the Snowbird resort near Salt Lake City and then to Denver, where he was performing at the famous Fiddler's Green Amphitheatre. It gave Glynis a glimpse into Tom's nomadic yet luxurious lifestyle.

They didn't stay in his suite, because Tom had a daily routine far removed from a normal person's. He was getting up in the late afternoon, as Glynis was finishing sunbathing. 'He slept through the day and he would be up all night. When he came off stage, he would have a shower and change and then if anybody had come backstage to visit with him, he would have a drink and be sociable. Then we would go and eat, usually at one of the restaurants in the hotel. We used to sit at a big round table just talking and reminiscing. Sometimes there would be a lounge show Tom wanted to see, so we would go and watch that. I don't think Tom knows what time it is in Las Vegas.

'I like the sun, so sometimes when we had eaten and Tom, Dave and Lloyd Greenfield were chatting, I would say, "I'll leave you to it. I'm going up." And they would walk me to the lift and then go back and have a few bevvies.'

After twenty-five years in Las Vegas, Tom had a daily, or more precisely nightly, routine that worked for him. He was over fifty now and long ago realised he needed to look after himself if he was going to maintain the high standards he had set himself as a young man. Glynis observes, 'He is disciplined. He got up at 4ish and exercised. Then he would breakfast – cereal and fruit – but would have nothing more before the show. He would never drink before a show.

'At dinner he would eat anything, but he always chose a nice wine. He is quite a connoisseur of wine. He would finish with a brandy and a cigar. Then out came the champagne.' He was never ostentatious about his wealth or fame – he wasn't a click your fingers at the waiter sort of star.

Dai and Glynis would either watch a show from a booth or stand at the side of the stage. The entertainment always began with a comedian, who would have the audience roaring with laughter – except for the visitors from Wales, who found the American sense of humour passed them by. Tom would sing at least twenty songs and come back and do three or more for an encore. Glynis recalls, 'As soon as he sang "Kiss", the audience knew they weren't going to get any more.' Her favourite from his show at the time was 'Walking in Memphis'. The song, a big hit for Cher, has often featured in Tom's stage act and he sang it during the final of the 2014 series of *The Voice*.

One night, Glynis turned round and saw Priscilla Presley sitting behind them, watching the show. On another, Liza Minnelli, who was in her own show further down the strip, came backstage and then joined them for dinner. 'She was really bubbly and friendly,' recalls Glynis. It was all a long way from Treforest.

The next time Glynis travelled with Dai to the US was when Tom was appearing in Atlantic City in 1995. She loved the hotel there, because it was right on the beach. Tom and Dai would put their bathers on, travel down in the lift and then walk across for a swim and a mess about in the sea – much to the surprise of other guests, who didn't expect to see Tom Jones in the surf.

Tom took the attentions of people desperate to have a picture with him or get an autograph with good grace. Glynis never saw him refuse a photograph, even if he was walking through the casino in the small hours of the morning. She asked Tom if the fans ever got on his nerves. 'No,' he replied, 'because when they stop asking me, I know I'm on my way down.'

One of the things that Tom liked about Dai and Glynis was that they didn't abuse his hospitality. If Glynis needed to phone home, she would do it from the lobby and not from the room, where it would be charged to his bill. Similarly, when she bought small items, like suncream, she would pay cash. Dai never gambled and hated walking past the slot machines and seeing people turning good money into bad.

They moved on from Atlantic City to New York and then Knoxville, Tennessee and Myrtle Beach, a resort in South Carolina. In New York, Tom took them to the renowned Harry

Cipriani restaurant on Fifth Avenue near Central Park. Glynis turned to Dai and said, 'Doesn't that look like Danny DeVito over there?'

Tom piped up, 'It is Danny DeVito. Watch now, he'll ask me for a cigar.'

They had acted together in *Mars Attacks!* and got along famously. Sure enough, Danny came bustling over and asked for a cigar, but had no luck. Tom only had the one in his pocket and he was saving it for himself.

While Linda liked Atlantic City, she didn't travel with Tom on this trip. He always made sure a ticket was bought for her wherever he was going, however, in case she changed her mind at the last minute and said, 'I'm coming.'

The third time Glynis and Dai went on holiday to the US, Tom and Linda were moving house. They had decided that the home on Copa De Oro Road was too large for them, especially as Mark and his family were now based primarily in England. Linda was also becoming more concerned about security and her personal safety, and wanted to move to a property where there was more protection. She had never been entirely happy there, initially struggling with feeling homesick and then feeling both isolated and exposed at the same time. It was years before Tom met his next-door neighbour, a lawyer, and then it was at an awards ceremony in LA and not over the garden fence.

Tom once amusingly remarked that the house, which had always been known as Dean Martin's, would only become Tom Jones' when he moved. He sold it to the actor Nicolas Cage for a reported $6.5 million and then proceeded to spend $2.7 million on a more modest five-bedroom home in a gated community off Mulholland Drive, not far from Freda and Sheila. The refurbishment and interior design were something Linda was looking forward to. Best of all, their new home had spectacular views across the San Fernando Valley. One thing the new home was missing was their famous red phone box. They accidentally left it behind.

Glynis and Dai were expecting to stay with the Joneses when they arrived in August 1998, but the new house wasn't ready yet, with many belongings still in boxes, so they stayed at an apartment in Santa Monica. In any case, Tom wasn't there at first. He was in Dublin, filming a small role in *Agnes Browne*, which starred Anjelica Huston as the title character. Huston plays a salt-of-the-earth mother of seven, whose secret passion is Tom Jones. Near the end of the film, her dreams are fulfilled when Tom pops up to serenade her with 'She's a Lady' – at least it wasn't 'It's Not Unusual' again.

The film was based on the book *The Mammy* by the Irish writer and comedian Brendan O'Carroll. He later began playing the part himself in *Mrs Brown's Boys*, one of the biggest television comedy hits of recent years. In 2014, the character Agnes returned to the silver screen in *Mrs Brown's Boys D'Movie*.

Tom was concerned about playing a younger version of himself. 'I was slightly nervous having to look as I did in 1967, but Anjelica told me not to worry as it was a "surreal situation".'

Linda, meanwhile, was happy to play host to Dai and Glynis in Los Angeles. Tom had arranged for them to have a driver, Kyle, during their visit, and he phoned ahead from the limo to tell Linda they would be arriving in five minutes, so she could be waiting outside to greet them. It was the first time Glynis had met her: 'I was a bit in awe of meeting her, but there she was in a long T-shirt and pumps, and, like me, her roots needed doing.

'We had been to Hollywood Boulevard earlier and bought loads of cheap T-shirts for the kids in our street back home. They were only $7 each. I told Dave that we should leave them in the car, because I didn't want her to think we were cheapskates. But he took them in to show her and said, "Look, Linda." And she told us that she liked to go to the thrift shops. She said, "Nobody knows who I am, so I can just browse." She was so down to earth. She made us lunch and we sat around a beautiful marble kitchen table that was as big as the lounge in our house.'

They also went to see Freda and Sheila at their home, which was just across from Barry Manilow's mansion. Freda was confined to bed, having become progressively weaker in the past couple of years after being diagnosed with breast cancer. She had always loved the climate in California, but hankered to spend her final years back in South Wales. Sadly, now eighty-four, she was too ill to make the journey. Her daughter Sheila became her full-time carer, even though Tom would have provided the best help money could buy for his mum.

Tom flew into Las Vegas after his commitments in Dublin and they spent time with him before coming home. Glynis asked Tom if he had spoken to Linda since he landed and he told her his wife had rung him that night. She had been out for lunch. Then he laughed, 'My wife is the only woman I know who would take the cook out for a meal.'

The couple who looked after the house and garden had been with Tom and Linda for years and they were her friends. Linda doesn't have any superficial showbiz friends and prefers the company of these ordinary people, whom she knows and likes. Glynis observes, 'Dai knew them. They are good people and they are loyal and that speaks volumes.'

They flew home to the UK happily unaware that it would be Dai's last visit.

'Tell me it's not true,' said Tom when Glynis came to the phone.

'I wish I could,' she replied, her voice catching in her throat.

Dai Perry, Tom's best friend all his life, had been found dead on the mountainside behind Treforest. It was January 1999, and he was just fifty-eight. He had died a morning walk away from Laura Street. Tom was devastated by the loss of a man he loved as a brother.

Glynis knew there was something wrong when she arrived home from work and Dai wasn't there. Every morning he would take Cassie, a neighbour's gun dog, for a walk up the mountain, so she dashed across the road to see if the dog was there. She was, and the neighbour told her that she had accidentally shut Cassie in the lounge, so Dai must have set off by himself when he didn't see her in the hallway.

Glynis ran back and discovered that his walking clothes and the binoculars that always hung round his neck were missing. Her last hope was that he was with Tom. Sometimes, out of the blue, Tom would show up at the house and take Dai off on a trip to London, but she knew he would have changed first. She decided to go and look for him, but when she opened the front door a police car had pulled up outside the house. Dai, who'd had a heart bypass operation four years earlier, had just keeled over while he was on his walk. He had been found by the local farmer.

Tom listened while Glynis told him what had happened. He then rang a couple of times a day to make sure she was all right and to find out how the arrangements for the funeral were progressing. He told her to keep her chin up, but was obviously very upset himself. She discovered that Lloyd Greenfield, Tom's great ally and friend for thirty years, had died in New York five days before Dai.

When Tom rang on the Sunday night, the day before he was flying in, Glynis asked him if he wanted to say 'ta-ra' to Dave in the Chapel of Rest. Tom said that he did. She recalls, 'I rang the undertaker and told him that a friend of Dave's was coming in the morning to see him before he was moved. The carpenters who were working there were just having their tea break, when a people carrier with tinted windows drew up and out stepped Tom. The undertaker told me afterwards they nearly choked on their sandwiches.'

After he had said his goodbye, Tom, who had Mark with him that day, went round to comfort Dai's mother, Elsie, who still lived in Laura Street. Then he went to the house in Lower Alma Terrace to see Glynis and set off for the funeral. It was the same house he had bought for Dai and his second wife Kay all those years ago. Glynis will never forget it: 'He just looked at me and he burst into tears and I did. And we were just holding each other and everybody just disappeared around us and left us.'

Then it was time for the funeral at the nearby chapel. Tom travelled in the car with Glynis, her son David from her first marriage, and Dai's daughters, Nicola and Gemma. A local councillor had arranged for them to have a police escort and in Treforest another policeman stopped the traffic to let them pass – something Dai would have loved.

At the chapel, Tom sat between Gemma and Glynis and 'sang his heart out', especially when it was time for his favourite hymn, 'The Old Rugged Cross'. Glynis recalls, 'That's the one he sang the loudest. You could tell by the tremor in his voice that he was finding it hard, but he kept going.' He had to lend Gemma, who was fifteen, a hankie to dry her eyes.

Afterwards, they went to the graveside for the burial and Cassie the dog sat patiently between Glynis and Tom while the vicar gave the blessing. On the way back to the cars, it was more like a wedding, with photographers taking pictures of Tom and Dai's family. They tried to take pictures of Tom and Glynis at the wake at the Wood Road, but she refused.

Tom stayed late at the club and made sure he spoke to everyone. He sat on a sofa next to Gemma, who told him, 'You smell like my dad.' They both used the same cologne, called Secret of Venus by Weil. He danced with her to the Aqua hit 'Doctor Jones', which made them both laugh. He danced with Glynis as well, to a song more fitting to end the saddest of days – 'Green, Green Grass of Home'.

# 20

# RELOADING

The inspired pairing of Tom and Robbie at the 1998 Brit Awards didn't lead directly to *Reload*. The publicity helped the public accept an album of duets as a good idea, but the impetus initially came from a satirical record called 'The Ballad of Tom Jones', which was an unexpected hit that year.

By a strange twist of fate, the song was written by a musician whose real name was Tommy Scott. He was the lead vocalist with Space, an indie band from Liverpool. They had made the charts a couple of years before with 'Female of the Species', a track Tom liked and included in his stage shows. Tommy had been inspired when he saw Tom in concert in Manchester, performing his song: 'All the housewives were screaming for Tom – but no one had a clue who I was.'

'The Ballad of Tom Jones' was a duet sung by Tommy Scott and the husky-voiced Welsh singer Cerys Matthews, whose band Catatonia were at the forefront of Britpop in the nineties, with hits including 'Mulder and Scully' and 'Road Rage'. Tommy and Cerys play a squabbling couple who stop short of murdering one another when they start listening to *Tom Jones' Greatest Hits*. Cerys memorably sang on the chorus, 'I could never throw my knickers at you.' She was voted the sexiest woman in rock in a *Melody Maker* poll, and Tom would probably have had no objection if she had thrown them at him.

The song was a huge hit, supported by an atmospheric video, and made number four in the UK charts. Tommy Scott described it as his 'Frank and Nancy Sinatra thing'. Tom was flattered to have a song named after him. He commented, tongue in cheek, 'You know you're doing something right when they start recording songs about you.'

After the Brit Awards, Mark Woodward was very keen for his father to record an album of duets. He wanted to take advantage while everyone was talking about Tom and Robbie. Independently, Gut Records, the label that had released 'The Ballad of Tom Jones', had been thinking the same thing. They wanted to make a record with Tommy Scott and Tom Jones together. That was the original idea and it grew from there.

Gut had quickly built a reputation as one of the leading independent labels under the direction of a former radio plugger called Guy Holmes, who had started his own company to release 'I'm Too Sexy' by Right Said Fred. He contacted Mark at exactly the right time and an album of duets was swiftly agreed over dinner with Tom.

The only surprise was that it had taken so long for the idea to be conceived. Ten years had passed since Tom's collaboration with the trendy The Art of Noise. Clearly the concept worked, as his duet with Robbie demonstrated. Now it was a case of deciding which artists to approach. That proved to be the easy part, because there seemed to be a queue around the block of credible artists wanting to perform with Tom. There was talk of All Saints joining him for 'What's New Pussycat?', but that never materialised. It might have breathed new life into the old song, but would probably have been a step back in time and Tom was anxious to avoid that. In the end, seventeen acts made the final recording.

Robbie didn't hesitate to sign up, even though he was understandably nervous about joining The Voice in the same vocal booth. They chose to record 'Are You Gonna Go My Way', a guitar-led track by Lenny Kravitz that was proving to be one of the highlights of Tom's current stage show. Robbie revealed how he handled it: 'I thought, "I know, I'll do an impression of him", so I did and I think I pulled it off.' The first time Robbie had sung the complete song was on their initial run-through. That was the only chance he got. After they had finished, Tom announced, 'That's it, then. Shall we go to the pub?'

Robbie was on his way to becoming an international superstar, but he never achieved notable fame in the US. Tom did his best by introducing his friend as a new British star at one of his Vegas shows. Robbie stood up and took the obligatory bow, but nobody really knew who he was.

Robbie's vocal concerns about singing with Tom were echoed by some of the other sixteen guests on *Reload*. Nina Persson, the blonde pin-up singer of The Cardigans, was scared she would sound 'like a little moth' next to Tom. She need not have worried, because Tom gave her the space to sing. The result was a quirky but memorable version of the Talking Heads song 'Burning Down the House'. It set the mood for an album that would include some unexpected song choices, which sounded entirely different from the originals.

The Australian singer Natalie Imbruglia was another talented female vocalist concerned she would be overwhelmed by the power of Tom's voice. After the first take, she felt like she had been caught in the path of a hurricane, but Tom subsequently reined back to give her a chance. They sang 'Never Tear Us Apart' by INXS, a poignant tribute to the singer Michael Hutchence, who had been found dead in November 1997. Tom had become friendly with Hutchence before he died and attended his funeral in Sydney.

Other singers were not so nervous. Mick Hucknall from Simply Red joined him to update the blues classic 'Ain't That a Lot of Love'. The two men enjoyed singing together so much that they sang a series of impromptu duets at a television party in September 1999 – 'Delilah' and 'Green, Green Grass of Home' featured, as well as Mick's number one hit 'Holding Back the Years'. It was like a night from the old days in Las Vegas. Tom thought Mick was one of the few singers who had 'got the pipes'.

Another who certainly did was Van Morrison, who provided his own song, the melancholic 'Sometimes We Cry', for the album. Tim de Lisle, in the *Mail on Sunday*, noted, 'The best guest, improbably, is Van Morrison, who has the lungs to keep up with the Jones boy and the clout to keep him under control. They deliver a touching, experience-tinged version of Morrison's own ballad.' Van shared one particular characteristic with Tom that made it much easier for the two men to work together: he liked to record things in one take.

Tom had seldom been inclined to follow Van's example and write his own songs. 'Looking Out My Window', however, was one of only a handful he had composed up to that point. Tom has always been too busy singing and performing to do any writing. As a young man, he was a gregarious figure and not one to shut himself away, finding meaningful chords on his guitar. He put his emotion into words other people had written. The poorly educated youngster had long ago grown into a well-travelled, entertaining man of the world with a lifetime of experiences he could put into composing – but he chose not to. He built the house, he didn't design it.

He had written 'Looking Out My Window', a funky jazz track performed with the James Taylor Quartet, while staring at the pouring rain from behind his car windscreen in the Cromwell Road, London. The lyric is about a man wondering why his love has left him, but there is no suggestion that there was anything autobiographical in the lyric. It had originally been the B-side of 'A Minute of Your Time', one of his lesser hits from 1968.

Tom was keen to surround himself with the cream of Welsh music for the new album. He was quick to sign up Stereophonics, Cerys Matthews and James Dean Bradfield, the lead singer with Manic Street Preachers – they were the only three Welsh acts he knew. He met the boys from Stereophonics when they came to watch him in concert in Cardiff. Afterwards, they joined him for a drink and he asked them if there was any chance of them taking part. He returned the compliment by going to see them at Wembley Arena in December 1998. They went for drinks and Tom spent three and a half hours telling them stories about Elvis, having a crack in Vegas and some legendary drinking. They were spellbound. When they left, Tom told them, 'Thank God, you're going. I've run out of stories to tell you.'

Tom enjoyed their company and their music. When Mark and his family travelled to Los Angeles to spend Christmas with his mother and father, he phoned the drummer Stuart Cable to tell him that at that very moment Tom was sitting by the pool, listening to the group's first album, *Word Gets Around*. In a sad postscript, Stuart died in 2010, aged forty, at his home in Llwydcoed, a village fifteen miles north of Treforest. He had choked on his own vomit after a bout of drinking.

With Tom, Stereophonics chose to sing an old Randy Newman song that had long been forgotten. 'Mama Told Me Not to Come' had originally been written for Eric Burdon and The Animals in the sixties, but was better known as a top three hit for an American group called Three Dog Night in 1970.

Stereophonics' lead singer, Kelly Jones, explained to *Melody Maker* why they were involved: 'Anyone in our position would jump at the chance to work with Tom Jones. He's a fucking legend. I don't give a fuck if we get slagged for doing a song with Tom Jones. I couldn't care less if in some people's eyes it isn't cool.' But the album *was* cool.

James Dean Bradfield joined Tom to sing an Elvis song from the fifties. Tom doesn't do too many Elvis covers, but 'I'm Left, You're Right, She's Gone' was transformed into a slice of Manic Street Preachers rock, complete with crashing guitar chords and exhilarating vocals from both men. The song was like an encore for a high-class pub-rock gig. It would have made a terrific single, but there were many other contenders on the album.

Cerys Matthews had a reputation of being a larger-than-life character, a self-confessed hell-raiser, who liked a drink and embraced the rock 'n' roll lifestyle. She wasn't too reverential where Tom was concerned, which he liked. She told the *Sunday Mirror*, 'You can't really fault a man willing to go on stage in a flamenco catsuit. But there was no Mr Big Time Las Vegas at all, apart from the tan ... and the fact that he had more jewellery than me.'

The song they chose to perform together was 'Baby, It's Cold Outside'. Their flirtatious interpretation managed to breathe fresh life into a song that was a staple of the Christmas season.

Cerys became part of Tom's entourage and was often seen with him on nights out around London and visited him in Las Vegas.

They have kept in touch over the years and were photographed enjoying each other's company at the after-party for the 2008 Q Awards at the Shepherds Tavern in Mayfair.

These days the Catatonia concerts, when Cerys used to bounce around on stage swigging from a bottle of chardonnay, are long forgotten. She has become a respected and popular broadcaster and a leading light of modern Welsh culture.

*Reload* is Tom's most successful album. After the blaze of publicity, including *An Audience with Tom Jones*, the lead single was 'Burning Down the House', which reached a slightly disappointing number seven in the UK. The album, however, went straight to number one at the beginning of October 1999.

Reviews were mostly positive. The Glasgow *Sunday Herald* enthused, 'Unlike embarrassing has-beens who think they can put on a black polo neck, do a cover version and revitalise their sagging sales figures, Jones is producing music that is fresh, innovative, popular and even credible.' *Reload* sold more than 1.2 million copies in the UK alone and in excess of 6 million worldwide.

Not everyone was completely gushing. BBC Online called the version of Iggy Pop's 'Lust for Life' 'toe-curlingly bad'. The *NME* reviewer clearly got out of bed on the wrong side, describing Tom as 'old leather face' and calling the album 'rubbish'. Arguably, the weakest song on the album was the collaboration he did with Tommy Scott. They sang 'Sunny Afternoon' by The Kinks, one of the great songs of the sixties. It was very hard to match the original, with the idiosyncratic vocal style of Ray Davies, but again it demonstrated that Tom was a risk-taker.

The album revealed a man still prepared to take chances in a year when he became more of an establishment figure. It began with him finally being awarded an OBE at a time when honours for tax exiles weren't as frowned upon as they once were. He forgot to take a hat with him when he formally received his award from the Queen. He joked with photographers, 'I didn't bring a hat because I thought it might mess up my hair.'

The award was also the excuse the now defunct *News of the World* needed to say that OBE stood for Order of Bonking Excellence. They ran a kiss and tell from a large-breasted lap dancer, who described a thirteen-hour 'romp' with Tom, which sounded nothing like as exciting as the headline suggested.

The media continued to be obsessed with Tom as a sex symbol, even though he was in his fifty-ninth year. It didn't help that the most memorable song from *Reload*, and the one that has become a Tom standard, was his collaboration with Mousse T, entitled 'Sex Bomb'. It was the natural successor to 'Kiss'. At Donna's wise suggestion, the lyric was changed from 'I'm a sex bomb' to 'You're a sex bomb'.

Mousse T seemed the most unlikely partner for Tom on the entire album. The German-born DJ and producer had originally written the track for inclusion on his own album and had wanted Tom to be the featured artist. He explained, 'I wanted to make the track a mixture between the sounds of the '70s and those of today's music, and so we definitely wrote it for Tom to sing.'

He had positive feedback from Tom after sending him a demo, and flew to London to make the recording. Tom told him, 'I'd really love to have it on *my* album.' Despite being the fourth and last single from *Reload*, after the duets with The Cardigans, Cerys and Stereophonics, it proved to be the biggest hit, reaching number three in the charts and propelling the album back to number one.

Mousse T enjoyed his experience of working with Tom: 'We did all the vocals in forty-five minutes flat – Tom is just incredible like that. He makes you want to cry – he is so good at what he does. All you can say is, "Thanks."'

# 21

# IN SEARCH OF
# CREDIBILITY

Tom had been around longer than the Brits. When they began in 1977, as the BPI Awards, he was nominated as Best British Male, despite being in the middle of his slump. The awards that year bore no relation to the prestigious annual prize-giving of today. They were designed as music's contribution to the Queen's Silver Jubilee and celebrated the best of pop during her reign. They weren't current: The Beatles won Best British Group, Shirley Bassey took the female award and Cliff Richard won Tom's category.

Five years later, in 1982, the Brits started properly and Tom was in the wilderness, as contemporary acts, including Adam and the Ants, Soft Cell and The Police, cleaned up. He might have won if there had been a category for Best British Vegas Entertainer, but this was a celebration of the performers who were fashionable and popular in music and he was neither. *Reload* changed that. While 'Kiss' had made it acceptable to like Tom Jones again, the album revived his commercial success. It was his first number one of original recordings since *Delilah* in 1968.

Surprisingly, *Reload* wasn't named in the album category in 2000, but Tom was again a contender for Best British Male, competing against David Bowie, Van Morrison, Sting and Ian Brown, the former lead singer of The Stone Roses. They must have been one of the oldest collection of artists ever nominated, with an average age of fifty. The *Guardian* unkindly described them as 'rock wrinklies'. Tom, the oldest, won his first Brit at the age of fifty-nine.

On the night at Earls Court, Tom roared through a performance of 'Mama Told Me Not to Come' with Stereophonics that left you wondering how on earth the bland pop act Steps won Best Live Act. Later in the evening, he received his award from the comedian and writer Ben Elton. Tom, who was dressed in sober black, thanked Mark, Donna and Gut Records and all the singers and groups on the album, before saying, 'I have won a lot of awards in my career, but this tops them all.'

When he celebrated his sixtieth birthday in June 2000, he qualified for a winter weather payment from the government worth £150. He didn't bother. Not only was he celebrating in the balmy heat of a Los Angeles summer, but his wealth had also topped the £100-million barrier, a conservative estimate in the *Sunday Times* Rich List.

Tom found passing sixty easier than reaching thirty. He was nervous then that he could no longer get away with pretending to be a kid in a pop world perennially obsessed with youth. He observed, 'When you hit sixty, you stop worrying. And people tell you that you look fantastic.'

Not for the last time Tom was asked if he was going to retire. His reply was an emphatic no. He would keep going as long as his voice sounded good in the shower. To prove the point, he sold out all six shows at the Cardiff International Arena and had to add an extra date. He had embarked on a huge world tour to cash in on his resurgence. It began in Washington on Millennium Night, after President Clinton asked him to appear at the celebrations in front of the Lincoln Memorial. He sang 'It's Not Unusual', before taking the lead during the finale with 'In the Midnight Hour'. In the latter, he was accompanied by the peerless rock guitarist Slash, as ticker tape rained down on an estimated crowd of 300,000.

The set list for the tours included songs from *Reload* without the guest singers, which proved that, while it was a successful gimmick, Tom didn't really need them. Mark, perhaps influenced by the success of the millennium show, decided that his father would reach a wider audience performing outdoors. If the crowds were bigger, then more people would buy the merchandise, particularly the T-shirts with 'Sex Bomb' or 'What's New Pussycat?' written on them.

Mark had also recognised that the demographic of a Tom Jones audience was changing. The original female fans were grannies now and they were there with husbands, sons and daughters and grandchildren. Trendy youngsters, looking as if they were ready for a night clubbing, rubbed shoulders with those dressed for an evening at the opera. It didn't matter who you were, *Reload* made it OK to admit liking Tom Jones whatever your age or sex.

By the summer of 2001, Tom was performing more open-air concerts. He played a series of gigs at the great castles of Britain, including Edinburgh, Warwick and Cardiff, which was a personal highlight. Vicky Allen in *Scotland on Sunday* was impressed that his voice seemed to be getting deeper and stronger with time: 'He sings his guts up, like an old lion who has lost his bite but can still roar.' The 'old lion' kept going for more than an hour and a half and sang twenty-seven songs, with the big ballads 'A

Boy from Nowhere' and 'I'll Never Fall in Love Again' retaining all their power.

The UK was seeing so much of Tom that inevitably there were rumours that he would be moving back to the country full time and buying a house near his son's. He had quietly sold Llwynddu House at the end of 1998, so he no longer had a permanent base. The problem with returning was that Linda was becoming more of a recluse in Los Angeles. That was soon to be an even greater worry, a week after he appeared in Cardiff, when she was badly affected by the 9/11 tragedy. Unusually, Linda was with him on a European tour at the time, and they both watched the drama unfold on television. She managed to make it home to California, but that was it for her. She hasn't flown since.

As a result, she spent more time in her million-dollar cocoon, where she felt safe. It was a turning point for her and, progressively as the years went by, she began to distrust people. She hates being called a recluse, but she didn't want to socialise. When Robbie Williams, who lived in the same gated community, popped round to say hello to Tom, she stayed upstairs and had to be coaxed down for an introduction. At the time, everyone thought she was shy of meeting somebody famous again, but it wasn't that; she had simply grown nervous of others. Tom explained, 'It makes her very anxious and she has to take tranquillisers and that.'

Though Tom worried about Linda, he has always been able to separate his home life and his work. His chief concern with the latter was how to follow up the success of *Reload*. At first there was talk of another duets album, but that was abandoned in favour of seeking more credibility through an alliance with the Haitian-born hip-hop master Wyclef Jean. He was formerly one third of The Fugees, who had achieved worldwide fame with their second album, *The Score*. It featured their reworking of 'Killing Me Softly', a song Tom knew well. 'I loved what Wyclef did with "Killing Me Softly". He stripped it down and turned it into something different from the original.'

They met in the summer of 2001, at the Party in the Park in aid of the Prince's Trust, when Wyclef told Tom he featured on his third solo album, *Masquerade*. He was reworking 'What's New Pussycat?' into a new R&B number called 'Pussycat'. Perhaps Tom might like the song after all these years.

The result was quite a catchy track that used Tom as a sample, driving the rap that included the unforgettable lyric 'Hey kitty, kitty, meet me in the city' – a line Burt Bacharach and Hal David forgot to include in the original. They enjoyed some nights out and then met again in December, when they performed a slightly surreal duet of 'It's Not Unusual' at the *Top of the Pops* Awards in Manchester. Tom was impressed enough to suggest Wyclef and his writing and production partner Jerry Duplessis steer his new album, *Mr Jones*. The major difference between this and former albums was that Tom would contribute songs himself – the next step on his path to solid credibility.

Wyclef encouraged Tom to write words that were true to his own life and experiences. Tom observed, 'He started bringing all these lyrics out of me that I wouldn't ordinarily have done. Every time I came up with an interesting thought, he would write it down.' He reminisced in 'Younger Days' that it was good in '65, '66 and '67, but it was also good now – which was true.

Tom left Gut after only one album and joined Richard Branson's V2 Records label, which had successfully handled the distribution for *Reload*. Fortunately, 'Tom Jones on Virgin' wasn't a headline that saw the light of day. He posed with the tycoon for pictures in New York, where he was finishing recording the new album. Branson was enthusiastic: 'Of all the legends out there, getting Tom Jones was the only thing equal to my signing The Rolling Stones.' He also managed to include a plug for the first single from the album. He said 'Tom Jones International' was so good 'it should be a number one worldwide.'

The single was a radical change in direction for Tom. It began with Wyclef shouting 'Refugee camp' and Tom, in a quieter vocal than usual, telling everyone that he was going to 'Blow up this party with this sex bomb'. It didn't make number one worldwide – nowhere near, in fact. In the UK, it stalled at a disappointing thirty-one.

The album wasn't even that successful. Whereas reviewers loved *Reload*, this seemed a step too far for the majority. Dorian Lynskey in the *Guardian* said, 'It's not that Wyclef isn't a capable pop-rap producer, nor that Jones doesn't still have a gutsy soul voice. It's simply that the twain should never have met.' Beth Pearson in the Glasgow *Herald* scoffed, 'Wyclef has tried to mould our troubadour into a Welsh Snoop Dog.' The general feeling was that this collaboration wasn't age appropriate. The critics couldn't accept a sixty-one-year-old man calling himself TJ and asking the house to bring it down. Tom did admit to some difficulty picking up the language of hip-hop: he said, 'Get the groove' to pick up the rhythm in the recording studio and nobody knew what he meant; Wyclef declared, 'Lay the beats' and they all nodded enthusiastically.

Commercially, the album was a flop, peaking at number thirty-six in the UK and performing equally badly in other countries. Tom said he was proud of it, even it didn't sell a single copy. It didn't sell many. Looking back on that failure, Tom believes one problem was that his core audience is white. If you go to a Tom Jones concert, particularly in Las Vegas, there are relatively few young black fans. His drummer, Herman Matthews, had a more concise reason for the album's failure when he mentioned it a few years later. He said, 'That was a pile of crap.'

While confirmation that he was going to be acknowledged at the 2003 Brit Awards for his outstanding contribution to music was a welcome tonic, Tom was left devastated when his mother Freda died after a series of strokes in February. She was eighty-seven and had been incapacitated by cancer for several years. He told her about his award before she died and she was, he said, very pleased: 'I could see she wasn't going to last long, but when it happens it is still a terrible shock.' He immediately cancelled a raft of concerts. His cousin Jean said simply, 'Freda was every-thing to Tom.' She was buried next to her husband in Los Angeles, so Tom and Sheila could spend quiet time at their parents' graves whenever they wanted.

He travelled to London to attend the Brits at Earls Court after the funeral. Robbie Williams sent a gracious message by video link, in which he said, 'I do believe that the duet with you at the Brits that year was the catalyst for my career.' Tom, in an immac-ulately cut blue suit, remembered Freda and Tom senior when he collected the award from the presenter Davina McCall: 'My mother passed away on the seventh of this month and my father passed away in 1981. They were my biggest fans and biggest supporters, and they would have been really pleased that I am getting this tonight. So this is for Mam and Dad.'

He sang a medley of hits, including 'What's New Pussycat?', 'Kiss', 'Sex Bomb', 'It's Not Unusual' (during which he seemed to choke back emotion), 'Black Betty' (a follow-up single from *Mr Jones*), 'You Can Leave Your Hat On', 'Delilah' and 'Green, Green Grass of Home'. He could have sung fifty more.

The most striking thing was that he looked different, now sporting a goatee beard dyed to match his hair. A cosmetic operation to remove fat from his chin – a problem he needed to address occasionally throughout the years – had left a scar. The goatee, which gave him the air of a musketeer, covered it. He could have had the scar dealt with by a laser, but decided he liked the goatee.

The Brit Award was the opportunity to produce a retrospective called *The Definitive Tom Jones*, a timely chance to banish the commercial failure of *Mr Jones* from public consciousness. Four discs spanned four decades of music, with some curios thrown in, such as a recording of him singing Otis Redding's best-known song, '(Sittin' On) The Dock of the Bay'. The first two discs were a canter through his classics. He even included 'Chills and Fever', which had aged remarkably well – better than some far more successful songs. The third and fourth CDs drew more heavily from *The Lead and How to Swing It* and *Reload*.

Tom would appear to have had at least a dozen greatest hits releases in some form or other. BBC Online said of the new collection, 'Slap on some Brut, put some chicken in the basket and prepare to throw your best new knickers; this really is the definitive collection from a much-loved legend.'

Tom's next original project was one dreamed up by a couple of mates over a late-night bottle of champagne. He had met the pianist and band leader Jools Holland at the latter's annual BBC Hootenanny in 1998 and they became great friends. When they went out for dinner after recording, they discovered they shared a love of old blues music. Tom started singing at the dinner table, which Jools loved. He realised they would have the chemistry to make an album together. He enthused, 'When Tom sings, it's like having a nuclear reactor at the end of the piano.'

The result was an album called, uninspiringly, *Tom Jones & Jools Holland*. It was like one big joyous jam at the end of a party. A couple of new tracks written by them mingled with classics from Count Basie and Willie Dixon. They closed with a version of the Jerry Lee Lewis song 'End of the Road', which Tom played to his hero. Jerry Lee was impressed by Jools' playing. He said it was 'so beautiful it could make a steel bow cry'.

One of the other numbers, which was released as a single, was an old Cliff Richard hit, 'It'll Be Me', although it didn't sound anything like Cliff. At least the album didn't include 'The Young Ones', still his least favourite track from the old days with The Senators. The album was an ideal stocking filler and sold well in the run-up to Christmas 2004.

For his sixty-fifth birthday the following year, Tom wanted to do something special. He decided to return to sing in Pontypridd for the first time in forty-one years. His last gig had been on 30 June 1964, at the White Hart, the night before he left for London with The Senators. This time, he came on stage in front of 20,000 people at Ynysangharad Park, known locally as Ponty Park, and a place he knew so well from swimming in the local baths there as a youngster.

It was the Saturday of the Whitsun bank holiday weekend, and the town shut down for the day. He told the cheering audience, 'I am going to be sixty-five in a few days and I can't believe it. I feel like I'm twenty-five again. I'll be an OAP and here I am singing in front of all of you.' Katherine Jenkins presented him with a birthday cake. She sang 'Happy Birthday' in Welsh and English. It wasn't quite a Marilyn Monroe moment, though. Tom said, 'There's beautiful, and she can sing as well.'

Tom didn't take a fee for the concert, his only one in the UK before he began a 139-date world tour. He made sure all his relatives were looked after in a separate marquee for the occasion. Margaret Sugar remembered Freda and how proud she would have been to see her son at home again. 'It must be terribly emotional for him,' she observed. That was clear on his face when he sang 'A Boy from Nowhere' and 'Green, Green Grass of Home', backed by images of the Valleys on enormous screens.

Tom was giving something back to his home town after such a long time away. Although he is fiercely proud to be Welsh, he left his home when he was twenty-four. Many people in Pontypridd and Treforest seem to think by some sort of divine right that he should do things for the area and the community without explaining why he should. Sentimentality? He was criticised in the papers for not supporting Treforest Primary School when it was set to close, but he couldn't possibly know the politics involved, living thousands of miles away in Los Angeles.

Tom could be forgiven for recalling how difficult it was for him, returning home when he first hit the big time. He advised Stereophonics to be careful: 'I'd do an American tour and we'd do six months straight, no trouble. We'd be playing these big places, going into all different nightclubs, meeting all kinds of hoodlums and nobody ever tried to take a pop. We'd go back home to Wales and some fucker would try and have a go.'

If Tom was back visiting, there would always be someone in the pub reminiscing about how they'd wiped the floor with him or telling him that they were at the first gig he ever played, even though they invariably didn't have a clue when or where that was. If he didn't buy everybody a drink, he was labelled mean. If he did, he was a 'flash bastard'.

After the concert in Ponty Park, Tom made sure that he was at home in Los Angeles on his birthday, so that he could spend the day quietly with Linda and tell her all about it.

He knew his wife wouldn't be with him when he was knighted by the Queen. Her absence from such occasions wasn't a surprise, so it didn't ruin the day for him. He was recognised in the New Years' Honours List in 2006. The timing meant that his grandson Alex had to rush back from competing for Wales in the full-bore shooting at the Commonwealth Games in Melbourne. Tom had taught Alex how to shoot with an air rifle when he was boy and had stayed with Tom and Linda at the house in Welsh St Donats.

The Queen conducted the ceremony at the end of March and remembered seeing Tom perform in the sixties. She asked him how long he had been in show business. He replied proudly, 'Forty-one years.' She told him he had given a lot of people a lot of pleasure.

Afterwards, he revealed he had been nervous at the occasion. He was worried that they would change their minds. He only relaxed when the Queen tapped his shoulders with the sword. This time, there was no lap dancer waiting in the wings to sell her story.

## 22

# THE ROAD

Tom and Linda celebrated their golden wedding anniversary in March 2007. They didn't go out. They had a quiet meal at the house in Los Angeles with Mark and the family, who had flown in from England. Linda no longer enjoyed dinners in fancy restaurants, because she hated the feeling that she was on show. She had felt that way ever since Tom had become so famous, but the digital age had increased her vulnerability – everyone had a mobile phone and could take her picture.

Occasionally, Tom persuaded her to go for a little drive with him. He recalled a conversation they had during one journey: 'She said to me, "I'm enjoying this. It's no big deal, is it?" And I said to her, "But I told you! People are only people." But then, well, then she gets frightened again.' Tom enjoys his wife's company. He always has and he doesn't want to give that up.

It's become fashionable for songs to be identified as autobiographical. They can gather easy publicity for a new album that way. Adele's timeless 'Someone Like You' is just one example of how the media likes to devote column inches to the who and the why in lyrics. No detective work was required to realise Tom's song 'The Road' was both a tribute and an apology to his wife. Tom prefers to regard it as a thank you for being there for more than fifty years.

Tom was proud of the song and would recite the lyrics in interviews: 'Felt the weakness when I was strong, Felt the sweetness when it was wrong.' Tom told Simon Hattenstone in the *Guardian* that Linda would never try to analyse it or ask him what he meant by those lines, but she did like the sentiment in the key line of the song, 'The road always returns to you.'

Unlike singing, which comes so naturally, Tom needs prompting and encouragement to write a song. He was discussing his marriage with one of the songwriters on the album *24 Hours*, Lisa Greene, when he observed, 'No matter where I have been or what I have done, the road always leads back to Linda', which immediately drew the response, 'Write it down: The Road!' The song began to take shape immediately.

The irony is, of course, that Tom has been on the road for so much of their fifty years of marriage, they have probably spent no more than ten years in each other's company. Their marriage is nothing like that of Freda and Tom senior, whose lives were completely intertwined. His parents were an important part of each other's daily routine, whereas Tom and Linda were apart for long periods of time, sometimes even living in different countries. Nevertheless, Tom has always insisted that he would never leave his wife.

Tom has never been shy of talking about Linda. She hasn't spoken of him for forty years, but he has been revealing her fears and feelings throughout that time. He is careful to present her as a strong and forceful woman and not a downtrodden housewife: 'We still have the same basic feelings and values and we are both Welsh, we come from the same place, so I can't bullshit my wife. She won't have it, which is great. I love that.'

Much of the publicity for *24 Hours* centred on 'The Road' and its significance, but the record itself again showed his desire to present the public with new material and not just rehash the old. In this case, Mark had enthusiastically played his father *Back to Black* by Amy Winehouse and told him, 'Listen to this.' The retro feel of that masterpiece was the sound they were hoping to achieve. They wanted to return to the brass-heavy soul sounds of the sixties, when Otis Redding ruled and you would go into a record store to buy the great singer's latest recording on vinyl. In the sixties, Tom sought to emulate the passion or 'soul' that Otis found in his songs. He was astonished, therefore, when he met the singer, who told Tom that black artists were trying to copy *him*.

For the new album, Tom and Mark enlisted the help of the production duo Future Cut, who were as fashionable as you could find. Tunde Babalola and Darren Lewis had made a name for themselves in the mid-nineties in Manchester's drum 'n' bass scene, but it was the Lily Allen debut single 'Smile', in 2006, that provided them, and her, with their breakthrough. They recorded it in a basement studio in Manchester for just £500.

Tom played a part in writing almost all of the songs on the album, with a few notable exceptions. He had been talking to Bono at Lillie's Bordello, the well-known Grafton Street club in Dublin, and asked him to write a song that he could record. Tom likes nothing better than sitting down and telling stories about his life. Bono listened and said he would write something that reflected that life and not his own – a Tom Jones song, not a U2 one. He came up with 'Sugar Daddy', probably one of the weakest tracks on the album, a dull rehash of Tom's old image as a sex bomb. The *Scotsman* described as an 'embarrassing misfire'.

Much more successful was Tom's interpretation of 'The Hitter', the Bruce Springsteen tale of a travelling boxer. He was in his most dramatic voice. It could have been Otis himself countering the controlled power of the horns.

The lead single from the album, 'If He Should Ever Leave You', was an underrated melodic slice of swing that harked back to the days when Les Reed and Peter Sullivan were in charge of Tom's recording career. It sounded as if it could be the next track on an album that began with 'It's Not Unusual'. He sang it on *Strictly Come Dancing*, but while the arrangement was perfect for that show and its sequinned twirls, nothing, it seemed, could make it a hit. The album itself failed to make the top thirty in the UK, although it was eventually certified gold. *24 Hours* was Tom's first US release in fifteen years. It flopped, despite tireless promotion.

The reviews were encouraging, but the sales were forgettable. It wasn't the hoped-for return to the spotlight that *Reload* had been in the UK. Tom was hugely disappointed. It seemed the public wouldn't allow him to find his own voice. They wanted him to be the Tom Jones they remembered and not the artist he wanted to be.

Tom was sixty-eight when *24 Hours* was released. His hair and beard were still dyed black as coal, but it was time for a change of image. How could he claim to be a current artist when his appearance was an ill-conceived throwback to more youthful days? It was time to go grey.

His plastic surgeon in Los Angeles had warned him to stop fighting the march of time. Tom's nose had been straightened and made smaller more than once; his teeth were capped; his hairline and scalp had been worked on to reduce the chance of him becoming as bald as his father; and the fat had been sucked out of his chin. Only recently, the inevitable heaviness had been taken out of his eyelids. He never made a secret of his surgery as some stars do, gamely maintaining that their looks are all natural when they look like something created by Frankenstein. Tom hadn't forgotten the wise words of his personal plastic surgeon many years before: 'He told me to be careful not to have too much done, or I'd end up looking like someone else.'

Tom didn't go grey overnight. His appearance on the Comic Relief charity single '(Barry) Islands in the Stream' was a silvery work in progress, as his colour began to grow out. The song, written by the Gibb brothers, had been a huge hit in the early eighties for Dolly Parton and Kenny Rogers. Since then, it had become one of the best-loved country duets, as well as a karaoke favourite.

In the Comic Relief video, which was more like a film short, Tom played himself – as usual. The stars were Ruth Jones and Rob Brydon, portraying Nessa and Bryn, the characters they played in the popular television sitcom *Gavin and Stacey*. They travel to Las Vegas to take part in the world karaoke championships. In the desert, their truck breaks down and they are rescued by Tom in his limo. Tom had apparently enjoyed a one-night stand that he had never got over. Nessa, he said, was an animal in bed. Nessa and Bryn's performance in the competition was woeful, until Tom stepped in to save the day by singing the last verse and chorus.

Tom had little to do, but it was useful being able to attach his name to the record, and it proved to be a huge success, becoming another number one hit for Comic Relief. The video was light fun, although, once again, it seemed acceptable to portray Tom Jones as a man who would casually have an adulterous fling. It was a subject guaranteed to produce knowing laughter.

Tom had gone completely grey by the time he played Glastonbury for the second time at the end of June 2009. The joke was that he finally looked as old as his son. He had slimmed down and for the first time looked distinguished – not an adjective normally associated with Tom, at least not during his medallion years.

He played a selection of old and new songs from the sixties, mixed with more recent tracks. As usual, the 100,000-strong audience responded best to the ones they could sing along with – 'Delilah', 'Green, Green Grass of Home' and 'It's Not Unusual'. The overall sound was very brass-heavy and funked up, reflecting the emphasis of *24 Hours*. He didn't seem to be sweating any less now that he was older and still wore black to ensure he wasn't covered in any unsightly perspiration patches.

Tom, who normally takes everything in a relaxed manner, was uncharacteristically annoyed to discover that, for the first few numbers, the people at the front couldn't hear properly because of a fault with the speakers. He wasn't used to staring out at blank faces. He blasted, 'Four songs I did like that. Four songs!' All was forgiven by the time he sang a vintage version of 'I'll Never Fall in Love Again'. He closed with 'Unbelievable', the EMF song that he had included in his first Glastonbury set seventeen years before. The *Guardian* praised a belting set of pipes.

His Glastonbury set was brimming with nostalgia, but Tom hadn't given up on finding a new musical voice. At the end of the year, he dropped his American band and replaced them with younger musicians. They were told that they wouldn't be required on his UK tour. Their shock was very similar to Vernon Hopkins' disbelief when The Squires were dispensed with unexpectedly. The drummer for the past seven years,

Herman Matthews, thought the timing of the dismissal was poor, especially as some of the band had been with him for eighteen years. He put the blame squarely on Tom's management: 'They seemed to struggle in finding the right tunes for his recent record *24 Hours*, like they didn't know which way to take him, and maybe this is part of that.' Matthews graciously called Tom one of the greatest singers he had ever had the pleasure of working with.

Tom's quest for musical credibility continued. He signed a new £1.5 million deal with Island Records, which was a good way to start the next phase of his career, and set about recording his next album. A vice-president at Island called David Sharpe was walking through the company's headquarters when he heard 'hymns' being played loudly. It was a weekday, but could have been a Sunday morning, he thought. He sent an email to colleagues, 'My initial pleasure came to an abrupt halt when I realised that Tom Jones was singing the hymns!! I have just listened to the album in its entirety and want to know if this is some sick joke????'

The email was leaked to the *Sunday Times*, which ran Mr Sharpe's comments in full. He continued, 'We did not invest a fortune in an established artist for him to deliver twelve tracks from the common book of prayer [*sic*]. Having lured him from EMI, the deal was that he would deliver a record of upbeat tracks along the lines of "Sex Bomb" and "Mama Told Me" … Who put him with this "folk" producer, and who authorised that he should go off on this tangent … for God's sake what are you thinking when he went all spiritual?'

Mr Sharpe was unrepentant when contacted by the newspaper. He commented, 'Shall we say we've paid for a Mercedes and ended up with the hearse.' Mark and Donna were taken aback when asked about the email, describing it as 'very direct'.

Tom was equally direct in his response. 'Who is this guy?' he asked. 'I don't even know who he is. I found out that he's some fella who signs cheques or something. I said, "What the fuck's he on about?" You can't go condemning a record. It's terrible to say "maybe Tom has made a mistake if the record company don't even like it." They've been apologising to me ever since. They can't apologise enough.'

While the controversy did provide much publicity for the album, entitled *Praise and Blame*, Tom pointed out that it was negative and misleading. The 'folk producer' was Ethan Johns, an acclaimed English record producer and musician, who had already been responsible for albums by Kings of Leon and Razorlight. The previous year he had produced Paolo Nutini's award-winning *Sunny Side Up*.

The suggestion that Tom work with him had actually come from Island. They met at Apple Studios in North London and Tom told Johns he was thinking of doing some spiritual music. He had never forgotten listening to Mahalia Jackson singing 'The Old Rugged Cross' when he was bed-bound with TB, or the late nights with Elvis singing gospel songs. He used to sing 'Danny Boy', not as a plaintive Irish ballad but as a black song from the cotton fields. He wanted to record an album of songs that said something and were meaningful. He wanted to return to the old days – not those when he wore a tuxedo in Las Vegas, but when he was a boy going to the Presbyterian chapel with his parents on a Sunday morning and hearing the sombre power of the organ playing when he walked in.

Ethan told him that they would go into the studio, play around with a couple of songs and take it from there. Tom observed, 'I liked what he said. "You sing 'em the way you feel 'em and we'll back you up."' Tom, in fact, thought they were still just rehearsing when Ethan switched on the tape machine and was amazed when the producer suggested they listen to what they had so far. He had managed to create an environment for the singer that took him back to the smoky back rooms of the Pontypridd and Treforest pubs where he had started more than fifty years before.

Tom wanted to sing the material not as soaring ballads that made your eyes water, but as songs that would move you: 'If my versions of these songs don't touch people, then I've missed the mark.' The very first track hit the target. It was a stripped-bare version of a Bob Dylan song, 'What Good Am I?', that Ethan had advised him to sing 'breathy'. Q magazine loved the track, saying, 'It's immediately clear his voice was made for such soul-bearing, sermon-giving, fire and brimstone-calling fare.' It was a perfect introduction to an introspective album from a man turning seventy.

Ethan astutely recorded the album live at the Real World Studios, Peter Gabriel's renowned recording complex near Bath. He used a minimal number of musicians, concentrating on an insistent bass guitar and a taut lead guitar, which he played himself.

The critics queued up to deliver praise and little-to-no blame. *MOJO* called it 'remarkable'. The *Mail on Sunday* found it 'surprising, brave and adventurous'. Andrew Perry in the *Daily Telegraph* said, '*Praise and Blame* is drenched in blues and Southern soul, and yet it sounds way more current than Jones's hi-tech latter-day flops.'

None of the tracks appeared weaker than the next, although the John Lee Hooker song 'Burning Hell' was memorable and would find its way into his live repertoire. The closing track, 'Run On', was one he used to sing in Vegas, not in the show-room at the Flamingo or Caesars Palace, but in Elvis's suite when they would duet late into the night. The public liked what they heard and *Praise and Blame* debuted at number two in the UK album charts.

Tom sang the album from start to finish at a special concert in the Union Chapel, a beautiful working church in Islington. He no longer needed someone to write his lines for him, telling the packed 'congregation' that the lozenge he popped in his mouth was Vocalzone and not Viagra. He also disarmingly explained the album title: 'If you take the praise, you've got to take the blame. People say, "Tom, he's got a lovely voice … but he's a bit of a naughty boy." You see?' As one reviewer pointed out, 'This is not hymn singing. If it were, then the churches across the land would be packed to the rafters.'

At last Tom had found the musical credibility he sought. The *Los Angeles Times* called it '*gravitas*'. His music had finally found a perfect fit with his rich and experienced voice. He really did sound black. The establishment loved him. The knighthood, the Brits, Glastonbury and *Desert Island Discs* were just some of the acknowledgements that here was an elder statesman to be celebrated. He was given a Music Industry Trusts Award 'in recognition of his achievement in being the most played Welsh artist of all time'. It is the ultimate accolade in British music – previous winners included Elton John, Andrew Lloyd Webber and George Martin, The Beatles' producer. Tom sang his old standards, as well as some new ones from the album, to invited guests at the Grosvenor House Hotel in London. Kelly Jones joined him to sing 'Mama Told Me Not to Come' and Cerys Matthews sang 'She's a Lady'.

It had been a year of huge celebrations for Tom, but on his seventieth birthday he was at home in LA, enjoying dinner with his wife ... The road always leads back to Linda.

# 23

# THE VOICE

---

Inevitably, the singer nicknamed 'The Voice' was approached to become a coach on a Saturday night television series called *The Voice*. You can imagine him being the first person the BBC thought of when they commissioned the show. For Tom, it was perfect timing. He had decided to give up his annual ten-week stint in Las Vegas, so he was looking for something not too strenuous.

Undeniably, even at seventy-one, it was a good career move for Tom, because these television talent shows are much watched and discussed. He would be the subject of many water-cooler conversations as a result. It would remind younger generations that here was one of the great British artists. The pay was also attractive. Picking up an estimated £500,000 for choosing a few promising singers and guiding them through to a final over a three-month period was easy money. The BBC, which paid £22 million for the show, offered a sweetener that clinched the deal for Tom. The Corporation agreed a special clause that he could swap his suite in Vegas for one at the Savoy, one of the great hotels of the world.

The television critic Kevin O'Sullivan observes, 'He has got a very superstar deal that gives him three months living in the lap

265

of luxury in London. It must cost a lot of money. After the show, he can go out to posh restaurants with his mates, like Jools Holland. He enjoys himself. *The Voice* is a nice little earner, which has let him enjoy London again.'

Tom was full of optimism when he was confirmed as a coach at the end of 2011. It wasn't obvious at the time that the Universal Music Group, which was providing a recording contract for the winner, was also the umbrella company behind Tom's record label. Jessie J was on the same label. Will.i.am was on Interscope, also a division of Universal.

Tom said the right things: 'It's exciting, competitive and compelling television. I look forward to being part of the team that discovers a great, new genuine talent.' He had to backtrack over a newspaper report that said he had criticised other talent shows. He apparently claimed, 'Some of the judges don't have the experience to be on talent shows – if you've only been in the industry two minutes, how can you offer advice?' He continued, 'Every time I see one of these shows I think half the decisions are wrong and it really frustrates me.'

The following day his Twitter account, which he doesn't write, stated: 'A comment of mine has been misunderstood by the press.' In truth, his remarks were only reflecting what most of the 10 million or so people who watch such shows are shouting at the television screen every week. It's part of the fun and makes the shows compelling.

*The Voice* began in triumphant fashion when a TV audience of 9.4 million watched the premiere in March 2012. The contest was at the chair-swivelling stage, also known as the blind auditions. Tom and his fellow judges, Jessie, Will and Danny O'Donoghue, the lead singer of The Script, listened to a contestant without being able to watch that person. They then dithered about whether to press their buzzer to turn their chair around so they could see the act. The beauty of this format was that it gave the opportunity for the coaches to be surprised to discover that the singer was old, young, short, tall, thin or fat. If Tom had sung on the show, everyone would have thought he was black until they saw him. In 2013, the surprise was that the angelic-voiced Andrea Begley, who won the competition, was partially sighted.

When more than one coach turned round, it was up to the contestant to choose whom they wanted to be their mentor. At first, Tom seemed to be the preferred choice, perhaps because he had the biggest reservoir of affection among the voting public, who ultimately picked the winner. That proved to be the case when one of his acts, Leanne Mitchell from Lowestoft, who initially hadn't been one of the favourites, won the series.

For her audition, she sang Beyoncé's 'If I Were a Boy' and all four judges turned round. Tom was the last to pitch for her to choose him as her mentor.

Leanne asked nervously, 'What would you like to do with me, Tom?', which reduced everyone to fits of giggles.

Tom laughed, 'I'm a married man, so I can't answer that question.' He said, more seriously, he liked the timbre of her voice and thought she could handle different sorts of material.

She chose Tom. As they hugged, she blurted out, 'You're a legend', and immediately wanted the ground to open up and swallow her.

Tom's team of chosen singers met him properly for the first time at the Hospital Club in Covent Garden. Just as he seemed to be enjoying himself, Mark, who is firmly in charge these days, told him, 'OK, Tom, we've got to go now', and ushered his father out. Leanne observed that you could see his face drop; she thought he would have been happy to stay out partying all night. Before the Battle Round, where two contestants have to duet against each other, Tom enlisted the help of a guest coach, or battle adviser, as they were called. He was joined by Cerys Matthews and the contestants could see they were good mates and happy to have a laugh together. Cerys told Leanne she had 'a fair set of lungs' on her.

During the live shows, Tom was surprisingly involved with helping his acts and advised Leanne about what songs might suit her. Behind the scenes, Mark, who had such an influence on Tom's own choice of material, interrupted rehearsals at the semi-final stage, when she was singing 'I Never Loved a Man the Way I Love You'. He told her it wasn't working and he thought they could do better.

Someone had the music to 'Run to You', the Whitney Houston song from *The Bodyguard*, so they tried that. It was the sort of big power ballad that had defined Tom's career, and it would win Leanne the competition. When she sang it for the first time, she noted in her book, *Finding My Voice*, 'Tom started to get a bit choked up, which really took me by surprise.' In the final, Leanne sang 'Mama Told Me Not to Come' with Tom. She gives an interesting insight into singing with him. Basically, he does what he likes – there was no point in giving him instructions on what to sing or where to sing it, because he would just ignore them.

Mark had decided that she should perform 'Run to You' again as her closing song, rightly gauging that she would win if she sang it. He wanted Tom to be the first winning coach. Both Tom and Jessie had tears in their eyes when she reached the soaring high notes. Tom had taught her to bare her soul in a ballad. He said, 'She knocks me out.'

Sadly for Leanne, her triumph didn't lead to a glittering prize. Her debut album, entitled *Leanne Mitchell*, wasn't released by Universal's Republic label until nearly a year after the show had finished. It sold less than a thousand copies in its first week. The fickle British public had forgotten about her. She did see Tom once more, when he performed at Newmarket Races in August 2012. He asked her how the recording was going and was encouraging.

Leanne made the perceptive comment that there is no handbook on how to be a celebrity. They don't give you one when you win a talent contest. She observed, 'For someone like Tom, there is a magic about him that makes it look so easy.'

Leanne was quietly dropped by her record label at the beginning of 2014 and was back appearing at the Potters Leisure Resort, a sort of modern Butlins, a few miles from her home, where she had been working since she was fifteen. She and Tom are not in touch.

Tom improved throughout the first series. Live television was not a comfort zone, but he eventually settled into his role as the elder statesman. When will.i.am mentions working with Michael Jackson, Tom counters with Elvis, or Aretha, or Janis, and his name-dropping became one of the best features each week. Kevin O'Sullivan observes, 'It has become a kind of ongoing joke, but it's not contemptuous. He is very entertaining. It's amusing, but it is bloody interesting at the same time. You name a superstar and he was mates with them and you know he is not bullshitting. It makes him very compelling and that is an important part of the show.

'He's got the talent, he's got the back-story and he's got the anecdotes. I've always thought he is the most important judge they have got. He could do with being a bit more articulate, but then live telly doesn't suit everyone. But there is a sense of *gravitas* whenever he is talking.'

Tom enjoyed it after he had settled in. He continued to find it difficult to send contestants home, however. The producers told him to drag out the moment for dramatic effect, but he hated being the one to end a person's dream. He explained, 'When I watched other talent shows and saw people getting emotional, I thought it was just show business. But when you're there, with the person in front of you, God, it is very intense and emotional. And you do cry.' He made a point of telling the contestants that only one person could win and that they should not let the outcome 'shatter their lives'.

*The Voice* confirmed Tom's newly acquired venerability. He could easily put his feet up for the rest of the year and go into semi-retirement, especially as he no longer had his 'pension', as he described his 140 shows a year in Las Vegas. He explained his decision to quit the desert: 'I was flogging a dead horse. When you've been somewhere a long time, you're taken for granted.'

Post-Vegas, Tom continued to choose projects that would stretch him. Finally, after talking about it for nearly fifty years, he had a proper, serious acting role. He played the title role in a bittersweet comedy called *King of the Teds*. It was a half-hour episode in the Sky Arts series *Playhouse Presents*. The writer, Jim Cartwright, was best known for the award-winning film *The Rise and Fall of Little Voice*.

The executive producer of the series, the comedienne Sandy Toksvig, arranged to meet Tom for lunch at the Savoy. She recalled, 'It turned out 1 p.m. was a little early for Mr Jones, so I sat with his son and daughter-in-law for a while before going up and knocking on the door of his suite. Tom materialised, wearing the shortest shower robe I have ever seen, and said, "Hello, Sandi" in that deep gravelly voice of his.'

Tom hadn't even seen a script by that stage, but his principal concern was to be treated with consideration in light of his inexperience. He didn't want to let anyone down because he had never acted in a drama before. He played Ron, a failed pop star in the late sixties, who dated two teenage girls when he was younger. He married Tina (Alison Steadman) when she became pregnant, while the other, Nina (Brenda Blethyn), leaves to become a career woman. Ron worked in a bottle factory, but now is a redundant has-been whom even his wife finds a bore.

*King of the Teds* obviously mirrored some aspects of Tom's own early life and his marriage to his pregnant girlfriend. Linda asked him how filming was going when they spoke on the phone. He told her, 'If I hadn't cracked it, Ron could be my life. There but for the grace of God.'

Tom's problem was a tendency to overact. He told the *Radio Times*, 'It's a Welsh thing. The camera records every expression, so you have to try to underplay. I haven't had acting lessons, but someone is helping me get the words right, because there are rhythms in the language and I have to be word perfect.' In some ways, he had the same difficulty when he started singing – he was always at full throttle.

Jim Cartwright knew that Tom would be a success in the role: 'Someone who had performed such dramatic songs as "Delilah" in such a real and moving way would be able to do it.' He was impressed that there was no ego or 'I'm the star' about Tom. He ditched his elegant and expensive clothes and sought out the tattiest cardigan to wear as Ron. He also mucked in with the rest of the cast during a week's filming in Surrey.

He sat on the catering bus with everyone, eating cottage pie and swapping stories, as he liked to do. 'He's a complete charm bucket,' said Sandi.

While Tom will always wish he had tried acting as a young man, he knows that it would never have replaced singing in his life. His follow-up to *Praise and Blame* was called *Spirit in the Room* and was his fortieth studio album. He is reported genuinely to have sold 100 million records worldwide.

*Spirit in the Room*, produced by Ethan Johns, was superficially more of the same. Tom was again in introspective mood, exploiting the richness of his older voice, but on this album he chose more contemporary songs from writers including Paul McCartney, Leonard Cohen, Paul Simon, Tom Waits and Bob Dylan. The *Daily Telegraph* described it as 'a beautiful album of great songs performed with taste and sung with tender resonance'. Amusingly, Tom, the man who has sung with all the greats, and known and drunk with many of them, has never met Bob Dylan.

If a contestant on *The Voice* had come on stage and sung one of the album's songs, Tom would have told him or her to lighten up. The opening track, Cohen's 'Tower of Song', is perversely autobiographical for Tom, including the lines 'My friends are gone and my hair is grey' and 'I was born with the gift of a golden voice'. Even Tom acknowledged that it felt as if he were singing about himself.

Tom could so easily have compromised and cashed in on his prime-time fame with *The Voice* and produced an album of familiar classics. Instead, again he challenged his audience. He would not be singing anything from *Spirit in the Room* on Saturday night shows like *Strictly Come Dancing*, however. They weren't party tunes. Even the Paul McCartney track is a lesser-known one, '(I Want to) Come Home', from 2010, a song the former Beatle hasn't included in one of his own albums yet. Andy Gill in the *Independent* noted that its theme of wearied resolution suited Tom's age and stature.

In *Praise and Blame* and *Spirit in the Room*, Tom is playing to his strengths. Some critics thought it a shame that he hadn't made such outstanding records earlier in his career. The simple answer to that is he wasn't ready then. These albums are autumnal.

The remarkable longevity of Tom's voice was abundantly clear when he was one of the stars on show at the Queen's Diamond Jubilee concert outside Buckingham Palace in June 2012. While others of his vintage, including Paul McCartney, Cliff Richard and Elton John, seemed to struggle to find their vocal power of old, Tom was the same as ever. His friend Rob Brydon introduced him as the 'King of Music' and the 'Rajah of Rhythm'. He sang 'Mama Told Me Not to Come' and 'Delilah' as if he were twenty years old. He performed them with such freshness and vigour, it was as if he were singing them for the first time. That is one of the great secrets of Tom's enduring popularity: he has sung his hits so many times, but he never looks or sounds for a moment as if he is bored doing so. The Queen arrived just as Tom finished, which was bad timing on her part.

Tom returned for a second series of *The Voice*. Despite disappointing ratings, which saw the show lose more than half its viewers as the weeks progressed, there was never any question of it being axed – the financial investment was too big. Kevin O'Sullivan observes: 'The first series could have got six viewers and they still would have made the second.'

Despite its grand ideal about being a singing contest, *The Voice* is primarily a television show. The problem that has yet to be solved was that the blind auditions were by far the most interesting part of the series and the ratings fell off a cliff when they were over. An additional difficulty for the programme will be if Tom decides to leave. They would have to replace him with someone of similar stature and there simply isn't anybody.

These days, Tom likes to do the unexpected. It is part of his enduring appeal. In December 2013, he interviewed Kate Moss for *Playboy* magazine. It was a bizarre gimmick, but strangely cool – more like a chat between buddies. Kate told him she was wearing a blue suede mini-dress that she had designed herself, matched with Yves Saint Laurent shoes. Tom responded that his cashmere jacket was from Smedley and his blue suede shoes were Jeffery-West. He was also sporting a Cartier Santos watch. Kate said, 'I've never seen one that big.'

By then, the auditions had begun for the third series of *The Voice* in 2014. Kylie Minogue replaced Jessie J, and Ricky Wilson of The Kaiser Chiefs took over from Danny O'Donoghue. The chemistry was much better. Tom observed, 'It's been fun to do it with people I know rather than ones I didn't.'

He was more comfortable during the series and was even able to offer Ricky advice: 'I told him to relax, go with the flow, go with his instinct and listen.' He didn't stop mentioning famous people he knew. In one show, he talked about Ray Charles, Jerry Lee Lewis, Little Richard, Frank Sinatra, Otis Redding, Prince and Elvis. An impressed will.i.am said Tom had worked with 'every legend ever'.

Tom nearly won again. His final contestant was Sally Barker, a fifty-four-year-old professional singer from Leicestershire, whose ethereal voice moved Tom to tears more than once. He joined some of the contestants for some impromptu – and carefully filmed – busking in Covent Garden. He sang 'It's Not Unusual' and 'Kiss' to the tourists. In the final, he sang 'Walking in Memphis' with Sally, but it wasn't enough to win her the competition.

Both Tom and will.i.am threaten to leave the show each year. It's almost part of the pageant. Tom hinted that he was definitely going if Kylie left. She went, but he stayed. It's a well-worn method stars use to bump up their fee. Tom is now earning close to £1 million for his annual trip to London. He doesn't need the money. The *Sunday Times* Rich List estimated his fortune at £145 million in 2014, quite an achievement for someone who writes very few songs and doesn't rely on publishing royalties for his income. A year later and the figure had risen to £150 million.

Tom has amassed much of his fortune through live performing. After the third series of *The Voice* finished in March 2014, he started rehearsing for a world tour. He played forty-four dates, beginning at the Ryman Theatre in Nashville at the end of April and ending six months later in Melbourne at the AFL Grand Final, the climax of the Australian rules football season. Tom's instinct for a cool alliance is still intact. This time, he shared a stage with Ed Sheeran for a duet of 'Kiss' in front of 100,000 people.

Tom did manage to produce some controversy when he was interviewed by a former Australian sports star called Campbell Brown, who, in a tired old gag, handed Tom a pair of underpants to mop his brow. At the end of the interview, Tom is heard to mutter, 'Dickhead.' He may have said 'take care'. It caused a big debate on Twitter. The Treforest Ted would definitely have said 'dickhead'.

Tom had one more responsibility to fulfil in 2014 before he could put his feet up in Los Angeles. He arrived in London for the first auditions of the 2015 fourth series of *The Voice*. Rita Ora replaced Kylie. She is signed to Roc Nation, who have a multi-million-dollar distribution agreement with the Universal Music Group. She proved a big hit, with her enthusiasm and winning smile. The new panel seemed to be the best mix on the show so far. Tom was more at ease than on any previous series – comfortable in his role as the legend.

Tom flew home for his Christmas break with Linda before the live shows began. They scarcely leave the house these days, because Linda doesn't want to, but Tom enjoys the quiet. Occasionally, he will go out to get fish and chips or their favourite steak and kidney pudding from a British food store in Hollywood. He reads history books by the pool. His *Desert Island* book is *The Rise and Fall of the British Empire* by Lawrence James. The books in his bookcases are all real now.

He is more careful these days about how much he drinks, mainly because he doesn't want to put on too much weight. When asked by his doctor how much he consumed each day, he told him he had a bottle of wine with dinner. He didn't tell him about the vodka martini aperitif, the cognac digestif or the bottle of champagne for the road.

Linda always knows when Tom is getting restless and it's time for him to go back on stage: he starts singing in the house. Tom isn't bothered about getting older: 'My voice is as strong as ever. Hopefully, when it's not, I'll stop. It can't be far away, but I hope it's a long way off. If you're making records that sell, and people want to see you on tour, there's nothing better.'

Every year he picks up a raft of awards, testimony to his longevity. His long-standing road manager Don Archell once compared Tom to two legendary drinkers, Richard Burton and Richard Harris. Tom has never matched their level of inebriation. If he had, he would be dead.

Tom won the Lifetime Achievement Award at the 2014 Silver Clef Awards at the London Hilton. He was amusing about it: 'When you get a lifetime achievement award, you think "Is that it?"' The best line, however, came from Rob Brydon, who introduced him. He said, 'Tom Jones has lived the life we would all love to live.'

# LAST THOUGHTS

Stow Hill is a very steep street in Treforest. At the top is the Central Guest House, where Tom's old secondary school used to be. He trudged up the hill with his best friends Brian and Dai every day from their houses a few hundred yards away. At the bottom is a bar, specialising in Indian food and pool nights, called The Red Lounge. This is the site of the much-missed Wood Road Non-Political Club, the venue for the first public performance of Tommy Woodward.

Tom wouldn't recognise the old home town any more. It doesn't look the same. At the end of Wood Road, the Cecil Cinema is now a snooker hall. In the other direction, towards Pontypridd, the Wheatsheaf pub no longer exists, replaced by a magistrates' court and some flats. The White Hart pub in the Broadway is closed, along with the County and nearby White Palace cinemas. The Polyglove factory, where Tom found his first job, is a bustling restaurant and bar called Barinis. It offers a 10 per cent discount for students. Next door is a Tesco Metro.

Some old haunts are still the same. The house in Laura Street has changed little, with a grating on the pavement outside and the gate at the back that his father would open to announce his arrival at the end of his working day down the mine. The streets are different, though. They are full of 'To Let' signs, advertising accommodation for students at the nearby University of South Wales.

The pride in the community has gone. The locals I spoke to complain of the litter and messy front gardens. They understand that the student influx has given their backwater a financial boost and energised the local retail trade, but the young men and women are just passing through. It's a movable population, far removed from the settled neighbourhood Tom knew so well. Nobody would be foolish enough to leave their back door unlocked now.

Tom Jones never lived in Treforest. He was Tommy Woodward when he walked these streets. He has returned only occasionally over the years for sad days, like the funeral of Dai Perry, or for happier ones, when he sang in front of 20,000 fans at Ponty Park in 2005. He can't, of course, just visit without it being a big deal, accompanied by a publicity jamboree. When he went back to the old Central School in 1983, he was presented with the school bell. It was a well-meaning but ironic gift, considering that, as a pupil, he would ignore the sound of its ringing whenever he could.

Not everybody I met in the Pontypridd area speaks highly of Tom. Some are weighed down by jealousy and the feeling that he has never given anything back to his birthplace. But others are hugely appreciative he has put the principality on the world map. He could justifiably claim to be the most famous Welshman of them all.

He is truly proud to be Welsh and can be sentimental about it, but in reality he has lived in tax exile in Los Angeles for forty years – far longer than he ever lived in Treforest. He may still sound Welsh, despite living so long in the US, but his lifestyle is decidedly Bel Air. He has spent so much of his adult life in impersonal hotel rooms that, inevitably, the people close to him have always been more important to him than places.

He has the reassurance that his beloved wife Linda is always waiting for him at their luxury home off Mulholland Drive. In April 2015, they celebrated their fifty-eighth wedding anniversary – an amazing length of time for a pop star. I wonder if it's a record.

Much has been written depicting Linda as some sort of down-trodden woman. The sacrifices she has made over the years because she loves her husband are not, in my opinion, those of a weak woman, but of a strong one. Her decision, all those years ago, to work in a sewing factory so Tom could pursue his dream, set the standard for the rest of their married life.

Tom has spoken candidly about his wife's fear of public places, meeting new people and travelling by air. She didn't make the journey across the Atlantic for his knighthood, so it doesn't seem as though she will ever be seen in the UK again. From time to time, stories have appeared in the press suggesting that Tom will move back, but that is increasingly unlikely as the years go by.

Linda has chosen to ignore his many and well-reported infi-delities, but she does not want to read about them in the pages of a tabloid newspaper. That, it seems, is her condition. All hell breaks loose if she suffers any public humiliation. One quote from her sums up this arrangement. When the Mary Wilson affair was getting too close to home, she reportedly told Tom: 'You'd better straighten it out, because you won't be able to do anything without your balls.'

Tom Jones the superstar has lived the champagne life of a famous man who enjoys the company of women. At home he is still Tommy Woodward, reading a favourite history book by the pool, eating fish and chips at the enormous dining table, and spending time with the love of his life.

Intriguingly, the female fans I spoke to find it easy to forgive his Don Juan tendencies. Young women in particular find it less easy to accept his failure to acknowledge his illegitimate son, Jonathan Berkery. The argument seems to be that a child cannot be held responsible for the circumstances of his birth and should not be punished for them. It is a moral dilemma.

Tom Jones was seventy-five in June 2015. He has more money than he needs or could ever have dreamed of having, so why does he bother? Why did he turn up to play a gig at Newmarket races on a drizzly August evening in 2014 – the last time I saw him in concert?

The simple answer is that he gets bored if he doesn't sing. It's the thing he's best at, so why would he want to while away his days wasting the gift he still has? Singing defines the man. He can't help the march of time and is looking greyer and older these days, but his voice doesn't seem to reflect his age. He still lit up the stage with his vocal majesty.

He has never wanted to be a headline act on a sixties nostalgia tour – they are ten a penny. I saw P. J. Proby on just such a tour a few years ago. They pay the rent, but are not going to thrill the crowds at Glastonbury.

As if to prove his current credibility, Tom's first number wasn't one the increasingly drunken audience could sing along with. Instead, the band launched into the brooding, guitar-led song 'Burning Hell', from his acclaimed 2010 studio album *Praise and Blame*. It was a statement of intent from an artist confident enough in the quality of his music not to need to get the crowd immediately onside with an old favourite. We would have to wait for 'It's Not Unusual'.

The song was a perfect statement: 'Listen to my voice, it's still strong and rich.' Tom may have lost his top range, but he has made up for it with greater depth to his bass notes. This is not a man performing in cruise control. The songs he chooses are too challenging for him to do that.

Much of the credit for his relevance today goes to the enterprise of his son Mark, who took over his management when Gordon Mills died in 1986. Mark has been guiding his father's career for many more years than his famed mentor ever did.

He revitalised his father's recordings and reversed a slump that might well have ended in a nostalgia tour, simply because there was nowhere else to go. Tom knows that his audience expects his sixties classics and he is happy to oblige them, providing he can showcase how much more he has to offer.

He is stately rather than dynamic around the stage these days, ambling about in an immaculate grey checked sports coat and a black shirt. He has never lost his love of expensive, well-tailored clothes. The familiar hand movements are still much in evidence. They haven't changed since the days of The Senators, when he punched the rhythms of the songs at the Green Fly in Caerphilly or the YMCA in Pontypridd.

'Are we gonna have a good time tonight?' he enquired at the end of the song. Banter between numbers has never been his strong point, but his crowd was enthusiastic. The audience at these summer racing concerts are a mixed bunch of folk: those just out to enjoy a drink outdoors, racegoers who decide to stay on and listen to some music and, as always, the diehard Tom Jones fans. The cheeky chappie who shouted 'Go on, Pops' was firmly in the first category, as was the drunken man who shouted 'We love you, Tommy' at the top of his voice.

Tom no longer plays exclusively to adoring women. I saw just a solitary pair of knickers – if you could call them that. A woman of uncertain age wearing a purple dress waved an enormous pair of granny bloomers every time he looked in her direction – which he seemed to do less and less as the concert progressed. She soon tired of the ironic gesture, especially as she was the only one making it.

Did Tom ever need the knickers? Musically, of course not. As part of a stage act, at a moment in time, they gave him an edge. Then they became an irritation, distracting from the serious purpose of his performance. Long ago they lost any point. Waving or throwing a pair of knickers became like waving a flag at the Last Night of the Proms – it was part of the whole experience.

On tour, he often tries new things. He sang a swing version of his hit 'Sex Bomb', which featured an excellent brass section that had the girls in their summer dresses dancing on the lawn in front of the stage. I couldn't see if he had a twinkle in his eye when he delivered the line 'Turn me on, girls'.

It struck me as ironic that Tom has been playing a number of racetracks in recent summers, but never has a bet. He will gamble with his voice, but not with his wallet. He took a risk by presenting new material. We were still waiting for 'It's Not Unusual' when he offered 'Tomorrow Night', a pleasantly old-fashioned melody that Elvis recorded in the fifties.

He followed that with 'Raise a Ruckus Tonight', a new version of an old favourite, which was good fun and contained the line 'I love my biscuits dipping in gravy.' 'Didn't It Rain' was another from *Praise and Blame*, while 'Evil' was his version of a Howlin' Wolf classic. Just when I thought that he might be losing the interest of the audience by overdoing the unfamiliar, the unmistakable first bars of 'Delilah' rang out. The drunks began to sing along and nostalgia filled the air.

Eventually, a piano accordion struck up the first few notes of 'It's Not Unusual' – always recognisable, despite an unusual presentation. Tom gave it a Latin flavour that breathed new life into the song. March 2015 marked the fiftieth anniversary of the week his signature tune reached number one. Quite frankly, it's so timeless, he could have sung it a cappella with the crowd. It again demonstrated that he isn't afraid to try something new with his repertoire.

These outdoor events attract big crowds, but they don't do justice to the music. It's a jolly atmosphere, but only part of the audience is there to listen to Tom. One of these days it would be good to hear Tom again in a more intimate venue like Ronnie Scott's.

The Newmarket concert was part of a relentless summer schedule that included dates across the US and Europe before finishing in Melbourne. Tom had been touring for six months. Before Christmas, he was recording the blind auditions for *The Voice* and then appeared at the inaugural BBC Music Awards at Earls Court.

This was a glittering affair, which saw Tom present the premier award of British Artist of the Year to Ed Sheeran, with whom he had shared a stage in Melbourne. Tom also performed on the night in a duet with the acclaimed retro singer Paloma Faith. They appeared together on the red carpet and in a special photo booth. They were larking about when Tom slipped and grabbed the nearest thing to steady himself. That turned out to be Paloma's left breast. She dissolved into a fit of giggles and the subsequent clip became an online hit.

It was probably better received than their duet, a version of the Beach Boys' classic 'God Only Knows', which closed the show. Their two voices didn't gel that well together, although Tom did his best to nurse them through the notoriously difficult song. The audience loved it, however. It would have been interesting to hear them sing the Paloma hit 'Only Love Can Hurt Like This' – the song, with its deep throaty verses, would have suited Tom. Again it proved how a duet with the great singer was a goal for any performer, however trendy they might be. Tom gives anyone artistic credibility. For a man who used to hate sharing the limelight on stage, Tom has sung more memorable duets than almost any other star I can think of.

Tom may well decide to pack it in and retire when another artist overshadows him in a duet. It hasn't happened yet. It seems to me he has finally reached the position he wanted. He appears content and comfortable in himself and his age. Both the record industry and the public have responded to his veteran status with respect and affection. He may need a bigger house to store all the awards he has received in recent years, and the critics have praised him more than any other performer at the big establishment gigs, like the Queen's Diamond Jubilee concert.

He is gaining full recognition for his status and his talent, applauded by young and old. It's cool to like Tom Jones. I began this book by declaring that even as a small boy, it was always about the voice. That hasn't changed, although he is now seventy-five.

Jones The Voice seems to be getting better with age.

# TOM'S STARS

It's not unusual to be a wonderful mimic if you are born with the Sun in Gemini. Developing his sense of identity is something Tom will have struggled with at times, but, from an early age, his talent for imitation helped him explore his own individuality. Versatility, charm and the ability to have fun are also well-acknowledged Gemini traits, along with the famous duality of Tom's Sun sign, identified by the symbol of the twins. The ruler of Tom's Gemini Sun, Mercury, is in family-loving Cancer, so it is very apt that he can sing about 'the green, green grass of home' while feeling perfectly well domiciled on foreign shores. Roots in two places – dual residence – equals happiness for this restless performer.

The presence also of the Moon in Gemini emphasises that this ability to combine two approaches to life is part of the very fibre of the man and is not in any way the debilitating conflict it might be for some. Tom is vitalised by such duality – both his heart and his head demand it and it influences many areas of his life.

To have both the Sun and Moon in Gemini highlights the importance of communication for Tom. However, it is the sign

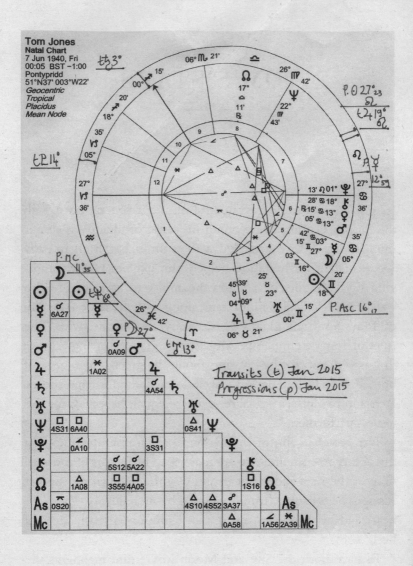

**Tom Jones**
Natal Chart
7 Jun 1940, Fri
00:05 BST −1:00
Pontypridd
51°N37' 003°W22'
*Geocentric*
*Tropical*
*Placidus*
*Mean Node*

Transits (t) Jan 2015
Progressions (p) Jan 2015

ruler, Mercury, and the fused planets of passion, Mars and Venus, in responsive, moody, sentiment-loving Cancer, that dictate his singing signature. Tom will be honoured and remembered for music of great emotional power and poignancy, songs of fierce love and tempestuous heartbreak – the stuff that pulls at the heartstrings of both genders equally. He is a musician who can communicate the volcanic feelings in us all.

What contributes more to the individuality of this gifted performer are the links made between the Sun and other planets in the chart: in particular, creative and compassionate Neptune and rebellious, break-the-mould Uranus. These two planets couldn't be further apart in the influence they wield upon a character, emphasising again the contradictions in the personality of a performer who is a champion in the realm of reinvention and originality.

The tight links from Neptune to Tom's Sun and Moon suggest an innate understanding of the importance of compassion. This wonderfully dynamic, smoulderingly charismatic and explosively sexual entertainer is, in fact, a very kind man – an extremely generous, sensitive man, with an ability to live out either end of the saviour–victim spectrum easily.

Neptune also creates a great yearning to be special. Tom early on will have idealised anything moving that had the slightest vestige of glamour and wanted to embody that quality. Sadly, this must sometimes lead to discontent. The ordinary has a way of bouncing back, breaking through the illusions built on shifting success in relationships or career.

The position of the heroic, quest-focused Sun in the chart area associated with roots and home suggests both love and loyalty to family, and the acceptance of a challenge. He is motivated by a desire to help those he is closest to. Family dynamics would have undoubtedly furthered his self-understanding, enabling him to find his role, perhaps as the one who entertained, brought harmony and fun to the everyday. The link between this Sun and sensitive, protective Neptune, prompts dreaming and belief in an ideal that might rescue him and others from none-too-welcome reality.

Neptune, long associated with creativity, gentleness and the spiritual, links tightly to the two planets that symbolise Mother and Father. It is likely that clever and clannish Tom saw what they could have been and appreciated the sacrifice of the life they might have had to do what good parents must. How could he not feel that he owed it to them to fulfil what was within him – that gift from his ancestors he will always honour ... the voice?

Mother had a vibrancy and quickness about her and would have promoted Tom's sociability, curiosity and rationality. She may have come from a line of healers, albeit the type who mended a person through supportive, sharing talk. It is likely, too, that she possessed a certain naivety, a childlike quality, so that at times she was less a parent, more a sibling. Although close to both parents, Mother wielded the greatest influence.

Father had strength of will, a degree of stubbornness and a fear of manipulation. Beneath a controlled exterior, he had a sustained faith in life and enthusiasm, which supported him and others in the family.

With Saturn influencing the chart area associated with siblings, Tom's sister will have provided a pragmatic influence during his early years. Perhaps she was something of a parent to him – Saturn often suggests an age difference. Her affection would have been very important to Tom, although there may also have been a degree of unpredictability in the relationship.

The importance of family to Tom, both birth family and present, can't be overestimated, because it was, and will remain, an environment in which he learnt and learns about his own needs and resources. He will be appreciative of his heritage and land, and feel honoured to shelter and protect family members.

A problem, though, with Neptune is that the loving closeness it can promote becomes something akin to enmeshment – a state in which it is hard to know if what you want is really your own desire or that of everyone you are trying to please. But this is a man who, with the dexterity of a magician, can have his cake and eat it too.

In parallel to the pleasures of a supportive home base, where he can be truly appreciated for what he is, this restless, adaptable performer will be drawn to the intensity of performance and the nectar of fame.

Two planets reveal the power and drive that have been fundamental to his resilience and stellar status. Pluto, the planet that governs death and rebirth, links positively with the chart area associated with public success. Instinctively, from an early age, Tom would be able to learn and develop the skills necessary for recognition, his facility to prioritise and work compulsively towards his goals never failing, no matter what the obstacle. These were not conventional academic abilities – the planet of delays and restriction, Saturn, influences the chart area connected with early education, hinting at failure here. But Pluto gifts both with the means to benefit from difficulties and great powers of regeneration. Together with the adaptability granted by the Sun and Moon in Gemini, Tom, like a Madame Tussauds waxwork, can embrace meltdown and reinvention, growing from the experience and finding new strengths in his talent each time. Crisis is at the very heart of his evolution.

Uranus, planet of rebellion, plays a distinct role in Tom's make-up too. This is the planet that preceded the Sun rising above the horizon at the moment of birth. It suggests initially that he came into his family at an unsettled time; it might even be that the pregnancy was a bit of a surprise. This is someone who will shake up the status quo. Linked beautifully to Neptune, planet of creativity, clearly there is then the capacity to stir things up on the music scene. Arguably, it is this that makes Tom not simply a great performer, but actually someone who shines with the brilliance of a true star – a man who connects with a wide audience and who is right for the time, heralding a new dawn.

A traditional family man in many ways, Tom will have played his part in the shifting of morals, the breaking down of taboos, and the more blatant acknowledgement of sexuality that marked the post-war era. It was not unusual to express love and emotion in popular songs; it *was* unusual to showcase the lust.

Neptune and Pluto, placed in the chart area connected with marriage, speak of closely binding and long-lasting links. In terms of relationships, Tom's default position is to be highly protective of his spouse, but he will need an escape clause. This is because of the position of Pluto, a planet that demands emotional intensity, but can also be repelled by prolonged intimacy. Pluto is reclusive by nature and often tries to kill that which it grows dependent upon – here, the love of his partner. It is the planet of control and power struggles. In the particular position it occupies, Tom, through the process of projection, will often feel that he is the one controlled – and this may not be groundless. Partly this is due to an innately empathetic heart (the redemptive Neptune to Moon influence), which will always be hooked by the desire to rescue should his partner need support. There are likely to have been many occasions when Tom has felt the need to redeem himself – that is, to restore his respected and loved partner's belief in his goodness. But Pluto is manipulative and control can be a two-way thing. Any partner of someone who has relentlessly pursued fame may well resent the restrictive and controlling invasion of privacy that is a consequence of egotistically sought popularity. So who has controlled whom? It is likely to take a long lifetime to settle this one.

The frequently acrimonious tussles that are the natural territory of this planet will challenge Tom until he lives by the non-negotiable Pluto lesson: to share power equally and employ honesty and integrity in all intimate encounters.

Tom will, in the past year, have experienced a number of challenges to relationships, not least involving those with a sibling role in his life. This could, for example, cover colleagues with whom he works closely on a day-to-day basis. In January 2015, the tough links between Pluto and Uranus moving in the sky and Venus and Mars in his chart suggest the climax to these contentions experienced in April 2014. Tom may have felt his goals and desires were thwarted and resented the demands from others to look at problems buried in the past. This period, early in the year, will revisit these problems, which will move towards resolution. Importantly, the passage of 'reap what you sow' Saturn at the pinnacle of Tom's chart means he will be held responsible both for errors in the past but hopefully also for years of ambition and effort that could pay off brilliantly in terms of personal achievement and public success. It is a period that reveals the consequences of how Tom has led his life, especially over the last twenty-nine years.

In May 2015, there is the progression of Tom's natal Moon into the feisty competitive sign of Aries, providing a resurgence of courage and self-esteem and an investment of time and energy in new projects, followed in June by returning Saturn positioned at the top of his chart for a second time. Tom should be able to accept the demanding responsibilities and hard work that accompany the opportunities presented now, which are the result of years of his own efforts.

There is a further period from July to September 2015 that heralds tension – all existing relationships may experience quite fundamental change and it is not beyond possibility that some may end and new ones begin.

Towards the end of September, Saturn, in a third and final hit, crosses the uppermost point of Tom's chart, promising a forthcoming period of great productivity. Tom will receive all that he deserves – acknowledgement of his status as a leader in his professional field and as a performer who has contributed his own individual brilliance to the entertainment of millions.

Madeleine Moore
February 2015

# ACKNOWLEDGEMENTS

One of the delights of writing this book was listening to the music of Tom Jones – revisiting old favourites and discovering new songs for the first time. As I found out more about his fascinating life, the music inspired me. You can't tire of hearing Tom sing, and *Praise and Blame* is now firmly established on my favourite CDs shelf.

Thank you to everyone who helped bring this story to life. I loved my trips to South Wales. Time and time again interviewees told me how much they enjoyed talking about things they hadn't discussed for many years – sometimes the stories were more than sixty years old. My particular thanks to Gill Beazer, Brian and Mary Blackler, Keith Davies, Donna Gee, Glynis McKenna, Gemma Perry, Tommy and Vimy Pitman, John Scanlon, Kay Tranter, and Tom's cousin Margaret Sugar and her husband Graham, who brought Laura Street and Cliff Terrace to life for me.

It's a small world, because John Scanlon and his lovely wife Denise run the Central Guest House in Treforest, where I stayed. It turned out that not only was the building on the site of the old Central School, but they were also the last steward and stewardess at the Wood Road Non-Political Club before it closed. And John was a pall-bearer at Dai Perry's funeral.

From Treforest, I drove over to Swansea for several enjoyable days spent with Vernon Hopkins, the original bassist with The Senators, and his daughter Tara, who proved to be a great help in hunting down people for the book. Good luck with those exciting projects, Vernon.

The great days of the sixties and the seventies were recalled with affection by Chris Hutchins and Les Reed. Glenna Stone has been a huge help in the US, and I love reading all her posts about her favourite singer. My old friend Kevin O'Sullivan, the best television critic in the country, again offered valuable insight into *The Voice*.

*Tom* is the start of a new era for me. This is my first book for HarperCollins, so it's been an exciting year. Sincere thanks to publisher Natalie Jerome for inviting me to join the company; editor Kate Latham for overseeing the project with enthusiasm and expertise; editors Simon Gerratt and Mark Bolland, and Dean Russell, who looked after production; Simeon Greenaway for the stunning cover design; Helen McFarland for her essential work researching pictures; and Virginia Woolstencroft for her deft touch with marketing in her role as communications manager.

Fortunately for me, Team Sean was able to join me. I would be lost without them: my brilliant agent, Gordon Wise, and his assistant at Curtis Brown, Richard Pike; my amazing researcher, Emily-Jane Swanson; Jen Westaway, who transcribed my interviews and somehow made sense of my ramblings; Jo Westaway, for listening patiently while I talked endlessly about the book in the pub; Arianne Burnette, the best copy-editor in the business;

and Madeleine Moore, one of my dearest friends, who once more produced a fascinating birth chart.

You can read more about my books at seansmithceleb.com or follow me on Twitter @seansmithceleb and facebook.com/ seansmithcelebbiog.

# SELECT BIBLIOGRAPHY

Eggar, Robin. *Tom Jones: The Biography*, Headline, 2000

Ellis, Lucy and Bryony Sutherland. *Tom Jones Close Up*, Omnibus Press, 2000

Hildreth, Stafford and David Gritten. *Tom Jones: The Biography*, Pan, 2000

Hopkins, Vernon. *Tom Jones: Just Help Yourself*, Iponymous, 2012

Humperdinck, Engelbert. *Engelbert: What's in a Name?*, Virgin, 2012

Jones, Peter. *Tom Jones: Biography of a Great Star*, Arthur Barker, 1970

Love, Darlene. *My Name Is Love*, William Morrow, 2013

Macfarlane, Colin. *Tom Jones: The Boy from Nowhere*, W. H. Allen, 1988

Mitchell, Leanne. *Finding My Voice*, BBC Books, 2013

Nash, Alanna. *Elvis and the Memphis Mafia*, Aurum Press, 2005

Powell, Don. *Pontypridd at War 1939–45*, Merton Priory Press, 1999

Roberts, Chris. *Tom Jones: A Life in Pictures*, Carlton, 2013

Savile, Jimmy. *Love Is an Uphill Thing*, Coronet, 1976

Schwartz, Bert. *Tom Jones*, Grosset & Dunlap, 1969

West, Sonny. *Elvis: Still Taking Care of Business*, Triumph, 2007

Wilson, Mary. *Dreamgirl: My Life as a Supreme*, Sidgwick & Jackson, 1987

# PICTURE CREDITS

Page 11: (top) Rex/Globe Photos Inc; (middle) Mirrorpix; (bottom) Rex/Huw Evans.

Page 12: (all) courtesy of Glynis McKenna.

Page 13: (top) courtesy of Glenna Stone; (middle) courtesy of Glynis McKenna; (bottom) courtesy of Glynis McKenna.

Page 14: (all) Dave Hogan/Getty Images.

Page 15: (top left) Montadori/Getty Images; (top right) Harry Langdon/Getty Images; (bottom left and right) Dave Hogan/Getty Images.

Page 16: (top) Rex/Beretta/Sims; (bottom) David M Benett/Getty Images.

# INDEX

# TOM JONES